THE WORLD OF COINS AND COIN COLLECTING

THE WORLD OF COINS AND COIN COLLECTING

Revised Edition

DAVID L. GANZ

Charles Scribner's Sons / New York

Copyright © 1980, 1985 David L. Ganz

Library of Congress Cataloging in Publication Data

Ganz, David L.
    The world of coins and coin collecting.

    Bibliography: p.
    Includes index.
    1. Coins.   2. Coins—Collectors and collecting.
3. Gold coins.   I. Title.
CJ76.G36   1985   737.4'075   85-10702
ISBN 0-684-18238-6

Published simultaneously in Canada by Collier
Macmillan Canada, Inc.
Copyright under the Berne Convention

1 3 5 7 9 11 13 15 17 19 F/C 20 18 16 14 12 10 8 6 4 2

Printed in the United States of America.

To Beverlee, who bought me my first coin album,

To Danny, whose writing I first tried to emulate,

To Sandy,

And for Scott, Elyse, and Sharon.

Acknowledgments

A number of people have made this book possible. For her encouragement with the preliminary draft, Doe Coover is thanked. At Scribners, Katherine Heintzelman has been a delightful assistant editor, and her response to queries, and persistence in obtaining replies from a too-busy author, even if not appreciated at the time, made for a much better book. To Patricia Gallagher, my editor, I can only say how much I appreciate the patient and skillful editing of the manuscript. Initial thanks must also go to Donald Young, an editor of the Encyclopedia Americana, who recommended my name to Charles Scribner's Sons when they first became interested in doing a book on coins and coin collecting.

Without the assistance of Margo Russell, editor of *Coin World*, and Ron Keysor, formerly news editor of the same newspaper, a substantial number of the black-and-white photographs would not have been available. Fred Reed, a former *Coin World* news editor, also assisted in yeoman spirit with last-minute illustrations. Thanks also go to Clifford Mishler and Arnold Jeffcoat, publisher and former editor, respectively, of *Numismatic News Weekly,* for their assistance with photographs.

Many of the leading coin dealerships were also of invaluable assistance when it came to obtaining black-and-white illustrations: Stack's Rare Coins; Bowers & Merena Galleries, and its predecessor, Bowers & Ruddy Galleries; Kagin's; Heritage Numismatic Auctions, and its predecessor, Ivy Numismatic Auctions; New England Rare Coin Galleries; Numismatic Fine Arts; Paramount; Rare Coin

Company of America, Inc.; and Superior are all thanked. Louisa Cahill Dittrich is also acknowledged for her assistance.

The very talented Carol Herman is thanked for providing some of the black-and-white photographs.

To Leslie A. Elam, director of the American Numismatic Society, and Dr. Richard Doty, associate curator, I greatly appreciate their valuable and timely assistance in permitting use of the ANS negative archives and their friendship.

With respect to the extensive discussion in this book on United States pattern coins and the early history of their issue by the Mint, I am deeply indebted to Miklos Lonkay, Esq., of the General Counsel's office, United States Treasury Department, and to Margaret Linzel Walker, of the Bureau of the Mint, for helping to locate old documents, papers, and regulations, which would otherwise have been relegated to the yellowing pages of time. Charles B. Holstein, formerly chief clerk of the House Banking Subcommittee on Consumer Affairs, must also be acknowledged for supplying me with pertinent copies of various committee reports, while his successor in the coinage field, Jackson O'Neal Lamb of the Subcommittee on Historic Preservation and Coinage, filled a similar role.

Early organization of this material was assisted by Barbara Bondanza, a Ph.D. candidate in American Civilization at New York University, whose historical approach to the data was useful. Margaret O'Connell, formerly my law secretary, spent many evenings completing the first of several drafts; my present secretary, Alice Gregory, deserves plaudits not only for dealing with the dictation of at least one of the chapters, but also for her tireless devotion to portions of this project and to the author. And my thanks to Barbara Karr, who lately has undertaken some of the secretarial responsibilities of this volume. Susan L. Cohen, who encouraged this project, is also thanked.

Since the first edition of this book was published, two major changes have made an impact on my life and the revision of this book. The first is my marriage to the bubbly, vivacious, and supportive Sharon Lamnin, who encouraged this revision despite the time it deprived her of. The second is equally momentous to me, at least, the birth of my son, Scott Harry Ganz. I hope he will not grow up resenting the hours I spent on the revision rather than devoting myself more fully to him.

I cannot close any acknowledgment without taking note of my two most ardent supporters since my love for coins began—my parents. My father has been an amateur writer for years, and in my own way I suppose that the three thousand articles and half a dozen books I've written through the years were a way of matching his own achievements. It was my mother who purchased that first coin album for me in 1959, explaining what a numismatist was, and encouraging me not to glue coins onto a sheet of cardboard, not to damage them, to read about them, and learn about what, I'm sure you'll agree, is a fascinating hobby.

Contents

Contents

Preface

Coin collecting is money. Not only is it the exciting study of coins, tokens, medals and currency, but it is part of a growth industry that yields high profits to its participants.

When I began to collect coins in the late 1950s, numismatics (as it is formally known) was a sleeping giant. There were a few monthly publications such as *Numismatic Scrapbook, The Coin Collector,* and *The Numismatist,* the American Numismatic Association's journal, and a biweekly periodical called *Numismatic News.* All helped collectors by publishing interesting articles about coins, utilizing paid advertising from dealers and classified buy, sell, or "trade" ads from other collectors.

Typically, Empire Coin Company, whose principals were Q. David Bowers and James Ruddy, might offer to sell a 1955 double-die mint error cent in pristine, uncirculated condition for $35. Or Stack's Coin Company might announce an auction sale where a set of ten proof coins made by the United States Mint in 1880 could bring $300.

Coins of some rarity could still be found in pocket change; my own impetus to start collecting came when I received an unusual worn 1906 Indian head coin in return for a bubble gum purchase. Silver dollars could be acquired easily at $1.00 each (their face value). Modern proof sets for the current year were available from the United States Mint for $2.10 each.

Investment first became a watchword in 1960. In that year, the small date error cent was discovered, and numismatists began investing in proof sets. By the time I became Washington correspondent for *Numismatic News Weekly* in

1969, the coin hobby was bordering on becoming an industry. In 1973, as assistant editor, I recall vividly writing the story about the first coin sold for more than $100,000—a 1794 silver dollar from the Charles Ruby collection, auctioned by Superior Galleries in Los Angeles and purchased by television producer Ralph Andrews for $110,000.

The 1960s was an exciting decade from a historical sense, for in 1965, silver was taken out of our coinage, and in 1970, the Eisenhower dollar was reintroduced. As the first member of the coin press to be a member of the Periodical Press Gallery of the United States Senate, I covered legislation that created a national, Bicentennial medal, and the introduction, hearings, and passage of the Hobby Protection Act, designed to assure that collectors would not be plagued with unauthorized reproductions. Still later came the battle to secure significant coinage commemorating America's Bicentennial. Although at least one weekly coin publication now maintains a full-time Washington correspondent, when I began weekly news coverage fifteen years ago it was largely an unexplored field. Since then, first as a journalist, and then as a lawyer, I have been in the thick of Washington's legislative and regulatory developments that have affected coin collectors in every way.

Prices altered dramatically following that 1973 six-figure sale of Dr. Ruby's coin. By 1980, Bowers & Ruddy Galleries, a "new" firm formed by two familiar names, had become a subsidiary of General Mills and auctioned a Brasher doubloon for $725,000 and an 1804 silver dollar for $400,000. Stack's then sold for one million dollars a set of eleven gold coins. New England Rare Coin Galleries began a pioneer effort in devising and marketing a rare coin mutual fund; the predecessor to the public offering actually yielded a 400 percent return on investment over a four-year period. Others to tap this lodestar market included Kagin's, Ivy, and later, Heritage and Neil S. Berman.

Inflation, in some measure, was the cause—for coins have long had a history of outpacing inflation. Even though each aspect of our life can be measured in inflationary terms, it can well be seen in the cost of a United States

Proof Set in 1980: $10. The differential from 1960 to 1980 amounts to more than 375 percent.

As a result of increases like these, which (when expressed in compounded interest terms) constituted impressive gains, members of the Wall Street community began to look at rare coins as an investment vehicle. Sharp rises in the price of gold and silver—to over $800 for gold and nearly $50 for silver—contributed in part to the remaking of the marketplace.

Objective analysts from the prestigious Salomon Brothers investment banking firm evaluated rare coins and other tangible assets. Not particularly to the surprise of those who have bought coins for many years, the Salomon Brothers survey showed coins a leader in investment return. Viewed over a fifteen-year period, the Salomon charts suggest an average annual return of more than 13 percent compounded.

In part, this attractive rate of return (which went higher in many instances than the Salomon Brothers average) caused many investors to place substantial stock in rare coins for their retirement. Individual Retirement Accounts (IRAs) and HR-10 (Keogh) plans began to place these tangible assets into long-term growth portfolios. In 1981, citing abuses in other areas, Congress amended the Internal Revenue Code to put the kabosh on placing any additional tangible asset (including rare coins) in a self-directed retirement plan. As a result, coin prices skidded, though anyone who had then held on to coins for five or more years still made a handsome profit.

This legislative shove, combined with efforts to regulate the sale of precious metals, galvanized collectors, investors, and dealers alike, each of whose interests were threatened by government intervention in the marketplace. The National Association of Coin & Precious Metals Dealers, of which I became the first general counsel, emerged from these events.

More governmental pressure came in the form of a proposal to eliminate capital gains treatment on collectables, and another reporting requirements by the Internal Revenue Service on the sale of certain gold and silver coins and bullion items. From this frontal assault was born the Industry Council for Tangible Assets, of which I am a founding member of the board of directors.

Even in the face of the threat of government involvement, coin prices prospered at previously unheard of levels. The predecessor to Bowers & Merena Galleries held a marathon sale of what had been the Louis Eliasberg Collection of U.S. Gold Coins—this virtually complete collection garnered over $10 million at public sale. In January 1984, Stack's auctioned the Amon Carter Family Collection for over $8 million to a room crowded with buyers, each of whom vied to acquire rare coins and common dates in superior states of preservation. A restored coin market seemed poised to go to new heights.

Coupled with this were the first rare coin issues in a decade, and the first commemorative coins in more than a quarter century: a half dollar for the bi-sesquicentennial of George Washington's birth, and two silver dollars and a $10 gold coin honoring the Olympic Games at Los Angeles in 1984. I was deeply involved as a lawyer in the Olympic coin issues, perhaps one of the most dramatic political confrontations in our time over a relatively minor issue.

Preface to the Second Edition

When the first edition of *The World of Coins and Coin Collecting* came out four years ago, I was told that coin books are nice on a coffee table but simply do not sell. That this book has gone through two printings and is now into a revised edition is a tribute to Scribners—and to the interest of the public at large in coins and coin collecting.

It is also in part due to the efforts of Robert Stack, a young public relations specialist who offered me invaluable advice about publicizing the book and who assisted in placing it on a number of television talk shows as well as national radio.

In this second edition, substantial revisions have been made at every material level. This is chiefly as a result of political changes, most emanating from Washington, which have both revised the minting and coinage laws of the United States and also changed existing Treasury policy with regard to the issuance of commemoratives and other coins.

When the first edition was written, between 1978 and 1980, the likelihood of commemorative coins being reissued seemed small. True, there had been a special Bicentennial coin issue in 1976, but the Treasury never retracted for a moment from its opposition to commemorative coins intended primarily for collectors.

Then new legislation, initiated in 1981 and intended to commemorate the 250th anniversary of the birth of George Washington, changed all that. With a certain irony, Washington continues to play the dramatic role in America's coinage that he had at the very beginning of our nation's history.

As the book notes, it was Washington who signed the first Mint Act of April 2, 1792, into law; it was his wife's silver service that provided metal for the first coinage (the half disme pictured on page 142); and he was the first President who refused to have his likeness appear on the earliest coinage issues of the Republic (though the patterns shown on page 139 indicate the desire on the part of others to do so).

The first commemorative dollar coin, issued in 1900, depicts Washington with his colleague Lafayette. In 1932, to commemorate the bicentennial of his birth, a coin intended for a single year's circulation—the Washington quarter—was introduced. Millions have been produced since then, of course.

There was considerable precedent, then, for honoring George Washington with a commemorative coin in 1982, and Congress did just that. The difference was that this time, the Treasury Department saw the project in a wholly favorable light, perceiving the revenue possibilities as exciting.

What followed next was the Olympic coin issues, which made the front pages of the nation's daily press as legislative maneuvering turned into a battleground. The result, however, was a gold coin (the first since 1933), a new mint mark ("W" for West Point), and two *real* silver dollars.

The success of these two commemorative coinage programs from a financial standpoint has already attracted the keen interest of members of Congress, who have various causes that could benefit from commemorative coins, as well as that of the Treasury Department. What is clear from all this is that the number of new coin issues is likely to increase in the coming years, and that the public at large is going to be tapped as a market for the collectables. This means that even more individuals are likely to become involved in coin collecting.

Coin collecting is exciting, historical, interesting, and lucrative. When I began collecting coins in 1960, common, uncirculated Indian Head cents—in much better condition than the "pocket change" specimen that I found—were selling for $7 to $9 each. A quarter century later, the average price is $200 or more, a more than twentyfold increase.

The reason I have collected coins has little to do with the profit motive (an investment in coins is not necessarily a collection) but, as I have found in the past quarter century, every collection of coins does constitute a substantial investment. Coin collecting, then, is a fun hobby, and also a very lucrative one—one that I hope many more Americans will share in.

Introduction

Coin collecting, or numismatics, is more than the accumulation of old money, medals, and tokens. It involves both art and investment, and it provides an enjoyable way to learn about a country and its people, past and present. Coins are now used as a form of exchange in most corners of the globe, and millions of people around the world collect them—for good reason. A coin that is common today could well become rare tomorrow. In fact, most coins that are now worth thousands of dollars were once made in relatively large quantities for circulation.

The value of a coin may escalate for a number of reasons, but the two most common causes are discontinued circulation and limited supply. As the quantity of any currency—metal or paper—decreases, its value to the collector increases. A 1955 Lincoln cent, for example, appears to be struck twice by the U.S. Mint at Philadelphia, so that the lettering on it appears to be doubled. That year its value remained 1 cent; but by 1958 the coin was scarce, and uncirculated or slightly circulated specimens were offered in newspaper advertisements for about $22. Today these coins sell for more than $400.

More dramatic examples of appreciation are legion. In the 1830s a well-known collector, J. J. Mickley of Philadelphia, obtained four 1827 quarter dollars as change after making a purchase. In the following decades, these quarter dollars proved very scarce—apparently less than a dozen were made—and their value rose steadily. At a public auction in 1946, one specimen sold for $2,400. Only four years later, another specimen of the same coin (part of the collec-

This 1955 double-die cent, which gives the appearance of being struck twice, was found in pocket change and is now valued at more than $300.

Price progressions on the 1827 quarter show a rise averaging 38 percent per year over nearly thirty years.

1

Frequently termed America's most beautiful coin, this double eagle was designed by world-renowned sculptor Augustus Saint-Gaudens. The 1931-D double eagle currently is worth more than $10,000.

tion of screen star Adolphe Menjou) brought $2,725. When the Menjou coin was resold a generation later at public auction, the winning bid was $16,000, and more recently, in 1977, it brought a whopping $31,000.

Artistic merit may also be the *raison d'être* for the coin collector. Some of the world's finest sculptors have been commissioned to create designs for American coinage. Augustus Saint-Gaudens, the brilliant Irish-American sculptor of such well-known works as the standing Lincoln in Chicago, the statues of General Sherman and Admiral Farragut in New York City, and the Shaw Memorial in Boston, was asked by President Theodore Roosevelt to design several new American coins. His double eagle, or $20 gold piece of 1907, is considered by many to be among the most beautiful American coins ever produced; in high relief, Liberty is depicted in a flowing dress against details of the Capitol.

Several years later James Earle Fraser, who sculpted "End of the Trail," composed a new design for the 5-cent piece to replace the classic Greek Liberty nickel that had been in circulation since 1883. Fraser depicted a bison on the reverse and a portrait of a weathered warrior on the face of the new coin. This fanciful piece of artwork, known to collectors as the Buffalo nickel, was made for many years, from 1913 to 1938, and is still affordable. To be sure, not all coins are as dramatic or artistic as the Saint-Gaudens or Fraser cre-

"End of the Trail" in a different medium — the Buffalo nickel.

ations; some are quite plain, but others have a life and vitality equal to that of any large sculpture.

Through the years, numerous economic crises and moments of national glory have been reflected in U.S. coinage. For example, the arrows on the 1873 quarter represent a diminished silver content in the context of an economic recession. On the other hand, the flowing-haired Liberty on the 1793 half cent depicts a time when America was young, vibrant, and confident. Plastic cents, dated 1942, have long been popular collectors' items, as have trial strikes and experimental designs for the 2-cent piece of the Civil War era.

Leaders have not been preoccupied only with the problems of coinage; a number of them have also collected coins as a relaxing hobby. President John Quincy Adams was an avid coin collector, making detailed records of the coins he and his son Charles Francis Adams acquired in their travels as diplomats for the United States. Nearly all the coins were common in origin but relatively diverse and well preserved. When the Adams family collection was sold in 1978 at public auction, the Greek, Roman, and foreign monies realized several hundred thousand dollars. Another American President, Ulysses S. Grant, acquired a magnificent collection of Japanese money during his travels. These coins, some of which are the finest of their type known to exist, are now on permanent exhibition for examination at the Smithsonian Institution.

Foreign rulers, too, have been attracted to coins. King Farouk of Egypt was a prolific collector of coins and other items, although it is questionable whether he was a serious student of what his curators were able to acquire. Victor Emmanuel II of Italy was a dedicated collector and skilled researcher of monies of his native land. After years of work, he produced a standard reference encyclopedia on Italian coinage, which is still considered a major work. The Duke of Windsor (formerly King Edward VIII of Great Britain) was also a coin collector of sorts. During the year that he reigned, coin patterns and dies were prepared with his portrait, but only trial strikes were produced at the Royal Mint. Following his abdication, the ex-king attempt-

Trial strikes of coins that would have shown the portrait of King Edward VIII had not the throne been abdicated "for the woman I love."

ed to collect a type set of specimens with his name and portrait—a seemingly easy task, but in fact most difficult, as the pieces were very scarce. Toward the end of the duke's life, a complete set of King Edward VIII coins was offered on the market for $1 million by an American dealer, but the duke apparently was unable or unwilling to make the purchase. Ultimately, the set was sold privately to an English dealer for later resale.

If coin collecting is the hobby of kings and presidents, it is also the hobby of commoners who collect kings and presidents in coin with great alacrity. In the United States, the hobby may be traced back to the middle of the nineteenth century. In 1886, the U.S. Mint sold fewer than nine hundred specially produced proof 50-cent pieces annually (slightly more for each of the lesser denominations). The total number of six-coin (cent through dollar) proof sets ordered annually today is over 4 million. In the 1860s, Sylvester Crosby wrote a book on early coins of America that was offered by subscription to interested collectors. Fewer than two hundred copies were sold. Nearly a century later, Richard S. Yeoman wrote *A Guide Book of United States Coins,* in which he listed all American coin issues, their mintages, and price valuations; by 1980, Yeoman's *Guide Book* was in its thirty-third edition. Counting previous editions, more than 13 million copies have been in print, making this coin book one of the best sellers in publishing history.

The scholarly *American Journal of Numismatics,* published in Crosby's era, had as small a readership as did his book; today *Coin World,* a weekly newspaper covering the numismatic field, has a circulation in excess of 100,000. When *Coin World* readers are added to those of other publications, there are probably between 1 and 2 million steady readers of news pertaining to the collecting of coins. Including those with interests in medallics, special tokens, or investment aspects, the number of enthusiasts rises to almost 10 million. Although the dollar investment of this total has never been calculated or even estimated, it seems clear that $500 million in sales per year on coins and subsidiary products in the United States is not unlikely and may be quite conservative.

Millions of people and dollars can't be wrong! There really is something to coin collecting for everyone, and perhaps this book will help you discover how coins can have their own niche in your life. For investment, historic, artistic, or cultural value, or even for relaxation, coin collecting can be very satisfying indeed.

Holding the $500,000 nickel—a 1913 Liberty head variety—is the late actor Victor Buono. The coin co-starred in a television series, "Hawaii Five-0," in an episode involving coin rarities. Note how he correctly holds the coin by its edges.

The History of Money: A Pedigree

MONEY OF A DIFFERENT SORT

The origins of money go back to the barter system; barter currencies, usually termed "odd and curious" by modern collectors, form the beginning of the numismatic legacy of civilization.

Cowrie shells from the ocean, plus cattle, sugar, spice, wampum, stones, and even tobacco are only some of the items that have served as currencies around the world. They are no less strange than plastic credit cards, paper checks, clearinghouse certificates, scrip, or gold, silver, and copper coins. With the possible exception of cattle and tobacco, just about all nonperishable objects that at one time

Typical cowrie shells. American Numismatic Society collection.

or another served as money are collected. In some instances museums compete directly with collectors for these exceptionally rare and unusual objects, which can be both fascinating historical and ethnological artifacts and works of art.

Among the earliest known forms of money is the cowrie shell, widely used in China, Africa, India, and even Europe. Unlike many other types of money, the cowrie was in virtually unlimited supply since the ocean itself was its source. In the Maldive Islands during the tenth century, historians of the period record that when the royal treasury was drained, coconut palms were thrown onto the sea. The mollusk inhabitants of the cowrie shells would crawl aboard the palms, and women of the islands would then drag the branches back onto the beach. There, the shiny, colorful cowrie shells would be abandoned by their occupants, and the natives would gather them up to add to the treasury.

The precise value of cowries is difficult to determine, but it is clear that their use was widespread. In Uganda, near the turn of the nineteenth century, two large cowrie shells could be used to purchase a wife; but, as with all currency, overabundance resulted in a decline in value, and by the 1860s a glut of cowrie shells brought the price of a wife up to some 10,000 cowries.

Today's collector seeking to acquire a cowrie usually chooses several individual pieces and a trading bead. A strand about a yard long is apparently a common length, though longer specimens are known. For most ancient societies, cowrie shells formed a basic unit of value, not unlike an American cent, which could be converted into other higher monetary units.

Beads, like cowrie shells, still are commonly used as money in tribal societies. In South West Africa (Namibia), ostrich egg shells were often cut into small disc-shaped pieces, which were then pierced (usually with an arrow) and strung. Copper beads, sometimes strung on vines, sometimes on leather, were also popular, especially in the Congo region of Africa. Nigerians seemed to prefer trading with a cast brass bead, complete with a loop for stringing.

Iron beads were also used. Most beautiful, colorful, and probably most widely used of all were glass beads, often referred to as "aggry" beads.

Two distinct types of aggry beads are known today. The first is those found naturally in the ground; the second, far more common type of bead, was artificially manufactured, first by natives and later by Europeans. That the ground is capable of yielding money should be no surprise, for in Western culture, gold and silver in placer form are similarly extracted and converted. The earth yields soft blue and yellow aggry beads, as well as some of a dull red. These three types combine to form a fourth, mosaic type. The variety of delicate shadings is almost infinite, and all are highly popular with collectors. For the modern collector of aggry beads, display is all-important. Some collectors have formal exhibition cases; more often the beads are mounted on an attractive wall plaque, either covered with glass or left freestanding.

Societies that used the aggry beads as money tended to regard them as something more than currency or art. Many tribal organizations attributed supernatural powers to the beads. The same magical mystique, coupled with their beauty, attracts modern collectors to the beads today.

There are other types of money that collectors term the "odd and curious"—a phrase that is something of a misnomer. The term betrays, first, a cultural bias toward money that is similar to what we use; it also ignores the fact that

Early Mexican spade money.

Chinese "shoe money."

Swedish copperplate money. American Numismatic Society collection.

when European monies began to circulate in primitive or evolving societies, the coin as a trinket (rather than an item of intrinsic value) was initially used by natives to facilitate trade and barter. Only later, when Western culture imposed a valuation fixed in a monetary sense, did the coinage cease to be interchangeable with monies of a different sort that were widely used by the indigenous population.

Bars of rock salt were used as currency in Abyssinia until the turn of the twentieth century. In the South Pacific, the teeth of whales were extensively used. (Some regions actually went so far as to specify the type of whale's tooth that could be used.) On the North American continent, the natives of Alaska at one time traded in fishhook money, while the Aztecs of early Mexican history made a currency out of copper hammered into the shape of a spade. China, the birthplace of paper money, also had more conventional primitive currencies in the form of jade and coral pieces, and in more unusual items such as the Sycee, or Chinese "shoe money"—silver that was actually cast in the shape of a shoe. The ingot varied in weight and size, but it was nonetheless effective, principally because it was an efficient means of exchanging precious metal. China, too, at one time made extensive use of the cowrie; interestingly enough, in the interior of that vast nation, imitation cowries were circulated when there were not enough genuine shells available. Some cowries were also covered with gold leaf.

In Scandinavia, Swedish copperplate money was used. Weighing an average of 6 pounds or more, these plates were actually minted pieces of solid copper the size of floor tiles. They circulated with fixed values (though these fluctuated with the price of copper). Even more astonishing, copperplate money circulated as late as the early eighteenth century. Each plate carried at least one official seal attesting to the weight of the coin; its copper fineness, or purity, was nearly perfect, owing to the large supply of the metal in Sweden. These pieces, too, are much prized by today's collectors.

In the United States, perhaps the best known of all the

Massachusetts wampum.

"odd and curious" currencies is wampum. The blue and white shells used by the American Indians were adopted almost immediately by the European colonists, who at first traded with the Indians in their own currency. The colonists swiftly perfected a means of manufacturing wampum and began to crank out specimens with regularity. The Dutch invented a lathe capable of perforating and polishing the shells with ease and exactness. Such a lathe may have played a part in the purchase of Manhattan Island for a total of about $24 in beads, wampum, and other primitive currencies. But overproduction of wampum brought about a decline in its purchasing power. While there was a parity, for example, between the money coined in Massachusetts around 1700 and native wampum, by the middle of the century the value of wampum had all but disappeared.

Museums abound with these unusual forms of money, and private collectors also have significant amounts of some items. An obvious problem is that of authentication. In the case of beads, for example, counterfeits were made more than a thousand years ago, and many beads used as currency hundreds of years ago are virtually indistinguishable from contemporary products of the fashion industries around the world.

These primitive monies seem unusual, but are they really so distinct from a modern credit card, paper check, or for that matter a coin made out of a base metal that has only fiat value? It is clear that there is a wide realm of items not ordinarily thought of as coins which have in fact served the purpose. From the cowrie shells used in different nations at one time or another to various types of metals, some of which were cast into objects such as spades or knives and then bartered, these monies of the ancients (and some modern peoples) are part of the expanding world of numismatics—fascinating to collect, interesting to display, and surely worth a story.

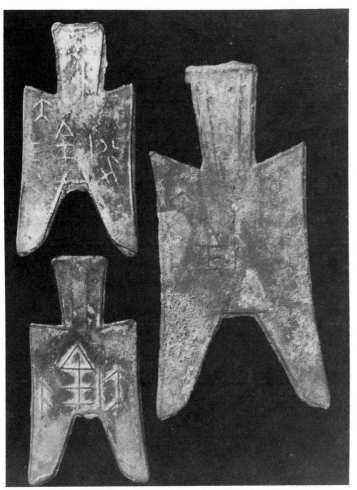

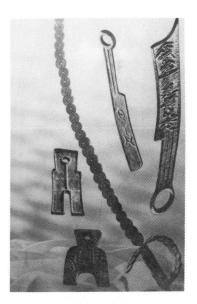

*A plethora of objects that our culture deems "odd and curious"
forms of money. American Numismatic Society collection.*

THE ORIGIN
AND EVOLUTION OF COINS

Traditional numismatics really begins with the creation of coins for the sole purpose of exchange. In Asia Minor, around 700 B.C., the Lydians produced what Herodotus, the Greek historian, two centuries later called the first gold and silver coins. Actually, the coins were little more than lumps of electrum (gold and silver alloyed in a natural manner), heated over a fire and then pounded and inscribed or stamped with the owner's insignia to guarantee their weight, authenticity, and fineness. A primitive anvil constituted the first coining press, and insignias were the first dies. Although these pieces were crude, the ancients recognized their importance: they were convenient and had precise value that was useful in a bargain or trade.

Ancient Coins

It was not the Lydians but the Greeks who perfected coinage and raised its manufacture, design, and use to an art. Skilled Greek craftsmen created coins of great beauty, with an artistic style that has been sometimes rivaled but rarely surpassed to this day. Exquisitely detailed portraits

A silver tetradrachm of Antiochus I (Seleucid king of Syria) minted around 280 to 261 B.C., at left; in the center, a moving portrait of Parikla, the last Lydian king (produced as a silver stater between 380 and 361 B.C.); at right is a gold distater with the portrait of Alexander the Great (made sometime between 336 and 323 B.C.). Robert F. Kelley Collection of the American Numismatic Society, New York.

of the gods were the specialty of the Greeks, and each city-state added its own symbol to the coins. For example, the owl represented Athens. These symbols themselves became important in the ancient world, for the quality of money varied from place to place. As a result, the symbol (analagous to a mint mark today) became a part of the standard of value, identifying the issuing authority that would redeem the coin. Aristotle himself noted that these symbols obviated the need for weighing and assaying, for the imprimatur acted as a guarantee.

In addition to portraits of deities, divine attributes were frequently depicted on Greek coins; grapes often accompanied Bacchus, the god of wine, while a lion symbolized Apollo. Different characterizations further depended on the locale of the city-state, the local gods (there were special gods for each of the city-states), and the talents of the artist who engraved the die and then produced the coin. The ancient mint masters were surprisingly expert, and their dies usually could be used to make between ten and fifteen thousand coins, all of them struck by hand in gold, silver, electrum, or bronze.

Nevertheless, the weight and consistency of these ancient coinages varied widely. As Athens gained preeminence among the city-states of Attica, it attempted, by decree, to standardize Greek coinage. Portions of the decree, issued in approximately 450 B.C., survive from reconstructed fragments; it prohibited the use of all but Athenian

Kimon, a noted Greek sculptor, created this Syracuse dekadrachm early in the fifth century B.C., shortly after the great victory over the Carthaginians at Himera. This specimen in extra-fine condition is valued at more than $15,000.

coins and weights, and required that "foreign silver coin" be melted and converted into Athenian coin. This monetary imperialism had the desired effect, for it permitted Athens to control the supply of money and to concentrate its resources and energies on expanding the state.

For the collector seeking to acquire ancient Greek coinage today, it is essential to read not only histories of the period but also the various treatises on its coinage. (A number of books that give general coverage, and some that are more specific, are listed in the Bibliography.) Although the Greeks rarely dated their coins in a direct manner, it is possible by using a decoding device almost always found in writings dealing with ancient Greek coinage to discover what the coin purported to reveal.

The Roman and Byzantine coinages also have distinctive history and appeal. Both are eminently collectable and highly valued, alike for their designs and their inscriptions. Roman emperors frequently used their coinage much like a tabloid newspaper of their tenure. When the armies of the Empire won a major battle or made a significant conquest, the coinage mottoes were altered to reflect the victory. As the Romans opposed personal deification in life up to the time of Julius Caesar, the portraits on the issues were of

Roman gold coins from the time of Commodus.

gods, not rulers, except for those who had died and achieved deification.

Caesar himself broke precedent around 49 B.C. when his so-called elephant coinage was produced, a pre-imperial series that showed his victory over Pompey in the form of an elephant trampling a snake. The coin was about the size of a dime (18 millimeters in diameter), but its impact was immense, for a consul had boldly elevated himself to imperial status, placed his name on a coin, and in summary fashion eliminated other proconsuls of the provinces. In 44 B.C., shortly before his assassination on the Ides of March, Caesar sat before the die engravers so that they could make a portrait of him for the coinage. Thereafter, all succeeding Roman emperors appeared in portraiture, along with deceased emperors who continued to receive deification and homage on coins.

The eastern half of the Roman Empire, centered at Constantinople, ultimately became the Byzantine Empire, with a coinage of its own. Constantinople was rebuilt in A.D. 330, which is sometimes thought of as the starting date for By-

Caesar's elephant coin.
(Photo courtesy of Coin World, *with special thanks to Fred Reed)*

Early Roman emperor.

This gold solidus of Justinian II (ca. A.D. 695), part of the Robert F. Kelley Collection housed in the museum of the American Numismatic Society, bears the earliest known coinage portrait of Christ.

zantine coinage. But the precise time at which Byzantine coinage began remains a point of conjecture, especially since Roman money was produced at more than one mint.

In contrast to the Greek and Roman portraiture, which was exquisite in detail, the Byzantine money was crude in design. Yet the coins, particularly the gold pieces, currently have value, in part because the romance and lore surrounding them has attracted many new collectors.

Medieval Coins

As coinage progresses from ancient to medieval times, a change is perceptible principally in the design—which becomes even more crude than the Byzantine, and totally

Typical Byzantine coinages include these gold solidus pieces: at the left, Zoë and Theodora, whose joint tenure as empresses lasted from April 20 to June 11, A.D. 1042; at the right, joint emperors Artavasdus and Nicephorus, who ruled ca. A.D. 743; and Alexander, A.D. 912–913, in the center. The style is distinctly crude when compared with earlier Greek and Roman issues. Robert F. Kelley Collection of the American Numismatic Society, New York.

lacks the sophistication and artistry the Greeks and Romans took for granted.

Despite the relative unattractiveness of many of these pieces, they are widely collected as type coins, generally on a regional basis or by country. Anglo-Saxon coinage is a drab collection of hammered pieces, usually with inscriptions rather than portraits, yet it is nonetheless revealing about life in Britain before the Norman Conquest of 1066. In the British Museum alone, there are more than six thousand specimens of these coins; most contain the marks of the moneyers who coined them, and some bear crude portraits of the kings who were enthroned at the time of their striking.

Coins in the region of the Franks, ruled by the Carolingian dynasty founded by Pepin, were somewhat more sophisticated, yet portraiture was totally lacking. The *denarius argenteus* (or *denier*), which became the basic monetary unit of medieval Europe, contained only abbreviations of the various titles of the king of the Franks. Charlemagne added his monogram to the coinage, along with a crucifix, and upon his coronation in Rome in 800 reinstituted the portraiture of the ancients. He was depicted complete with laurel wreath.

Skilled late medieval coin design from the Germanies.

Renaissance Coins

The Renaissance, which gave birth to new art forms in all disciplines, moved coinage from the Dark Ages into modern design. Portraiture returned, both in medallic art and coin of the realm. Coinage, still hammered on an anvil as in ancient Greece, was produced with regularity, and designs became more sophisticated and larger. By the 1480s, a 35 millimeter coin (nearly 1½ inches in diameter) was produced in Germany. Coinage of papal Rome also bore portraits of the popes (Sixtus IV was the first pope so commemorated); and in the German states, skilled engravers created exquisite portraits and vignettes.

Perhaps the most interesting thing about Renaissance coinage was the use of old-fashioned inefficient methods of production. The great master Leonardo da Vinci attempted to remedy this, and his journals show designs for a coining press to replace the hammer and anvil. Several years ago, International Business Machines Corporation provided a grant to build such a machine from Leonardo's sketches. In 1977, a hand press was constructed from the plans and presented to the museum of the American Numismatic Association (the largest educational nonprofit organization of coin collectors in the world). The museum, located in Colorado Springs, on the campus of Colorado State College, keeps a working model of the press on display. Visitors can see how the die is brought up by a hand crank and then left to fall and cut the planchet by sheer weight. A test of the model with modern dies shows it to be an effective coining tool.

Medallic art of this period is a separate phenomenon, discussed in the chapter "Collecting Medals and Tokens." It is important to note, however, that the portraiture techniques of the modern Renaissance medal did translate to the smaller coins, and the same methods, to a large degree, are in use today.

While Europe developed its sophisticated coining techniques using gold, silver, and copper in alloyed form, the Orient had another distinctive money form—paper currency. Marco Polo reported its existence to a skeptical Europe at the end of his first voyage to China in the thirteenth century. The paper money, his journal said, had no intrinsic value of its own, yet it circulated and was widely accepted. The fact that China was a closed society and that the emperor had mandated that failure to accept paper currency was to be met with death may have hastened its acceptance. In any case, it was centuries before this Chinese invention gained acceptance in Europe.

The Renaissance marked the commencement of the age of exploration, and with it came colonization by the great powers. First the Spanish and Portuguese, then the English and Dutch, made exploratory sailings, and the inhabitants of the colonies they founded soon needed money.

Colonial Money

Spanish colonialism in the New World initially prohibited the coining of gold or silver in this hemisphere, as virtually all the metal was shipped back to Spain and the royal
treasury. However, a royal mint was established in Mexico
in 1536 to pay the conquistadores, who were demanding reward for their services. Earliest of the coinages was a copper
maravedie, which apparently met with a poor reception
from potential users. Gold and silver continued to be exported back to Spain until the middle of the seventeenth
century. Throughout the rest of Spanish America, there

*Spanish pillar dollars once circulated widely in the United States; today,
the laws of the nation still provide that "the pieces commonly known as
the quarter, eighth and sixteenth of the Spanish pillar dollar, and of the
Mexican dollar, shall be receivable at the Treasury of the United States,
and its several offices, and at the several post offices and land offices at
the rates of valuation following: The fourth of a dollar, or piece of two
reals, at 20 cents; the eighth of a dollar, or piece of one real, at 10 cents;
and the sixteenth of a dollar, or half real, at 5 cents."*

were various mints responsible for the manufacture of coinages. (Each was identified by a mint mark.)

The basic coin produced throughout Latin America at the time of the American Revolution was the Spanish pillar dollar, or piece of eight. This coin was broken or cut by users into various portions—up to eight in all. Each "piece of eight" was called a "bit," which was valued at 12.5 cents. A quarter of the dollar consisted of 25 cents, or two bits—a legacy continued in American slang even today. These coins were used throughout the American colonial period, but after the Revolution, when the United States lacked sufficient coin of its own, the pillar dollars enjoyed an extraordinary circulation, which was not ended by law until just before the Civil War. Today a reminder of this coin's role is found on the statute books, which still require the U.S. Post Office to redeem all Spanish pillar dollars tendered.

THE MAKING OF COINS

The earliest designs on coins were created by an engraver, who took a piece of soft metal, carefully etched an image in reverse form, and then refined the portrait in minute detail. The reason for making the image in the reverse is that the die is concave; when placed upon the planchet, or blank coin, that would become a coin once struck, its image would be transferred in the reverse. By placing the reverse image in the die, a positive version emerges in final form.

As time progressed, hammering became an inefficient way to produce coins, especially by the nineteenth century, when more and more pieces were required. To provide adequately for the growing population, there was a need for new technology. The screw press evolved in the Middle Ages. It utilized dies at both top and bottom, with the top lowered by a screw until it met the bottom and a planchet or coin blank in between. By trimming the planchet, it was possible to obtain a round coin, as opposed to the cruder and less geometric designs from the hammer and anvil.

Even the screw press proved too slow for mass manufacture, however, and in the 1830s the steam engine was used to run coining presses. At the U.S. Mint, the conversion to the steam press was considered so important that a special medal was produced for the occasion and struck on one of the new presses installed at the Philadelphia Mint.

Manufacture of the dies actually involved an engraver or die-sinker rather than a sculptor. The basic process consisted of taking a piece of flattened metal, which was "incused," or stamped, with a design, lettering backward, so that when it made contact with the flan, or blank, piece of metal, the image was projected above the surface of the coin. The process was time consuming and, while an engraver could copy a design with some degree of similarity, the likelihood of exact duplication was minimal. Consequently, among the earlier issues produced in this manner, a number of varieties are known to exist.

It was not until the middle of the nineteenth century, when a combination engraving-reducing machine was invented, that it became possible for transfer engraving to be

Frank Gasparro served as chief engraver of the U.S. Mint from 1965 until his retirement in 1982. Here he is shown examining die reduction operations in the U.S. Mint at Philadelphia.

undertaken. Initially, this enabled an artist to make a positive image, which could then be transferred onto a negative impression on the die as though engraved. Subsequently, the technique was refined so that the original design could be reduced. Through levers and a sophisticated tracing device, it became possible for an artist to create a copper or master positive image of the design 12 inches in diameter, filled with detail, and then reduce it to the size of a dime on the reducing engraver.

This is largely how coins are created today. The major difference now is that a dateless galvano—or large copper model from which a die is made—is generally used as a master, and a duplicate original is made, to which the year of coinage is added. Fine-line engraving may be executed later to strengthen the impression of a date or other detail on the die.

A large plaster is utilized to create a galvano, which is in turn reduced and made into a die. Depicted is Frank Gasparro's exquisite version of a flowing-haired Liberty, intended for a small-size dollar coin. Susan B. Anthony was ultimately chosen instead, and some believe if the more beautiful design had been used, it would still circulate today.

This $20 gold piece contains 0.9675 troy ounces of gold. U.S. Mint records confirm that over 39% of these coins were melted after the gold recall of 1934. Historically, the coin has sold at a premium of at least 40% over the bullion value, in part because of the beauty of Saint-Gaudens's design, in part because of desirability to collectors.

MONETARY STABILITY

The stable value of both gold and silver was an important part of all coinage during the nineteenth and twentieth centuries. From 1837 until 1933, the price of gold was, with some minor exceptions during wartime, valued at $20.67 per ounce. American gold coins all contained their full measure of metal; a $20 gold piece, for example, contained 0.9675 troy ounces of pure gold, valued at $19.998. (To contrast with Standard Measure, there are 12 troy ounces in each pound.) In the 1930s, however, gold began to disappear from the circulating coinage of various countries. President Franklin D. Roosevelt ended its use in the United States by executive order in 1933, a decision ratified by Congress with the passage of the Gold Reserve Act of 1934. When gold coinage was suspended in 1933, the price of the metal was artificially increased (by devaluing the dollar relative to gold) to $35 an ounce, where it stayed until 1968. This fixed level permitted governments to issue gold coins without fear that the content of the precious metal would exceed the face value of the money. The same was generally true of silver, except that until the 1960s the price of silver was substantially below that of the bullion content in coinage, so that the government made a profit, known as seigniorage, on every silver coin it produced.

In the early part of the 1960s the price of silver began to rise in the United States, and the federal government guaranteed a price of $1.29 an ounce by offering to sell silver bullion to all prospective buyers at that level. This price approached the rate at which the silver content of the dime, quarter, half dollar, and dollar equaled face value, based upon their bullion content. But until the price exceeded $1.38 an ounce, there was no fear of dimes being melted down for their silver content. Nonetheless, the demand for silver finally succeeded in raising the price of the metal worldwide. Consequently, the decision was made to eliminate silver from circulating American coinage, as well as from circulating coinage in other nations where it was still used.

The United States, at first, opted for a dual system in which one coin, the 50-cent piece, retained a nominal amount of silver, while the dime and quarter were made entirely of a copper-nickel cladding bonded together and then made into coin in the conventional manner. Later, even the silver in the 50-cent piece was eliminated.

What emerged was a monetary system that is essentially a fiat currency order, in which the value of the currency and its legal tender power are derived not from the base metal content of the coin but rather from the faith, integrity, and economic power of the issuer. The actual cost for the government to produce a small-sized dollar coin made of copper-nickel is only about 3.2 cents; the balance is seigniorage. To produce a piece of paper money (without regard to denomination), according to the Bureau of Engraving and Printing of the Treasury Department, costs slightly less than 2 cents. The 1-cent piece is least profitable for the government; in 1976, a private consultant to the Treasury Department calculated that the government actually lost money on each 1-cent piece it produced, when the costs of the copper metal, labor, die charges, and storage were included. This resulted in a recommendation to eliminate it which Congress ignored. Instead, Congress voted to produce the coin in zinc, plate it with copper, and continue to strike it at the rate of over 12 billion per year. The 1984 Grace President Commission Report again recommended an end to the denomination's production as a cost-saving measure, but a consensus appears to believe this is not yet politically feasible. So the "copper cent" continues like our other currency—a shadow of its former self.

Time passed it by.

Still, this is the currency we all use without question. The reason is the financial integrity of the U.S. government. With American currency, there is little that cannot be purchased—not only in the United States but anywhere in the world.

Over the years, demands have arisen for the end of low denominations. The reason is clear: the demand to eliminate the American half cent pieces was so high by 1857 that there was simply no reason for the denomination to continue. When in 1976 the Research Triangle Institute, the private consultant hired by the Treasury Department, recommended that the American cent be eliminated for a similar reason, a controversy arose. The resolution initially remained unclear until 1982, when a zinc cent was authorized. Still, it appears likely that in the long run the cent is doomed unless a political solution permits the U.S. Mint to produce billions of coins at a loss to the government for each piece manufactured.

SPECIAL COLLECTOR COINS

With the demise of silver and gold from coinage and the use of copper-nickel substitutes, special collector coins struck in precious metals were produced specifically for sale to numismatists and investors. The United States undertook such a program with its silver-clad Eisenhower dollars and Bicentennial coins (in which the silver content far exceeded the face value of the coin). Of all these noncirculating, legal tender items, those made by the Franklin Mint, a large private concern, are probably the most popular among collectors.

There are numerous other instances of special commemorative coins. In 1976, the Montreal Olympic Games offered a series of twenty-eight silver coins (to which two gold pieces were later added) to raise money for the Olympics and aid each of the participating national teams. Almost all of these special commemorative coins are legal

Eisenhower dollar struck in silver for collectors. Here, a unique 1970 galvano. The actual coin was not struck until 1971.

Some of the Olympic commemorative coins struck by various minting authorities from the time of ancient Greece to the 1976 Montreal Games.

tender in name only; although attractively designed, they rarely if ever circulate in the country of their origin, whose citizenry often is unaware of their existence. Yet people continue to collect them for a variety of reasons, and if coin collecting really is based upon personal preferences and desires, there is nothing wrong with this. Many of these special commemoratives are indeed beautiful, and if produced in limited quantity in years to come may grow in value. But the likelihood of growth potential is probably small, and pieces produced especially for collectors are far more likely to retain their issue price than a scarce, regular issue.

Selling commemorative coins to collectors is clearly big business. The Canadian Olympic coin program was followed in the next Olympiad by forty-five Soviet coins, ranging from a copper-nickel 1-rouble piece to silver, gold, and platinum pieces. The set fit neatly into the scope of Russian history, since platinum coins had first been produced 140 years earlier. It also set the stage for a watershed in American coinage history, the first commemorative coin issue since 1954.

Surprisingly, to those who are close observers of the Treasury Department and Congress, there was little opposition to a proposal by Representative Doug Barnard (D-Ga.) to strike a commemorative half dollar to celebrate the 250th anniversary of George Washington's birth. Decades of truculent opposition by the U.S. Mint melted away, and Washington again appeared on the half dollar, this time in an equestrian pose designed by new chief engraver Elizabeth Jones. Over four million pieces were sold as proof and uncirculated issues.

The Treasury's agreement to the Washington commemorative removed the lynchpin in its written and oral testimony which had so devastatingly defeated scores of proposed commemorative coins in the past and nearly derailed the three Bicentennial issues. This in turn set the stage for a proposal to issue a series of twenty-nine coins designed to commemorate the 1984 Los Angeles Olympic Games.

By late 1983, the gold $10 coin and silver dollars were struck in anticipation of the Olympic Games and sales commenced. As predicted by the chairman of the full House Banking Committee, Representative Fernand St. Germain (D-R.I.), they were flat—fewer than 800,000 silver dollars of a possible 50 million pieces were initially sold. Ultimately, 525,000 gold coins and about 5 million silver dollars were produced. Gold coins were also a long way from a sellout. But collectors everywhere seemed glad that new coins had been issued, for that suggested a promising future for other commemorative coins. Those other commemoratives might include a tribute to the centennial of the Statue of Liberty (1986) and the Constitution's bicentennial (1989) (details on commemoratives and other modern American issues are found in the chapter on the History of American Coinage).

One thing is clear: from our earliest monies to the most modern, coinage has run a full cycle. First coins were made of precious metal, then they were debased. Now, to attract collector appeal, they are being struck in precious metals again.

THE IMPACT OF CREDIT

Concurrent with the rise of collectors' coins has been the increasing use of credit cards, which in the early 1970s seemed to point toward the ultimate—a cashless society. Collectors got into the act early; many began to collect expired credit cards, sometimes keeping their own, sometimes trading and buying used specimens from others. But as we approach the year 2000, it has become apparent that a cashless society is, at least for this century, unlikely.

Although coins form a relatively small part of the nation's money supply, the number of coins in daily use is startling. The National Automatic Merchandising Association, an industrial group, calculates that there are roughly 84 million transactions with vending machines every day. Nevertheless, in large measure, checks have greatly reduced the amount of money actually handled. Whereas two or three decades ago it was often necessary for an employer to make a payroll in cash, most now distribute a payroll check that can be either cashed or deposited directly into the employee's bank account. Except for spending money, the employee may not see any real monetary evidence of a salary.

The changes that have occurred in the history of money are striking. From coins that reflected their true value in bullion, society has promoted those valued at a mere fraction of their stated worth. And from collections of coins that began as a means of study, the progression has been made to coins produced specifically for collectors.

Building, Organizing, and Displaying a Numismatic Collection

HOW TO BEGIN

Numismatics is the science of acquiring coins, medals, tokens, and paper money, and organizing them in a coherent manner so that they can be studied and appreciated. As with a piece of art, sculpture, or decorative furniture, the enjoyment of a collection comes in acquiring and displaying it, in the knowledge gleaned, and, for an increasing number of collectors, in the profit made from it. Once you have begun to collect coins, another pleasure is derived from sharing what you have acquired with fellow collectors or friends interested in history, art, and related disciplines.

Closely examining coins in a coin dealer's store is one way to learn about coins — and to acquire them.

To the inexperienced, there may not be a real difference, but to the collector, the condition matters. Here are three $20 gold pieces in extremely fine—45 condition, mint state—65, and proof—65+. The 1854 coin is just short of uncirculated, with minor bits of wear evident in the field and hair. The 1870 is a beautiful dazzling uncirculated coin. The 1901 has mirror surfaces. Each is priced accordingly.

Before You Collect

Grading Coins

The condition that a coin is in helps to determine its worth and desirability, and also its aesthetic value. The top of the line is *uncirculated* (which on a 1 to 70 numerical scale ranks as 60 to 70), meaning that the coin is as fresh as the day it left the mint, with all the sheen and luster of a new copper penny obtained from a fresh bank roll. At the lower end of the scale is a coin in *good* condition (10 on the scale), which means that it has seen extensive circulation, is worn in appearance, with the lettering merged together and the design not at all clear. In between are many different conditions, which include *very good* (12 to 15, a bit better than good, with slightly less wear); *fine* (15 to 25 on the scale, the average circulated condition); *very fine* (30 to 35 on the scale, a bit better than average circulated); *extremely fine* (40 to 45 on the scale, much better than average circulated, but still worn on the high spots of the design, which prohibits it from reaching the uncirculated status); and finally *about* or *almost uncirculated* (or 55 to 60 on the scale, a coin that has had only the most minimal circulation and thus contains some slight markings on the metal as a result of friction).

To give more than the most general description of coin grading would require extensive analysis. Fortunately, the American Numismatic Association in 1978 published a major book, fully illustrated, in which the grades of every U.S. coin series are set forth at length. This *Official Guide to Grading* after revised editions has now achieved a good measure of acceptability. From novice to expert, collectors can readily utilize the guide simply by identifying the series or denomination, then placing the specimen coin next to the drawing until a near-match is found. In addition, several other guidebooks to grading are available.

The Counterfeit Coin

For the modern collector, there is perhaps no single scourge greater than that of the counterfeit coin. Particularly for those who collect gold coinage, the number of spurious specimens available for purchase is nothing short of incredible.

Part of the reason for the prevalence of gold counterfeits has to do with the laws of the United States, which between 1934 and 1975 made it illegal to own gold bullion but legal to own gold coin, then selling at a premium above the price of bullion. Individuals abroad who could own gold had the bullion turned into counterfeit coin, then exported it to the United States and sold it to collectors at a price far in excess of the bullion's worth.

Counterfeits of this type are usually excellent and difficult to detect. Common and rare coins alike are the subject of this invasion; only with skill and diligence can one avoid getting stuck.

For the collector who is serious about making purchases of gold coins—particularly expensive ones—the best solution is to try to test the coins for their counterfeit status. This involves substantially more than the suggestion of the Secret Service that the coins be examined for excessive grease or dropped for their ring. In the first place, counterfeiters are sophisticated and produce their coins from presses every bit as good as their counterparts at the various American mints. Secondly, if the coin is good, the nicks and scratches that result from this treatment will make it less desirable to other collectors and hence less valuable.

In some instances, scientific instruments used by authentification agencies are needed to detect a phony coin. There are private certification services available that offer a guarantee of sorts as to the genuine status of coins. The oldest is the American Numismatic Association Certification Service (at 818 North Cascade Avenue, Colorado Springs, Colorado 80901), which charges a fee based on the estimated worth of the coin to determine whether the coin is good or merely a good phony. Others include the International Numismatic Service, P.O. Box 19386, Washington, D.C., and Kahlindoor, which also grades diamonds, located in New York City.

Acquiring Coins

One means of acquiring coins, tokens, medals, or paper money is obvious—purchase from a reliable dealer. Coins can also be acquired by trading or barter with other collectors, by purchase at public auction, or by the exciting, if unpredictable, alternative of using metal detectors to hunt for "buried treasure."

The seller can be a coin dealer, another collector, or simply someone with an item of interest to you as a collector. Prices can be low or extraordinarily high, and are not always dependent on how rare the item is. The critical factor is usually the relative knowledge of both seller and prospective buyer.

Dealers

Aside from the "junk box" approach, a number of coin dealers across the country maintain offices or shops. A visit to them is often instructive, and most dealers are qualified to purchase or sell at fair prices the rare or unusual coin you desire. Two weekly coin publications, *Coin World* and *Numismatic News,* also contain advertisements from hundreds of dealers and collectors. *COINage Magazine,* which has the largest circulation of any coin periodical, is a monthly sold chiefly on newsstands, as is *Coins Magazine.* Each contains stories about coins, news of interest, and advertising. These advertisements usually encourage mail purchases, and most collectors I know who have purchased coins in this way are entirely satisfied. Both newspapers have strict advertising standards and investigate people placing ads in an attempt to police potentially disreputable sellers. Terms of sale usually permit buyers to return any goods purchased within a reasonable time.

To find a coin shop near you, start with the Yellow Pages of the telephone directory. You may wish to seek out a member of a major hobby or trade organization with a code of ethics and other protection. In alphabetical order, these organizations include the following, whose addresses and telephone numbers appear in the section on Sources: American Numismatic Association; Industry Council for Tangible Assets; National Association of Coin & Precious Metals Dealers; Professional Numismatic Guild; and Retail Coin Dealer's Association. Then write to one or more of these organizations to ask for a list of dealers in your area who are members of their organization, an assurance that you are doing business with a reputable coin shop. Coin shows or conventions are also excellent places to learn more and to build your collection. Dealers come from all over to sell their wares, and collectors to swap, buy, and sell. The ANA convention has the largest gathering and is held in a different section of the country each year to ensure maximum participation.

Most dealers of coins have what they call "junk boxes," usually an old cigar box containing hundreds or even thousands of coins, tokens, and medals. For a nominal sum one can search through the box and pick out anything that suits one's fancy. A number of key specimens, genuinely rare pieces, have been found in this way. In some instances, the pieces were picked up because the dealer simply did not know what they were (most people cannot be familiar with all areas of coin collecting) or because a distinctive piece, though little known to most people, was detected by a specialist. In any case, "cherry picking" has long been a favorite pastime of collectors and remains an important means of acquiring tokens, medals, and coins—often at a fraction of their true value.

Trading

Trading or swapping coins is perhaps the single most challenging aspect of collecting. Here, traders match wits—not to mention key pieces they hope other collectors will be interested in. Conventions or coin clubs often provide the settings for collectors' meetings. Sometimes one collector seeks out another who is believed to have a desirable piece; others may take a more organized approach, based on knowledge of the locale, colleagues, and items generally

Comparing a coin to its catalogued description, which here includes a photograph.

traded. It is also possible to exchange coins for medals, tokens for coins, or paper money for medals.

Among the numismatic publications, *Coin World*'s "trading post" classified advertisement section regularly carries ads from collectors (or in some rare instances dealers) who will consider swapping coins. To be sure, there are bargain hunters everywhere, but the essence of a swap is a fair deal for both parties. So long as this is considered the key element, it is hard to lose from this method of acquiring coins.

Public Auctions

A public auction is an important means of purchasing coins and selling collections. A number of auction houses in the United States deal almost exclusively in coins. All have regular monthly or bimonthly auctions of coins thoroughly described in their catalogues. Mail bids are welcomed, although of course attendance in person can be desirable.

Generally, a catalogue for an auction lists a number of lots, each containing a single coin or set of coins, and adds a full description of date, mint mark, condition, and other identifiable features. Sometimes a photograph of the coin is

Prospective bidders line up to examine lots on which they contemplate bidding.

included, especially if it is of particular quality or rare.

It is not unusual for six hundred or more persons to attend three or four sessions of a major auction, and for more than a thousand persons to send in mail bids on individual items. Auctioneers do not generally permit "unlimited" or "buy" bids to be placed through the mails—meaning that the prospective purchaser is willing to go to any limit to acquire a particular specimen. For those who are so inclined, attendance either in person or through an agent is the answer. The auction sale is conducted like any other public offering. The lots are called out consecutively, and bids are solicited from the audience and those who have bid by mail (their bids have been entered in the bid book). Bidding usually begins with the highest mail bid less 20 percent. If there is no bidding, the coin is sold to the "book" for the initial price announced. Otherwise the floor bids against the book until all the mail bids are surpassed. Thereafter, the floor bidders compete with each other until there are no further bids. The auctioneer will "knock down" the coin for that price with the standard cry, "Once, twice, sold."

While the terms of sale may vary, depending on the auction company, most auctions in the coin field are conducted

This 1907 ultra-high-relief sold for $242,000 in 1982. Another specimen sold for $200,000 in 1974, and a virtually identical specimen for $3,800 in 1950.

without reserves. This means that when a coin is placed on the block, the auctioneer must accept bids at any level. For some, the system can provide the bargain of a lifetime; it occasionally happens that bidders much interested in a piece are absent when it is placed on the bidding block, and as a result a nominal bid from another person can take the coin. The reverse is equally true, for nowhere in coin collecting does the adrenaline start to flow as in an auction room. The very air becomes electrified and the crowd senses it. Unlike the practice at most auctions, it is rare for a coin sale auctioneer to watch bidders for secret signals, such as a twitch of an eyebrow or a flick of a lighter. But it is not uncommon to see discreet bidding from those present, for usually more than one person wishes to acquire the coin.

Coins placed on the auction block range in price from nominal to expensive, and the realized price can run anywhere from $10 to several hundred thousand dollars. For the person newly interested in coin collecting (and even for the experienced), a coin auction dramatically brings home the excitement of acquisition. Consider, for example, a May 1974 auction by Stack's, a leading New York City coin dealer and auctioneer. Compared to most auctions the number of lots was small, but the quality was outstanding. The star attraction was a 1907 double eagle in extremely high relief, produced as a pattern, which had been given to President Theodore Roosevelt and to a dozen other people.

The $20 gold piece was placed on the bidding block as part of a 676-lot sale consisting entirely of gold coins. The crowd was prepared for spirited bidding. The auctioneers had supplied a two-page description of the coin, consisting of a photograph enlarged several times, its full history and pedigree, and prior sales of other specimens. Two earlier auctions were mentioned: a comparable piece from the J. F. Bell Collection sold by Stack's in 1944 had brought $2,800; and in 1950, B. Max Mehl sold composer Jerome Kern's specimen for $3,800. It was reported that earlier in 1974 dealer Abe Kosoff had negotiated the private sale of a specimen for $125,000. For their part, the cataloguers anticipated a price in the range of $125,000 to $150,000, which would have been the highest price ever paid for a coin at a public auction.

The bidding opened at $110,000, and in short order a number of individuals began to speak for the piece. The audience of several hundred listened in dead silence as the auctioneer recognized the hands of those bidding. When the $150,000 mark (the previous record for a coin sold at auction, an 1804 silver dollar) was passed, the crowd gasped audibly. A few bidders dropped out, but the bidding continued as excitement intensified to near-pandemonium. Finally, the auctioneer called out $200,000, and a sole bidder raised his arm ever so slightly. "Once," said Benjamin Stack; "twice," then "last call at $200,000, sold to 'M.' "

There was spontaneous applause, an outburst of "Recess, recess," then a five-minute break in the proceedings as dozens of individuals went up to Luis Vigdor, representing Manfra, Tordella & Brookes, the purchasers, who had been prepared to go as high as $300,000 for the coin. Meanwhile, the auctioneers, in the words of Harvey G. Stack, stood by speechless. Later, in assessing the entire sale, which grossed $2.3 million, they spoke of the enthusiasm and determination of the bidders and wondered whether any future auctions would equal it.

Auctions historically have been the way that major collections are disposed of. They attract a maximum audience of prospective bidders and, generally, a price determined by the marketplace. Coins from more famous sales bear pedigrees for life; sometimes this adds to their value. The catalogues of great sales of the nineteenth and twentieth centuries are themselves collected and form an invaluable research tool.

In recent years, some "name" sales have been more spectacular than others. In 1979, four old-line firms initiated a joint venture that has continued annually ever since: a once-a-year sale with a common catalogue in which each firm has a 500-lot limit. The two thousand coins in the "Auction '79" included the Coin & Currency Institute's specimen of the fabled Brasher doubloon. No Brashers had been on the market in more than a half century and a spirited contest developed. The $435,000 realized pleased Arthur Friedberg, who declared it a "historic price for a historic coin." Yet within eighteen months, another Brasher was in a dramatic bidding contest between dealer Art Kagin of Des Moines and New York attorney Martin Monas, bidding for a Long Island–based client who is a private collector.

As the bidding edged to where no coin had ever gone before, Kagin was urged on by the crowd, many of whom knew him as a dealer of some fifty years in the field. "Go, Art, go!" they chanted. But Kagin was bidding for his own account, and Monas took it at $725,000—a figure which remains the most ever paid for an American coin at public sale.

The Garrett triumph was quickly followed by the Bowers organization's sale of the U.S. Gold Coin Collection, which knowledgeable observers immediately identified as being the collection formed by the late Baltimore industrialist, Louis Eliasberg. In stellar fashion, it brought over $10 million in less than a week of sessions in New York. Prices included a $625,000 bid for a unique 1870-S gold dollar, plus the ubiquitous 10 percent buyer's premium that has emerged as an industry standard.

To be sure, not every auction is this dramatic. But the excitement of acquiring a coin—even at $20 rather than $200,000—is something that every collector appreciates from attending a first auction sale. Once hooked, beware. Auctions can become a most tempting way to sell (and buy) coins.

The former rule that the seller, not the buyer, pays a commission of up to 20 percent to the auction house for cataloguing, advertising, and merchandising the sales no longer applies. Most firms now charge nominal buyer's fees of about 10 percent; all have catalogues for the various sales at minimal charges. In the Sources section at the back of this book you will find a list of the various firms that regularly conduct coin auction sales. There are of course many other sources for this information. By reading *Coin World* or *Numismatic News* it is possible to keep up with auction sales as well as the prices realized.

Randall hoard cents — uncirculated, of course — were found in a keg.

Conventions

A number of state, regional, and local organizations hold conventions periodically. Perhaps the best way to keep track of these is to consult *The Numismatist,* the ANA monthly journal, which lists a calendar of shows, or the comparable (though expanded) listings in the two weekly coin newspapers. Most are listed by city, not region.

"Antiquing" and searching for hidden treasure are among the fastest growing hobbies peripherally connected with coin collecting. Those who hunt strictly for numismatic items call themselves "coin shooters" and use metal detectors to comb beaches and remote areas of desert or barren land in hope of finding relics from the past. Some people seek to examine the ocean floor for treasure that may have been left by the Spanish Armada or other lost ships, and they can be extremely successful. However, before undertaking such an endeavor at great expense, one should become familiar with the laws of several states. Texas and Florida, for example, which are known to have offshore wrecks from colonial days, have laws that automatically deed to the state portions of any treasure found. In England, all gold or silver treasure or hidden riches belong to the Crown.

For modern collectors, it would appear at first blush that the law of treasure trove has little application. Yet in the past few years it has increasingly moved to the forefront, particularly with respect to finds in the coastal waterways from eons gone by. In Florida, for example, treasure salvors have rescued the hoard of coins from the *Achoca,* a Spanish man-of-war. Mel Fisher conceived of the dive, and expended substantial sums in locating the treasure, which included a number of numismatically significant pieces, as well as many pieces of eight that were in the vaults of the Spanish galleon.

The state of Florida sued Fisher for possession of the hoard, claiming that the treasure divined to the state. The case went all the way to the United States Supreme Court, which ruled that Fisher, and not the state, was entitled to the bulk of the booty. The mystique of the *Achoca* appears limited to noncollectors, however. Pieces of eight are relatively common, and available, and those left under brine and seaweed for three centuries or more are not the best of examples. Nonetheless, it demonstrates clearly that even as the twentieth century draws to a close, there still remain vast repositories of coins for the aggressive finder who is willing to take on the elements and (increasingly) the courts.

Throughout coin-collecting history there have been fascinating stories about such finds. The so-called Randall hoard cents—approximately twenty thousand uncirculated large cents that were found in a discarded keg in a Philadelphia basement in the mid-nineteenth century—have been sold and resold for more than a hundred years by the finders' heirs and others. Other examples from the Civil War period show that both Southerners and Northerners buried coin against the possibility of defeat on the battlefield and subsequent financial ruin. Today these coins are greatly prized by collectors, as much for the tales that can be spun about their possible origin as for their value.

ORGANIZING A COLLECTION

The next step in collecting coins is to plan and organize them in a coherent manner. Ultimately, this avoids needless duplication and, by not flooding the marketplace upon resale to other collectors or dealers, seems to foster higher prices from purchasers seeking a well-rounded collection.

Many collectors begin by acquiring coins of a particular series or type. They usually purchase the type of coin album available in department stores and then fill the holes date by date, mint mark by mint mark. Perhaps the most popular series collected in this way is the Lincoln head cent, which has been produced at the Philadelphia, Denver, and San Francisco mints since 1909. It is the longest running series in the history of American coinage. For convenience, a collection of Lincoln cents is usually divided into two or more parts. This division has been influenced by commercial album makers, who for reasons of size, weight, and bulk split the series into two albums. Most dealers sell (and collectors buy) an "early" Lincoln set, from 1909 to 1940, and a "later" series, from 1941 to date.

Commercial albums have also been prepared for other series, providing relatively easy storage and viewing. Most albums are about the size of a standard sheet of $8\frac{1}{2}$ by 11 inch letter paper and contain slots the exact diameter of the coins to be displayed. Thin sheets of plastic above and below the coins permit viewing without handling. Fingerprints, oil, and grease deposited on the surface of an uncirculated specimen by too much handling can cause damage. For other types of complete collections, custommade holders of Lucite may be used, all readily available from dealers and distributors of numismatic supplies.

Collection of coin types is another popular means of acquiring rare and unusual coins. A type collection usually consists of one specimen of each type of coin produced for a specific denomination. The quarter dollar, for instance, has at least fifteen types (described in the accompanying chart), and they are worth examining.

Some of the fifteen types of quarters struck since 1796.

QUARTER DOLLARS

First Date of Issue	Design Distinction or Type Marking
1796	Liberty obverse, "puny" eagle reverse
1804–07	Same obverse, heraldic eagle reverse
1815–28	Liberty facing left, eagle pose changed
1831–38	New reverse without E Pluribus Unum ("Out of Many, One") motto, size reduced from 27 mm. to 24.3 mm.
1838	Seated Liberty design introduced
1853	Weight reduction, arrows placed at date to signal change; rays added to reverse for same purpose.
1866	"In God We Trust" motto introduced on reverse
1873	Weight reduction, arrowheads at date
1892–1916	Barber-designed Liberty introduced (Greco-Roman interpretation by chief engraver)
1916	Liberty design standing, introduced with exposed breast and thigh
1917	Mail chain placed on Liberty breast, thigh covered
1925	Date recessed for better wear
1932	Washington quarter design introduced
1965	Clad coinage (copper and nickel instead of silver) begins
1976	Bicentennial commemorative design with dual date 1776–1976, silver-clad quarter produced with copper–nickel-clad issues.

Robert W. Cornely, a collector and a dealer in coins, holds a proof set in his hands. On the desk in front of him are currency in holders and coins encased in plastic.

In acquiring a type collection of quarters, or coins of any other denomination, remember that you alone as the collector set the bounds of what is to be acquired. Twentieth-century type sets are growing increasingly common and now consist of many coins in a variety of designs and denominations. To give one example, the cent pieces include the Indian head cent, made from 1859 to 1909; the Lincoln head cent, produced between 1909 and 1958; the 1909 "V.D.B.", with the initials of the designer, Victor David Brenner, boldly included on the reverse; the 1943 steel cent; the Lincoln Memorial reverse in 1959; and, for the purist, the compositional changes of 1944 and 1962.

It is also possible to collect first date of issue for particular series, types, or denominations. The key is not the scarcity of the coin but the collector's perception of what he or she wishes to acquire and display.

Most collectors wisely begin by limiting themselves to one particular area and then expand to another specialized field. The first move is sometimes to another series but more often to a type collection of some kind—denomination, mint marks, or even the coins of a particular designer. From there, the limits are set only by the collector's imagination. Perhaps the one rule is that there must be organization of some sort, for cataloguing, sale, and appreciation of the collection all become easier if there is some order to the way in which it was assembled.

DISPLAYING A COLLECTION

Most collectors feel an overwhelming desire to display some of the coins, medals, currency, and tokens they have acquired. Whether the exhibition is mounted professionally, as in a museum, or simply for enjoyment at home, several rules should be observed to preserve the pieces from damage or ruin.

First, care should be taken that no foreign substance, from cigarette smoke to furniture polish, comes into contact with a silver or copper coin. Oxidation readily results, and

Reverse of a 1909-S VDB cent with an Indian head cent also struck at San Francisco the same year. The "VDB" is hard to locate, but is at the bottom between the wheat chaffs; the mint mark on the Indian cent is beneath the wreath. Both coins are scarce today.

the tarnish, though it can be removed by experts, may leave an unattractive patina that damages the coin value. Certain cloths used in mounting museum displays prevent oxidation while providing attractive background color and texture.

How Not to Clean

A novice collector may be very tempted to take an older coin in circulated condition and try to "clean" it, in an attempt to make the coin appear to have the luster of an uncirculated specimen. The sad thing is that if a collector yields to this temptation, the likely result will be a coin worth substantially less after the experiment than at the beginning. Most experienced collectors and dealers respond with a single word when asked the familiar question on how to clean coins: "Don't!"

Any attempt at cleaning a coin—whether by polishing it with a metal cleanser or dipping it in a special solution—has the identical effect: the cleaner will eat away at the metal, though perhaps only microscopically, and create a distinctively unaesthetic appearance that can be seen under any magnifying glass utilized at 10 power (ten times the viewing resolution of the naked eye).

Skilled dealers and collectors do clean some coins, of course. A cotton swab dipped in alcohol solution and rubbed gently over the surface is usually sufficient to remove some top dirt on uncirculated coins without actually damaging the surface or leaving a permanent reminder of the impression. Olive oil has also been used successfully to float dirt free.

If you feel that you must try cleaning coins, the best method is to experiment on nonvaluable pieces. And at that, *leave copper coins alone.* They can almost never be cleaned properly, even by an expert, and damage to them is virtually irreparable. Silver coins can be retoned in time to give an attractive sheen or appearance, but copper, for some reason, retains its "cleaned" look for years.

Mounting and Display

In mounting coins, museum wax or beeswax available from art supply stores is preferable to some commercially prepared items, which can permanently scar the surface of a coin; the museum wax can be removed later without leaving so much as a mark on the top layer.

For home display, there are a number of methods possible, ranging from self-contained stands to coffee tables with space under glass tops for coins and medals. By modifying certain "how to" book plans, it is possible to create a coin-display board of your own. The essential tool is a drill bit capable of boring a hole into the plywood board slightly larger than the coin or medal to be displayed. A thin felt covering then can be placed on the board and the coin fit snugly into the hole. For wall mounting, Lucite holders purchased commercially can be used.

In recent years, a number of pieces of "collector furniture" have been manufactured for those who want professional pieces to display their prizes; some of the finest factories and craftsmen in the nation have produced furniture that blends well with interiors ranging from colonial to contemporary.

Mounting. American Numismatic Society collection.

The beauty of displays reached a new height with the American Numismatic Society's "World of Coins" exhibit, unveiled in late 1983 at the organization's building on Audubon Terrace in upper Manhattan.

An entire wing of the downstairs exhibit area was gutted, and an exhibition that traces money from its earliest origins to contemporary credit cards was mounted at a cost of over $100,000.

What is particularly interesting about the ANS exhibition is that it is so well thought out. Not only are coins easily viewed, but the descriptions of them are mounted close to the glass; the items seem to be floating in space, to magical effect—and the delight of the viewer.

According to Leslie Elam, director of the ANS, the exhibit is intended to be a permanent one and will probably be displayed for the next decade or so, giving both young and old (the serious collector, and the beginner) a totally new awareness of what the world of coin collecting is all about.

In a similar vein, the American Numismatic Association in Colorado Springs has also revitalized its exhibition and visitor facilities. The downstairs Stack's Galleries now display a rotating series of exhibits, which in 1984 proved to be timely: the coinage and medals of the Olympics, honoring the 1984 Games at Los Angeles, but covering ancient coinage issues as well as modern ones, and medallic tributes since the 1896 revitalization in Athens. There was also a marvelously interesting show featuring coins and autographs of American presidents in a distinctive blend of history and politics.

Regardless of the method you use to display your coins, the pieces should be secure, so that a slight jarring or bump will not send thousands of dollars worth of rarities against the surface of the display area, where damage might occur.

For the most part, a fine display requires imagination and a sense of what is artistically pleasing. A strategically placed medallion can become a striking work of art. So can a grouping of several coins in a wall plaque. The key to displaying coins or other numismatic items, just as in hanging pictures, is attractive presentation that makes the pieces stand out. Whether you use furniture, wall displays, or bookcases to exhibit your numismatic collection, your aim is to create an aesthetically pleasing display while also safeguarding your collection.

Mounting. American Numismatic Society collection.

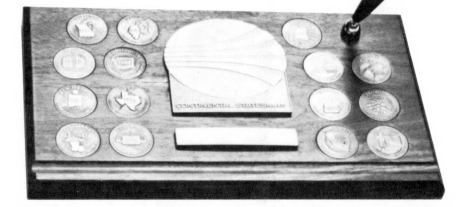

Coins for Investment

Probably the goal of nearly everyone who decides first to collect coins and then to invest in them is a $100,000 coin collection. Unlike many daydreams, this one can be realized through careful, judicious investment in coins over a period of years. It takes dedication, persistence, time, and systematic purchases. It also requires an understanding of what coin collecting and investing are all about and why a coin achieves the rarity that virtually ensures increasing value.

There are no rules for successful coin investment, but certain points should be carefully considered to convert a hobby into a long-term profitable investment. By heeding them and using common sense, the collector can produce a fine collection of coin rarities that is bound to increase in value, usually at a rate substantially higher than that of inflation.

INVESTMENT GUIDELINES

First and perhaps foremost, it is essential that the prospective purchaser of coins learn something about what is to be acquired. This involves learning how coins are collected (by type or design, date, series, or other means), how they are generally sold (at auction, by trade, at conventions, over the counter, and other methods), the quality or grade of coins (which can vary greatly) and, where applicable, the provenance or history of a particular piece. This basic rule of primary study is no different for the purchaser of a stock or bond, real estate, or any other investment: the potential

Acquiring Athens city-state coins such as this one is a good beginning.

investor should enter the market with some knowledge of the fundamentals.

Once the basics are mastered, the next step is to choose an area in which to collect. As a buyer, your real edge in dealing with sellers will be the knowledge you have in a specific area that a generalist may not have. For example, rather than choosing the broad category "ancient coins," it would be wiser to narrow the field to coins of ancient Greece, and perhaps to narrow it still further by concentrating on the monies of the city-state of Athens. A modern collector could begin with twentieth-century type coins or even Lincoln head cents.

JUDGING RARITY

A brief period of time spent reading about your chosen field is essential. From books on American gold coins, for example, one learns that although the U.S. Mint produced 351 million gold coins between 1795 and 1933, it is likely

This 1889 half eagle, with a mintage of 7,565 pieces, is valued at more than $700 in uncirculated condition. The 1798 half eagle, with a mintage of 24,867 pieces, is worth more than three times as much in about uncirculated condition.

that a substantial quantity of those coins (perhaps as much as three-quarters) was melted either by the U.S. Mint itself for recoinage or during the 1933 recall, or by individuals who sought to take advantage of the bullion content of gold coin. Moreover, despite relatively high mintage figures, very few American gold coins struck prior to 1834 are extant. The bullion value of these coins was substantially greater than their face worth, and consequently the coins went abroad to melting cauldrons. A 1798 half eagle, or $5 gold piece, with a recorded mintage of 24,867 pieces is thus worth substantially more than an 1889 $5 gold piece from the Philadelphia Mint, of which just 7,565 pieces were produced.

The federal government melted nearly a third of all 20-cent pieces ever made.

Melting of this type is not limited to gold coins. While it is widely known that all but about a dozen of the 10,000 20-cent pieces produced at the Carson City Mint in 1876 were melted soon afterward, additional research and reading reveals that the government itself destroyed nearly one-third of all the 20-cent pieces ever minted. Records of the Bureau of the Mint (reprinted in the *Annual Report* of the director of the U.S. Mint, a publication of the Government Printing Office) show that more than 390,000 20-cent pieces were melted by the government between 1895 and 1954; just 1,355,000 pieces were minted during the four-year lifetime of the series. This fact makes the 20-cent piece especially rare.

Recorded mintage figures are always a good starting place, and they are conveniently listed in several *Annual Reports* by directors of the U.S. Mint, as well as in several of the guidebooks listed in the Bibliography. It must always be remembered that, in addition to the gold melting and odd-denomination destruction, a massive recall of silver coinage by the government in the 1960s decimated the population of even common-date coins that predate 1965. Thus, a significant portion of what should be common-date coinage is actually scarce and one day might even reach true rarity status.

In some early mint records, the figures listed may be deceptive. The case of the 1804 silver dollar is illustrative.

Mint records show 19,000 pieces coined; in fact, no more than a dozen or so were made — and those were produced thirty-two years later. This 1804 silver dollar is today valued at more than $500,000.

Elaborate research by two dedicated scholars revealed that the 19,000 pieces listed in early U.S. Mint records for silver dollar production in 1804 were actually for the 1803 dollars. In the early part of the nineteenth century, the mint practice was to use the previous year's dies until they were no longer workable but to record coins produced as if they were dated in the year that they were struck. The result for the twentieth-century collector is a key rarity, valued into the six figures, which shows a recorded mintage of 19,000 pieces.

All this undoubtedly forms a confusing maze for the novice investor and points up the importance of buying the book before the coin. The lessons to be learned and money saved are staggering.

GRADING

The grading of coins, once a mysterious art, has been vastly simplified over the past decade. Several books that teach a step-by-step method for learning about wear and tear on coins—which can differ widely among series—are now available (and are listed in the Bibliography). The importance of grading cannot be overlooked by the investor, because plainly a coin value is determined almost as much by its condition or state of preservation as by its mintage and subsidiary factors. The price differential can be seen in a typical example, an 1860 quarter eagle (mintage 22,675). At the Theodore Ullmer sale held by Stack's in May 1974, a proof specimen (or special, highly polished coin produced at the mint for collectors) brought $4,100 in a spirited bidding contest after opening at $1,250. In contrast, an uncirculated specimen (or a coin produced for commerce but never used), sold at the Winter Collection auction by Stack's in February 1974, realized just $300. At the George Scanlon auction held by Stack's in October 1973, two 1860 specimens were offered: one a proof piece, with a slight "rub" on the surface, a defect that brought the price down to $675. An about uncirculated specimen went for about $140. The price difference between the about uncirculated and the uncirculated is substantial (more than 50 percent). At the 1975 convention sale of the American Numismatic Association, conducted by Superior Galleries, Los Angeles, an *extremely fine* specimen of the coin brought $95, again showing that pieces in poorer condition bring proportionally lower prices.

Although it takes time to learn grading standards, the guidebooks on the subject are excellent tutors. It may be difficult at first to understand why a double eagle from the Carson City Mint can be termed choice, about uncirculated, when its surface is pockmarked and scratched. It turns out, however, that the Carson City Mint (CC) production methods were so primitive that nearly every coin of large size emerged from their presses in that manner. Further inquiry reveals that the rarest of gold coins from the Carson Mint, an 1870-CC double eagle, is totally unknown in uncirculated condition, and that even the experts do not know whether to define the best piece known as extremely fine or about uncirculated.

The different approaches have to do with the probability of mint-created damage to the surface of the coin. But most pieces do not have this problem, and the use of a grading guide can greatly simplify the novice investor's troubles, as

Unknown in pristine uncirculated condition, nearly all 1870-CC double eagles were badly scuffed and bagmarked at the mint.

53

can making purchases from reputable dealers who describe their wares accurately.

EVALUATION

Researching which coins are "ripe" for purchase, not unlike charting a stock prior to taking the plunge, is common in coin investing. Many coins, particularly those sold at public auction, have established pedigrees, and through these it is possible to estimate the potential value of a particular date, series, or type. Those interested in doing research on coins without a pedigree can chart their progress through back issues of coin newspapers and magazines, nearly all of which contain advertising offering thousands of coins for sale. Where there is an upward price trend, the odds are strong that it will continue into the future. There is an established market in the United States for sale of second-hand auction catalogues and books that pertain to numismatics—a gold mine of information for the serious researcher and investor wishing to track price changes over periods of time.

This 1794 silver dollar became the world's first $100,000 coin, at an auction conducted by Superior Galleries, Los Angeles, in October 1973. A prior pedigree history shows that of 1,758 coins struck, only about 50 are extant today. At the same sale in which this uncirculated specimen realized $110,000, a very fine piece brought $12,500—demonstrating the importance of condition.

This Hawaiian 1883/3 "overdate" was discovered as a result of the close scrutiny of dealer Tom McAfee. Note the slight doubling of the last digit.

Examining coins themselves is another important clue, for it inevitably leads to the discovery of varieties and oddities. Many of these finds are relatively recent; not until the mid-1960s were silver dollars examined comprehensively, and it was not until the mid-1970s that a comprehensive catalogue and encyclopedia was published listing the different varieties of silver dollars struck from 1878 to 1935. Other fields are equally ripe, and valuable varieties and types (such as overdates, where the mint has punched one year's date over another and both show through on the coin) are still waiting to be discovered in the case or even the junk box of a dealer who is too busy to sort out the coins for proper identification.

TIMING

Another important element in the decision to invest is timing. This is no different from any other purchase with prospective growth. The useful adage, "Buy low and sell high," applies to coins as well as stocks, but unlike the investor who trades in stocks and is provided with a daily composite index (the Dow Jones), how can an investor in coins know whether there is flux in the market? One answer is provided by *Coin World,* which publishes news and trends for various coins. On a monthly basis, the whole body of American coinage in virtually every collectable condition is covered. As a supplement for collectors and investors, a composite index of coin prices (usually done series by series) is included in the price trends. This enables an individual to examine Indian head cents (struck between 1859 and 1909), for example, and see how that series has progressed over weeks, months, or even years since 1960, when *Coin World* was first published. Another publication is the *Coin Dealer Newsletter,* or "Grey Sheet," which charts key areas of investor and collector interest. This Monday morning report of the coin market keeps close tabs on dealer teletype transactions and the pulse of the marketplace.

Other elements of timing concern the state of the national economy, the price of gold, silver, and other precious metals, and additional investment factors that daily find their way to the financial pages of the newspaper. When the market price of gold jumps, the value of most gold coins will also increase. Since a sizable number are of relatively common vintage, much of their value resides in their bullion content. Thus, when a common-date $20 gold piece, or double eagle, is purchased, a substantial percentage of the cost is not its numismatic value, or worth to collectors, but rather the valuation of 0.9675 troy ounces of gold (there are 12 troy ounces in 1 pound of gold). When that metal was priced at $20.67 an ounce, the official rate from 1837 to 1933, the double eagle contained $19.99 in gold; at $35 an ounce, the official rate from 1934 to 1971, the double eagle contained $33.86 worth of gold and was usually sold for about $48. That means that 70 percent of the purchase price consisted of bullion, and the remainder was a numismatic premium. With gold at $400 an ounce, the same double eagle would have a bullion content worth $387.00, and at the same ratio the numismatic worth would carry the coin's value up to $567.04. The bullion value of commonly available gold coins has increasingly taken over the major portion of their worth, especially in higher denominations.

Perhaps because silver is considered to be a less noble metal, the price correspondence so apparent with gold cannot occur in quite the same dramatic manner. If silver prices on recognized commodity markets were suddenly to increase by 8 or 9 percent, they would surely make headlines, but the effect on most coins would be minimal. These leaps would really affect only the relatively common-date or readily available coins issued before 1965. In the early 1960s, Roosevelt dimes were frequently offered to collectors in choice uncirculated condition for a bare 5-cent premium over their face value, or 15 cents, at least for the most common dates. A circulated specimen was sometimes offered for a mere 12 cents. By the middle of the 1970s, the price had jumped past 60 cents, and as silver climbed to $17 and beyond, a $1.50 asking price for that same Roosevelt dime was commonplace. If the gain seems small, consider it in percentage terms—as a return on investment. If that 15-cent coin purchased in 1960 brought $3.50 today, a 2,233 percent return on invested capital is achieved. In quantity purchase, the result is the same.

There is something extraordinary about such an occurrence: although 1,357,517,180 Roosevelt dimes were produced at the Denver Mint in 1964, they still have a dollar value equal to that of uncirculated Mercury head dimes of common vintage in the late 1940s. This example points out that the astute collector and investor should be looking at other economic price trends—such as the rising prices of copper and nickel—to ascertain whether or not a similar event might precipitate the withdrawal from circulation of copper pennies and 5-cent pieces.

One must also take into consideration the size of the investment and whether to make steady purchases over a period of time, as well as the length of time it takes to build the collection, and which purchases to keep rather than sell. Return on investment is the obvious goal for anyone seeking to make substantial gains. It is far more preferable to have a dozen $100 coins that gain 18 percent per year than to have a single coin costing $1,200 that returns 12 percent.

It is necessary to monitor the coin investment almost constantly and to keep track of the rates of growth.

DIVERSIFICATION

Investors should also consider diversified portfolios. This has more to do with the psychology of price increments than with anything else, but through careful diversification the rates of growth may increase at a faster rate. One is far more likely to purchase a coin that has risen in value from $250 to $400 than one that has increased in value during the same period from $4,500 to $7,200. Moreover, if a collector owns a dozen or even two dozen coins with a total worth of one prize specimen, the odds are strong that the diversified portfolio will gain more over the long run. To be sure, there are exceptions; the superstars such as the 1804 silver dollar, the 1913 Liberty head nickel, and other "sexy" coins disprove the rule. But they are exceptions.

A "sexy" coin, but difficult to increase at high percentage rates for prolonged periods. This 1907 pattern coin struck from dies executed by Augustus Saint-Gaudens was the capstone of the Dr. John Wilkison pattern collection acquired by Paramount International.

Once a coin's value exceeds $10,000, the number of potential buyers diminishes significantly. To a lesser extent, the same holds true at the $1,000, $2,500, and $5,000 levels. Ability to raise capital partly explains this, but sophisticated investors also know that coin prices can go down in a cyclical manner; hoards can be discovered, collecting interests can change, and a series can become unpopular and difficult to sell; or, if a specimen is scarce and generally unavailable, several dealers may independently decide to sell at the same time. A 20 percent "correction factor" is a good rule of thumb to go by, for a potential "bottoming out," although cases exist where higher drops have occurred.

APPRECIATION

When a rarity is placed on the auction block and two or more collectors are equally interested in obtaining it, the bidding war can send the price significantly higher than if it had been negotiated privately. Moreover, in times of economic stress, when the dollar is under attack, for example, or there is general fear for the health of the economy, unnatural price increments can occur. A case in point is the gold market of May 1974, when it was apparent that Americans would be able legally to own gold bullion by year's end and the dollar was under acute stress. Stack's conducted an auction sale of Theodore Ullmer's gold and other coins, all of which realized record prices. The chart on page 61 shows some of the prices realized at that sale and prior pedigrees where applicable. The results were somewhat astonishing, even a few years later. They show an unnatural growth in price that for the most part could not be sustained. Some of the coins were later resold for less than the record price of the Ullmer auction.

In the late 1970s, as economic inflation steadily depreciated the dollar's purchasing power, the Ullmer records were again shattered in nearly every case. The $200,000 paid at that sale for a 1907 ultra-high-relief double eagle designed by Saint-Gaudens—the highest sum ever paid for an

This coin had a public auction sale of $21,000 in 1967, and rose to $150,000 in May 1974.

American coin—was dwarfed by Donald Kagin's 1979 purchase of another ultra-high relief for $225,000, the sale of Capitol Coin Company's Brasher doubloon for $430,000, and the negotiated sale for $1 million of an 1834 proof set (containing an 1804 silver dollar) by Lester Merkin.

The chart on selected coin prices shows that as a *general* rule, coins advance in value over a period of years. There are exceptions, however. The 1875 $3 gold piece that sold first as part of the Grant Pierce Collection in 1965 and then resold as part of the Charles Jay Collection in 1967 proves the point. The Pierce coin was purchased by Mr. Jay for $21,000 and held for a relatively short period of time for numismatic investments—a bare two years. The time was insufficient, and as a result, on resale, a net loss accrued.

The 1974 Ullmer sale, despite inflated prices that sent the price of the 1875 $3 gold piece to $150,000, does demonstrate the potential increment in value. Prior to the sale, the cataloguers, in an interview with the author subsequently published in *Coin World,* predicted that a $65,000 price would be realized for the coin in question, which would have been a healthy increase from its last sale price.

Some growth is steady, if not spectacular, especially in the short to intermediate run, generally defined as the first three years of holding. During that time, the changes in the coin's value do little more than generally recoup the dealer's profit. Beyond that period, however, the general rule is that unless coins have been bid up in a war between two determined collectors and investors, the value will increase dramatically—sometimes 18 percent annually or more.

Perhaps the best way to visualize the growth in value of coins held for a period of time is to examine a single specimen of some rarity and then compare the prices of similar coins that have been auctioned over a number of years. One coin that lends itself well to this practice is the 1838-O half dollar, a specimen proof coin that was produced in the New Orleans Mint during the first year of operation. To be sure, no two pieces are ever identical, and price comparisons are bound to be faulty or flawed in some manner. But as an illustration of the sustained growth in the numismatic market since the early 1950s, this coin is a fine example.

SELECTED COIN PRICE RECORDS FROM PUBLIC AUCTION SALES WITH PEDIGREE HISTORY

Date	Denomination	Additional Data	Condition	Sale Date	Sale Title & Collection	Price	Subsequent Sales History of Identical Coin					
							Sale Date	Collection & Sale	Sale Price	Sale Date	Collection	Sale Price
1797	$2.50 gold		About uncirculated	5/65	Pierce (S)	$3,600	10/68	Miles (S)	$4,500	5/74	Ullmer (S)	$10,000
1875	$3 gold		proof	5/65	Pierce (S)	21,000	10/67	Jay (S)	20,000	5/74	Ullmer (S)	150,000
1878	proof set	9 coins	proof	3/68	(M)	1,875	12/75	Kensington (B)	4,850	7/77	Lewis (P)	5,500
1854	3 cent	silver	proof	2/72	Carson (M)	575	8/77	ANA (K)	1,800			
1859	half dime	transitional	proof	11/54	DuPont (S)	525	11/73	Rothert (B)	5,750	8/75	ANA (Su)	7,250
1838	dollar	Gobrecht	proof	9/68	Ostheimer (M)	2,200	2/72	(S)	4,300	4/75	Dalton (S)	7,000
1838-O	50 cents		proof	11/55	Baldenhofer (S)	3,200	3/59	Pelletreau (S)	4,000	10/67	Jay (S)*	14,000

Sellers' abbreviations: (B) — Bowers & Ruddy, Los Angeles, Calif.; (K) — Kagin's, Des Moines, Iowa; (M) — Lester Merkin, New York, N.Y.; (P) — Paramount International, Englewood, Ohio; (S) — Stack's, New York, N.Y.; (Su) — Superior Galleries, Los Angeles, Calif. * refers to subsequent chart on page 62. XF: Extremely fine, just under uncirculated. On the Sheldon scale (1–70:70 = perfection, 60 = uncirculated), extremely fine is 40 to 45. WGC: World's greatest collection, comprising gold and silver coins of Fred C. C. Boyd, sold by A. Kosoff, Abner Kreisberg, Numismatic Gallery, in 1945–1946.

SPECIMENS OF THE 1838-O HALF DOLLAR—
AUCTION SALES CHART

Sale	Date Sold	Prior Sale	Price Realized
F.S. Guggenheimer (S)	Jan. 1953	World's Greatest (N) (1946) at $1,600	$ 3,400
DuPont (S)	Nov. 1954	No prior pedigree	3,500
Baldenhofer (S)	Nov. 1955	No prior pedigree	3,200
ANA (F)	Aug. 1957	No prior pedigree	4,450
Empire (S)	Nov. 1957	No prior pedigree	4,000
R. Pelletreau (S)	March 1959	Baldenhofer—1955	4,000
R.E. Cox, Jr. (S)	April 1962	McAllister	9,500
Charles Jay (S)	Oct. 1967	Pelletreau (S) and Baldenhofer	14,000
ANA (S) (XF)	Aug. 1971	Guggenheimer; WGC 1945	13,000
Reed Hawn (S)	Aug. 1973	Atwater (BMM) 1946 $2,200	41,000
James A. Stack (S)	March 1975	Will W. Neil (BMM) 1947	50,000
E. Yale Clarke (S) (Proof)	Oct. 1975	Jay-Pelletreau- Baldenhofer (S) (1967)	43,000
Auction '83 (Proof)	Aug. 1982	E. Yale Clarke (Jay, Pelletreau, Baldenhofer)	47,500
Robison (Proof)	Feb. 1982	R. E. Cox, Jr.	70,000
Oviedo (XF)	Sep. 1983	1971 ANA Sale	40,700

Abbreviations: (BMM) — B. Max Mehl, the late Texas dealer active in the first half of the twentieth century; (F) — Federal Brand Coin Co., formerly of Cleveland, Ohio; (N) — Numismatic Gallery (Kosoff–Kriesberg), formerly of Beverly Hills, Calif.; (S) — Stack's, New York, N.Y.

Even though the coins are not identical (and some of the proof specimens are in fact impaired), it is clear that the 1838-O half dollar has grown in value from under $4,000 in the early 1950s to $40,000 and beyond today. Advertisements offering for sale several of the specimens listed in the chart have quoted prices above the $60,000 mark; but since the sales are private and lack public record, there is no means of corroborating these figures. Yet even assuming that the $4,000 to $40,000 price is the only valid one, the 900-percent gain over a period of a quarter century is impressive, amounting to an increase of 36 percent annually, or 3 percent per month, a simple (not compound) growth rate. It is equally clear, however, that to sustain such a level for the next quarter century, the coin's price would have to rise to $400,000—which is unlikely, though conceivable.

An 1838-O half dollar — courtesy of Stack's.

WHEN TO SELL

The ideal holding period for any collection is at least a dozen years. It affords the collector an opportunity to acquire coins, watch their values increase, and then sell them at a profit. There are exceptions, of course; some people put their collections together and sell them in a shorter period, while others acquire coins over a lifetime.

If a particular coin shows a sharp increase in value, it may be wise to sell off the coin and use the proceeds to buy several lower-priced pieces with similar value potential. Thus, if one coin were suddenly to decline in value, as sometimes happens, the diversified investor is protected. The collector whose whole investment is tied up in a single specimen is powerless except to take the capital loss or wait.

The tax laws are another reason to diversify, since the "like kind" exchange (permissible under Section 1031 of the Internal Revenue Code) has been held applicable to rare coins. This means that when rare coins are exchanged, there is no tax on the conversion, although there would be tax on any ultimate sale.

The question remains, can a $100,000 coin collection be built on limited investment? Through systematic purchases of even modestly priced coins, it is a distinctly possible goal. Consider the purchase of Indian head cents in uncirculated condition. In early 1970, each coin would have cost about $9. Suppose one purchased ten coins every month at an expenditure of $90, between 1970 and 1974, for a total of six hundred coins. During the last two years of the term, the price rose from $9 to $15, so that the investment would have gone from $90 per month to $150 a month. At the end of the five-year term, the coins were put away and not sold until 1978—a total holding period of eight years from first coin purchase. At $90 per month for thirty-six months ($3,240), plus $150 per month for twenty-four months ($3,600), the total cost of the investment would have been $7,000. In 1978, the average asking price for a choice uncirculated Indian head cent was $70; the investment of $7,000 would now have a value of $42,000. If a decision had been made to invest $2,000 per year, the holding would have been in excess of $63,000; and a longer holding period would bring the sum of $100,000 well within reach.

Most collectors would not, of course, buy this many Indian head cents, but instead would acquire different types of coins—perhaps a type collection or series. Since each coin has a separate price progression, the likelihood of realizing a six-figure collection is even greater through diversification.

By way of contrast, if the same sum had been placed in an interest-bearing account at the rate of 6 percent per annum, or in a long-term certificate of deposit, the gain realized would have been considerably less. Saving $90 per month yields interest of a comparable figure over a one-year period and over a three-year period, and less than a $400 gain is achieved. However, as the investment rises to $150 per month, or $1,800 per year, the return amounts to a comparable figure over a two-year period. By simply placing funds into interest-bearing accounts for a period of five years, a net gain of under $2,000 is achieved, or $9,000 on the original investment. This contrasts with the $42,000 figure quoted for the Indian head cents.

The question frequently is asked whether or not coins are a liquid asset, which a savings account is presumed to be. The answer is decidedly yes. Coins purchased today can be readily converted into cash tomorrow—provided that the item acquired is not obscure, is readily collectable by others, and is in a superior state of preservation.

In order to dispose quickly of a coin, a person need only go to a dealer and strike the bargain. Sometimes, if the coin is of particular interest to other collectors, the dealer may suggest that it be placed at auction, and may even advance part payment of the projected sales price. In other instances, the dealer may have a ready buyer for the coin and simply pay cash over the counter for the specimen. Or a number of other exchanges in whole or part are possible, including the taking of part of the worth of the rarity in other rare coins (which qualifies as a tax-free exchange) and the balance in cash (a capital gain if the investment had been held for a year or more).

There is an even more compelling reason to collect and invest in rare coins, and that has to do with its success relative to other investments. The Wall Street investment banking house of Salomon Brothers in late 1979 produced a study that was reprinted in the Federal Reserve Bank of Boston's prestigious journal *New England Economic Review.* In summary it demonstrated that when viewed over a period of more than a dozen years, the return on investment in rare coins has averaged well over 10 percent per annum on a consistent basis. By contrast, stocks, bonds, and other seemingly "liquid" assets performed well below this percentage.

Salomon Brothers has annually surveyed coins and other collectables, together with more traditional vehicles for investment. The study has been going for seven years, and the results of the latest survey show that for the ten-year period ending June 1982, coins had an average annual return of 22.5 percent, compared to stocks (which averaged 3.9 percent during the same period), Treasury bills (which had a 10.8 percent interest rate factor), and the Consumer Price Index, which moved up marginally to nearly 4 percent.

Over a longer period, coins came out in even better stead. Only petroleum had a higher ranking than coins when looked at over a fifteen-year time frame. Then, coins averaged 17.9 percent annually, compared with silver at 12.6 percent per year, Treasury bills at 8.8 percent (recalling that fifteen years ago money was less expensive), and even high-flying gold, which weighed in at only 16.6 percent.

The chart appears below:

SALOMON BROTHERS
SURVEY OF COLLECTABLES, 1982
(released June 1983)

Item	Annual Rate of Return (1982)	15-Year Average Rate	Rank
Silver	109%	12.6%	6
Stocks	51.8%	5.7%	14
Bonds	39.0%	6.4%	13
Gold	28.6%	16.6%	4
U.S. Coins	16.8%	17.9%	2
Treasury Bills	10.8%	8.8%	9
CPI	3.9%	7.3%	12
Housing	2.1%	8.6%	10
Old Masters	1.8%	7.8%	11
Diamonds	0.0%	10.1%	7
Chinese Ceramics	0.0%	14.2%	5
Foreign Exchange	−4.3%	3.1%	15
Farmland	−5.7%	10.0%	8
Stamps	−6.2%	16.8%	3
Oil	−14.78%	20.4%	1

As part of the tax revolution of 1981, a little noticed provision was slipped in at conference which had the effect of preventing investments into individual retirement accounts with rare coins and other collectables. Incorporated finally as §408(M) of the Internal Revenue Code, this provision does not act as an outright bar to the use of coins or collectables in all retirement accounts, but does prevent their use in any self-directed plan. Where a fiduciary or trustee still believes that coins are a solid investment, and one which a reasonably prudent person would utilize, then it is still permissible under narrowly drawn circumstances to have coins and other collectables in this medium.

In considering any investment, whether for pension or other purposes, it is essential to define the growth goals you have in mind. And there are a number of other factors, in particular what types of coin you should include.

The rate of inflation, and consumer prices, have diminished substantially over the past few years, yet coins have continued to be surprisingly strong. In fact, coins have outpaced inflation by over four times, as have other collectables. The reason is not hard to figure out. When money is scarce, inevitably interest rates rise, and a guaranteed return is more attractive than the more speculative nature of any return on a collectable. However, if the interest rates decline, the speculative return possibilities on a coin are always more interesting.

In June 1984 a new survey by Salomon Brothers showed an equally impressive result. Coins increased 21.4 percent annually over that term (ranking as the number one investment). Over a fifteen-year period, at 17.3 percent annual growth, coins were second only to oil.

The largest denomination (and size) gold coin ever contemplated for the United States—a $50 gold piece. This pattern is about 2" in diameter (52mm). Photo courtesy Bowers & Ruddy Galleries.

In reviewing the Salomon Brothers survey, Harvey G. Stack, a partner in Stack's, commented that the study shows that rare coins have been a good investment when held for a minimum of five to seven years. This seems not only to be accurate but to be having a profound effect in the marketplace.

A number of other marketers (principally in the savings bank field) evidently thought so, and took action to prevent the spread of the use of coins in individual retirement accounts and pension funds, particularly HR-10 (Keogh) accounts.

As to your portfolio of rare coins, a sampling might arbitrarily include U.S. type coins, or a series of gold issues. The keystone throughout, however, is to choose issues that do have an existing demand and that in the future will be disposable should the need arise.

Finally there are, as we have seen, no true rules for investment, yet common-sense adages help not only in coin collecting but also in investing. First, read the book before buying the coin. Then make a thorough investigation of the item or series of coins to be purchased. Next comes timing, followed by systematic purchases and diversification. To be sure, there is no foolproof method. But with careful planning and investment, a six-figure coin collection can be yours—and the fun of an excellent hobby along with it.

Since 1970, the Krugerrand has proved to be one of the most popular means of buying bullion in the world. Over 38 million pieces have been sold, nearly half of them in the United States.

Collecting Gold

Glittering gold in the form of coins, ingots, and even bullion has been desired by acquirers of wealth since ancient times, when Jason searched for the Golden Fleece. Historically, gold coins are a traditional storehouse of value that is obtained from their precious metal content, and their record of price appreciation has been unparalleled.

In the 1980s, gold as a medium of exchange between world governments has a diminishing role. But to consumers searching for a way to prevent the further decline of the purchasing power of their currency, to collectors looking for new outlets of acquisition, and to the investor seeking a means that historically has worked to the advantage of the holder, gold remains an attractive property.

A 1907 $10 gold piece, by Saint-Gaudens. Photo courtesy Stack's.

THE GOLDEN PAST

The use of gold in international commerce has a long and ancient history, dating back to the coinage of the Lydians centuries before the birth of Christ. The ancient Greeks, the Romans, and the Byzantines all produced pieces in this medium; in fact, the earliest known portrait of Christ in metal is on a Byzantine gold coin. The remarkable, lifelike portrait of the spiritual founder of Christianity is revealing both as a dramatic sculpture and for what it represents. It is interesting to note that a coin of this type, or a scarce piece, is still obtainable, though at a high cost.

Gold coins were issued by nations of the world in a rather haphazard fashion, at least prior to the start of the nine-

American double eagle $20 gold piece designed by Saint-Gaudens. Photo courtesy Stack's.

teenth century. Columbus's voyage to the New World, as well as those of other Spanish, Portuguese, and English explorers, were all basically in search of gold.

If the English were unsuccessful initially in their venture, and the Portuguese similarly were less than lucky, then it is clear that the Spanish succeeded beyond anyone's wildest dreams. Indeed, the conquistadores not only discovered vast quantities of the precious metal in the New World, Hispaniola, but mined it extensively and shipped it by convoy from New Spain to the mother country, where it was turned into coin or retained in the world treasury.

Unfortunately, there were no early gold coin issues in the Americas. The reason was that the Spanish government explicitly forbade production of gold coinage from the mints established in the viceroy provinces in Mexico and South America. All gold was to be shipped back directly to Spain; as a result, many of the Spanish galleons were the subject of attack by pirates. Inevitably, the weather also played havoc with this transportation of bullion from the New World to the Old. Today it is estimated that billions of dollars worth of gold bullion (and the struck silver coins known as Spanish pieces of eight) lie encrusted in the marine life of the Atlantic Ocean and the Gulf of Mexico along the route the treasure-laden ships took in the 1500s.

Man's quest for gold has been well documented. The *Concepción* was one sixteenth-century Spanish galleon whose treasure was eagerly sought both by contemporaries and later explorers. The treasure was finally raised in 1979, yielding millions of dollars worth of silver pieces of eight and gold. Other wrecks have yielded many artifacts, including much-prized bronze cannons recovered in the mid-nineteenth century, and coin rarities.

That adventurers should seek out the billions of dollars that lay on the floor of the ocean is not unusual; what is extraordinary is the pristine condition of the recovered gold, which had been virtually untouched for more than three hundred years, and the fact that it is considerably more valuable today.

THE AMERICAN GOLD EXPERIENCE

When the United States began to issue gold coins, in 1795, the gold was given a value fifteen times that of the silver contained in a standard $1 coin. This ratio, carefully calculated by Alexander Hamilton as first Secretary of the Treasury, was substantively correct when his report was issued, fully reflecting the existing conditions of the daily gold and silver markets in London. However, the problem with Hamilton's plan (which would continue to plague American financiers and also those from other nations that issued gold and silver coins) was that the value of gold and the value of silver do not remain constant. The fluctuations were caused by existing supply and demand, availability of the precious metals, and increases in their use for jewelry and for other commercial and industrial purposes.

In the case of the United States, the ratio became so far out of line that it became profitable for gold coins produced by the nation to be exported abroad, where they were melted down by individuals who had purchased them at face value and destroyed them for the profit realized in the difference between their bullion worth and their face value.

Mint officials were unable to reduce the content of the gold because this would have constituted a serious crime of currency debasement, for which they were personally liable for any difference and even, under the original legislation, punishable by death.

Shortly after the turn of the nineteenth century, the coinage of all gold was suspended, as was the coinage of silver dollars, due to their overvaluation in the world market. For today's collector, there are two interesting results of this coinage suspension. First is the creation of a great American rarity known as the 1804 silver dollar—a pseudo-coin, apparently produced three decades later to represent what coinage of the earlier period should have been. Second, and more important, is the realization that the mintage figures of all these early coins are unreliable because of the vast meltings that took place. An examination of any

A 1795 $10 gold piece. Note the "puny" eagle, heralding America's first gold coin. Photo courtesy Stack's.

An 1807 $5 gold piece, a coin of the people, showing Liberty wearing the Liberty cap. Photo courtesy Bowers & Ruddy Galleries.

guidebook listing mintages and prices of coins confirms that the mintage figures of pre-1834 coins, especially gold coins, bear no relation to the prices or the demand. With so many pieces being melted, few were available for collectors of that time, and on a percentage basis, even fewer are available for the collector today.

If America was to become a world power, it was essential for its money to obtain parity, so that its gold and silver coins could be convertible the world over. The Coinage Act of January 18, 1837, did achieve this effect, creating a stable situation that would last nearly one hundred years. Gold was valued at $20.67 an ounce, and on that basis the eagle—a $10 gold piece—was produced, containing 0.4837 troy ounces of gold. That same year, the United Kingdom introduced the sovereign, a gold coin weighing 0.2354 troy ounces. Larger by almost half, the eagle would compete with the sovereign, although clearly the British coin was the more desirable. It was more widely circulated throughout the world and was produced at British imperial mints in South Africa, Bombay, Sidney, Ottawa, and elsewhere. While the U.S. eagle bore the head of an imaginary and symbolic Liberty, the sovereign featured the portrait of the reigning monarch, and for most of the nineteenth century that was Queen Victoria. Victoria, who reigned for sixty-four years, is seen in four distinct periods, ranging from her youth to her diamond jubilee.

GOLD AS COMMON DENOMINATOR

As stability came to the American monetary system of the nineteenth century, the price of gold (except in times of war, when it fluctuated wildly) made gold coinage relatively common, though never to the extent of rendering it readily available to the common man. The quarter eagle, or $2.50 piece, was perhaps the most widely circulated coin in the United States. But when gold was discovered in California, it became apparent that coins of larger denominations were required to bring the gold from the mines to the

Treasury, and also to permit their circulation on a wide-spread scale. The double eagle, or $20 gold piece, proved to be the solution. It contained 0.9675 troy ounces of gold, nearly 1 ounce, and with gold valued at $20.67 an ounce, the precious metal content of the coin accounted for $19.99. Thus, any individual who deposited gold at the mint could have it turned into coinage of equal value. In one sense, the double eagle of the 1850s was what the Krugerrand and its counterparts are today—a convenient way to own and hold gold in increments of approximately 1 ounce.

By the latter part of the nineteenth century, gold in the United States occupied the preeminent place that it would retain until 1934. In that year, President Roosevelt over-night revalued, with Congress's approval, the gold weight of the dollar. A double eagle no longer contained $19.99 in bullion but $33.86; under these circumstances, of course, the gold coin could not circulate—though interestingly enough it still retained its basic face value of $20, as indeed it does today. If you were to take a $20 gold piece to a bank, the U.S. Post Office, or a Federal Reserve Bank, they would be obliged to give you $20 in coin of the realm or paper currency in exchange for this piece of bullion impressed with American seals and labels. (Obviously, this is not something that will be done so long as gold has a value substantially above the face value of the coin.)

As America was about to depart from the age of gold, this 1930 eagle ($10 gold piece) was struck. Photo courtesy Bowers & Ruddy Galleries.

Building a collection of gold coins in the 1980s is a difficult task for many reasons. First and foremost is of course cost. The problems collectors had in acquiring gold a generation ago are compounded by the dramatic price changes that have placed gold coins on a level at which the bullion content is fifteen to twenty or more times the nominal value of older dates. Once the numismatic value is added to the coins, the cost becomes prohibitive.

In the past, very few individuals collected gold coins the way cents, nickels, or even quarters were acquired—by both date and mint mark. Rather, because of the complexity and the cost, gold coins traditionally were acquired in narrow specialty areas, such as a particular mint mark, a type set consisting of one specimen of each portrait of Lib-

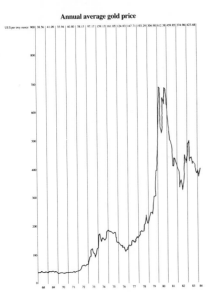

Annual average gold price

Monthly average London gold price, 1968–84. From "Gold 1984" by Louise du Boulav. Courtesy of Consolidated Gold Fields PLC, London.

erty, or some other readily distinguishable means. This way a collector could satisfy his or her interest without taking out substantial mortgages.

As the price of gold continues to fluctuate, and as new coinages of the precious metal are produced, the collector today is faced with several choices, which come down essentially to the age-old question of what to acquire and under what circumstances. The prohibitively high prices of American gold coin issues seem to mandate a change in collecting style. Type coin collecting, especially, becomes very attractive. For example, instead of striving to acquire one of each of Saint-Gaudens's eagles produced at the Philadelphia, Denver, and San Francisco mints between 1907 and 1933, it might be prudent to acquire one specimen of the later issues, for example a 1932. In terms of Saint-Gaudens's exquisite double eagle piece, a realistic alternative to acquiring the many specimens—some of which are genuine rarities selling in a five-figure price range—might be a choice of circulated "common date."

Even in attempting to purchase some of the half eagles and quarter eagles, a substantial investment in bullion content is at once necessary. In the case of the $1, $2.50, and $3 gold pieces, the bullion content does not play as significant a role in the overall cost as it does in the higher, more weighty, coins. However, it is useful to consider that even the lowly $1 gold piece has a bullion value that must be taken into account, as the chart shows:

Price per Ounce of Gold

	$20.67	$200	$400	$600	$800	$1,000
Bullion Value	$1.00	$9.67	$19.35	$29.02	$38.70	$48.35
	$20.00	$193.50	$387	$580.50	$774	$967.50

NOTE: $20.67 an ounce was the official price of gold from 1837 to 1934. Other prices are selective and designed to reflect recent market prices and projections.

MODERN GOLD

As to new issues, there is a plethora of pieces to be considered. Between 1933 and 1980, with the exception of specially authorized congressional gold medals for presentation purposes, or the Bicentennial medal authorized in 1976 by Congress with prices ranging from $100 to $5,000, the American government steadfastly refused to produce gold coins or medals that its citizens could use. As a result, a number of foreign governments and private commercial mints acting on behalf of foreign governments began to produce gold coins not necessarily of the realm or for circulation, but intended specifically for the collector. Many of these noncirculating legal tender pieces are exquisite in design, composition, and even collectability. In some cases, the very limited editions have risen substantially in value simply because low mintages made them highly desirable to a collector of a particular series or type.

During the 1960 to 1979 period, more than forty different countries issued gold coins at a time when the gold market was rising but not at abnormally fast, high, or unusual levels. To be more specific, between 1968 and early 1979 the price of gold meandered slowly upward, until in the latter part of the 1970s an explosion took place.

Interestingly enough, the effect of the dramatic rise in the price of gold from $200 an ounce to $400 an ounce within a twelve-month span seemed to support the theory that not only was gold a tremendous storehouse of value but all gold coins were a good investment. Later rises to $600, $750, and beyond seemed to confirm this. In fact, this theory does not hold up under sound analysis. Some gold coins have a keen numismatic value; others must be viewed apart from the value of their gold content. If a coin is struck for collectors and contains $\frac{1}{4}$ ounce of gold, and if gold is valued at $200 an ounce at the time the coin is issued, then the bullion weight of the coin is $50. If that same coin is sold for $125 or $150, substantial ground must be made up either in terms of numismatic value or bullion gain before any kind of a return can be realized on that investment.

What has happened, of course, in the case of coins purchased in a world where gold is $400 an ounce is that $\frac{1}{4}$ of an ounce coin purchased for $150 suddenly contains $100 gold content. If gold were to rise to $600, that coin would in fact have its nominal weight fully covered. To the extent that the coin sells at a substantial premium above its bullion weight, this is a reflection of its numismatic value. To the extent that the coin remains available, even after the series has been sold out at or near its original issue price, this is an indication that the numismatic value obviously is minimal and the coin's worth is tied into the bullion content. In such instances, it is not unheard of for a coin to be resold below its issue price by its owner, who is seeking to make some return, or even suffer a loss, rather than indefinitely hold onto a gold coin that has questionable future value.

In order to determine what gold coins have in them by way of value, only two things are necessary: a pocket calculator and a chart giving the troy ounce weight of the coin. By simply multiplying that weight by the daily price of gold as published in the financial section of most newspapers, the bullion worth of any particular coin can be ascertained immediately. The following chart lists many of the coins popular with collectors today:

In the eighties, the U.S. government has begun to market medallions of 1 ounce denomination, plainly a challenge to the South African Krugerrand and its domination of bullion sales around the world. More than 6 million Krugerrands,

Type	Troy Ounces	Type	Troy Ounces
U.S. $20	0.9675	100 francs	0.9334
U.S. $10	0.4838	(France, Belgium,	
U.S. $5	0.2419	Switzerland)	
U.S. $2.50	0.1209	Colombia 5 pesos	0.2333
U.K. sovereign	0.2354	Germany 20 marks	0.2305
20 franc	0.1867	Hungary 8 florins	0.1867
(France, Switzerland,		100 corona	0.9802
Belgium)		20 corona	0.1960
10 franc	0.0933	Mexico 50 pesos	1.2057
(France, Switzerland,		20 pesos	0.4823
Belgium)		10 pesos	0.2411
Austria 4 ducat	0.4438	5 pesos	0.1206
1 ducat	0.1109	2.5 pesos	0.0603

each representing 1 troy ounce of gold, were sold in the United States in 1979. As a result, the American Congress approved over the opposition of the Treasury Department the American Gold Arts Medallion Act, which requires that at least 1 million $\frac{1}{2}$-ounce medallions and 0.5 million 1-ounce medallions be struck annually for a five-year period. These attractive medals, which will be designed, produced, and marketed by the U.S. Mint, mark the entry of the United States into the field of modern collectable coinage. Because the purchase price must be at or near the market price of gold, these pieces represent a substantially better buy for the individual seeking to acquire bullion—or any other type of foreign coin.

It is clear that gold will still play a dominant role in coin investing throughout the 1980s. While no one is quoting what the price of the metal will be with any certainty (some seers project $1,000 an ounce by 1990), it seems clear that the fortune of rare gold coins as well as modern issues will be closely tied to the price trends of that precious metal.

Gold's aura has not diminished in the first half of the 1980s. The price of the metal ran to a high of about $800 an ounce during the first year of the decade, and then settled in at about half that level—running sometimes high, sometimes low, but generally providing a good storehouse of value.

Interestingly, some of the coins that had previously been linked closely to the bullion price began slowly to divorce themselves. American double eagles, for example, historically traded at a premium of about 48 percent above the spot price on any given day. This is the pattern that had existed since the early 1960s.

Yet in 1984, the price of the coins jumped dramatically. With gold wavering in the $400 an ounce range, the double eagles were trading (even for common dates in MS-60 condition) in the $850 to $900 range, and up.

One explanation offered was that there was a general lack of confidence in other gold coins, ranging from the Krugerrand to the Canadian Maple Leaf. This seems to belie the facts, however.

Mexican gold coins originally struck forty years ago still have intrinsic value, and jewelry interest. Photo courtesy of the Banco de Mexico.

A more likely explanation is that the perception has finally hit home that these coins are in fact not of limitless supply. There are truly few hoards left. Some central banks may have minor stocks, but the majority of the great hoards have been dissipated. Even rumors in 1984 that a major European hoard had been discovered did little to bring the price down. Rather, the perception of the marketplace seemed to be that there were few left, certainly not enough to meet available demand.

One added feature to all this is the "hard money" discovery of coins and other numismatic assets as an investment vehicle. "Hard money" is essentially a philosophy which holds that only tangible assets can protect against a decline in the purchasing power of a currency (whether the dollar or any other unit of value), and that the first among these is gold, silver, and coins.

Recognition that this was a significant element in the marketplace came about in 1981 when Congress was called upon to consider the tax reform legislation of that year. "TRA '81" legislated that it was no longer permissible to invest retirement funds into tangible assets, and defined these so as to include coins, stamps, diamonds, and a host of other items.

Some perceived this as the ultimate reaction of the savings and loan industry, which had hemorrhaged badly when interest rates went as high as 21 percent per annum and many people left their depositories for money markets and other investments. Others believed it was the government acting to force savings and retirements to stay in the marketplace where they could be loaned and reloaned.

Regardless, the effect on pensions, IRAs, and Keogh accounts was devastating—and the long-range effect on coin prices was downward. Yet in place of this came the discovery of hard-asset investors, people who were not looking, necessarily, for pension plans, but rather were seeking a means by which they could acquire assets that were relatively safe from seizure while likely to grow in value.

In considering coins, these buyers undoubtedly had examined studies like those of Salomon Brothers, which since its pioneer survey in 1979 has annually examined the short- and long-term investment possibilities of coins.

Of keen interest are the 1983 and 1984 surveys, which showed that over the course of fifteen years retrospectively, coins had outperformed virtually every form of tangible assets with the exception of oil. Gold, silver, stocks, bonds, and even real estate fell by the wayside; rare American coins jumped out in the lead with a better than 17 percent annual return.

Put another way, that means that if $100 was invested fifteen years ago, it would now be worth $1,053.87. Since investments are usually done in multiples of that number, the results are even more impressive; certainly they must be an allure to those looking for a tangible way to beat out inflation in a sure-fire winner.

Throughout all this, a number of gold bullion–related products have also come to the forefront of the marketplace. In terms of gross sales, the South African Krugerrand certainly merits mention. Since 1970, more than 38 million pieces have been produced (representing 38 million ounces of gold), and some 3 million pieces, alone, are sold annually in the United States. Close competitors include the Canadian Maple Leaf and the Mexican Onza, each of which apparently utilizes South African gold at least in part of their production schedule, and all of which mimic the South African one ounce, half ounce, quarter ounce, and tenth-of-an-ounce denomination. The United States entered the bullion coin market with the American Arts gold medallions in an unambitious way, initially designed not to compete with any other nation. When J. Aron & Co. won the right to market the product, the strategy seemed to change. The pieces resembled coins more, and had a reeded edge. They bore the appellation of origin, "United States of America," and the year of coinage. Nonetheless, they persistently sold for less than the Krugerrand or any other legal tender products. As every marketer who has entered the field has found, there is something magical about legal tender—even if a U.S. government product, sold by the mint, is exempt from the collection of sales tax.

The imposition of sales tax was something that also

emerged as a major issue in the sale of gold bullion in the 1980s. As states hungered for more and more revenue, and as each of them sought out various areas to tap, bullion coin sales seemed logical. Yet, organizations such as the National Association of Coin & Precious Metals Dealers, and the Industry Council for Tangible Assets, repeatedly testified before state legislative bodies that bullion was an investment in the same way that a stock or bond was, or a contract on a commodities exchange for silver or gold.

By the end of 1983, some fifteen states either had no sales tax at all, or had agreed that coin and bullion sales (usually termed "monetized bullion") ought not to be taxed. And with some states vacillating against taxation, the pressure on the remaining states grew to conform to the still-minority mold. This was because bullion or coin sales made through the mails (and in interstate commerce) are not legally subject to sales tax, and the evasion of taxation in this area had apparently become rampant.

Treasury Department officials nationally gave this credence when they endorsed legislation that would remove from capital gains status the acquisition or sale of any of the American gold bullion coins. Treasury's unabashed aim was to cut out tax cheating, which they believe is costing taxpayers millions each year in uncollected revenue. They theorize that a buyer of bullion who sees the price of the metal go down sells, on the record, and takes a capital loss. The gains, they believe, are unrecorded.

Partially in order to record these coins, 1983 saw an attempt by Treasury's Internal Revenue Service to alter rules and regulations within the tax code to require reporting of any and all bullion buys and purchases. While the newly formed Industry Council for Tangible Assets appears to have beaten this back, most people believe that in the forthcoming years, such purchases will increasingly attract the attention of revenue authorities—who try to plug the gap in government spending policies with the earnings of those who have hedged against the inflation of yesteryear and today.

Paper Money

Collecting paper money is probably the newest aspect of numismatics. Today, there is a paper money rainbow on display, with thousands of collectors dazzled by the vast spectrum of colors and hues. While coins have a history dating back several centuries before the birth of Christ, the use of paper as currency is far more recent, at least in Western culture. Yet paper money has tremendous collector appeal, based in part on its colorful and exotic designs and in part on the fact that acquiring once-used legal tender notes can be very inexpensive.

In medieval Europe, wealth was measured in such terms as livestock, spices, silver, and gold. Plundering and the ravages of war placed value on objects that could be converted or exchanged upon demand. Animals, land, and precious metals proved satisfactory items of barter and exchange in this materialistic society.

The first European exposure to paper money came upon Marco Polo's return from Cathay (modern China) near the end of the thirteenth century. This adventurer to the Orient told of paper money accepted without question throughout China, with a value equal to a specific amount of gold or silver and redeemable at Peking. The keystone to the use of paper money was the political and economic structure that centered on the powerful khan, who decreed that the paper promissory notes be accepted on pain of death. In the homogeneous Chinese society, where the khan ruled absolutely, money could be used; in Europe, however, it was possible that a coinage of one nation, even

Thirteenth-century Chinese promissory notes, which Marco Polo unveiled to a disbelieving Europe. Collection of the American Numismatic Society, New York.

though of precious metal, would not be accepted at par in another.

It was not until the eighteenth century that Europe seriously began to experiment with paper money, and not until the twentieth century that paper currency gained true acceptance in the United States. In most instances before then, paper money served as a promissory note that could be converted into coin or other precious metal. When issued by a government, paper currency was backed by a reserve of precious metal that usually amounted to only a fraction of its face value, the theory being that it was most unlikely all of the citizenry would redeem its currency at the same time.

Today in the United States there is more than $80 billion worth of paper money in circulation, most of it in $1 bills. Yet, unlike earlier times in our history, there is nothing to

All money is now equal, but at one time in our history some money was more equal than others. Note the superimposed half eagles in the lower left — which theoretically were worth the same as the paper money, but in practice were worth a lot more. Today, the scarce paper money issue is worth more to collectors than the common coin.

back up the value of the dollar except the economic and political strength of the government and the nation itself. At one time, U.S. paper money was convertible into gold and silver; for every dollar bill the government printed, a comparable amount of precious metal was kept in reserve. A $20 bill could be converted into a double eagle coin, or a $1 bill into a silver dollar or an ounce of silver. That of course is no more. Surprisingly, however, as recently as 1968, silver certificates were convertible into silver bullion upon presentation to the Treasury Department; and until 1971, foreign governments claimed entitlement to redeem all American dollars abroad for gold at either the Fort Knox bullion depository or the Federal Reserve Bank of New York.

Because the experience of the United States with paper money so closely parallels that of other nations, the humble origins of the earliest attempts to use nonmetallic currency in the colonial period are relevant here. For many people, moreover, collecting colonial currency is among the most interesting (and profitable) aspects of American numismatics.

AMERICAN PAPER CURRENCY

The origins of paper currency in the English colonies date to 1690, just five years after the first recorded use of paper money in North America, in French Canada. In Canada, playing cards were cut into parts as a means of paying soldiers, whereas Massachusetts experimented with a bill of credit that, while used to pay soldiers, also had a legal tender value for the populace. As a means of securing widespread use, the government granted a premium of 5 percent when it was used to pay taxes.

Colonial Paper Issues

Before the Revolutionary War, eight colonies were using paper money in various denominations. The need was

Pine Tree shilling "backdated" to 1652.

acute, for the king refused to grant the colonies the right to coin money (though some, such as Massachusetts, backdated coinage to 1653 in order to get around the requirement), and Parliament first forbade the creation of banking institutions in the New World and then withdrew New England's right to use bills of credit by making them all immediately due and payable, regardless of the due date printed on them. By 1764, because of uneven valuation and overissue that caused inflation, Parliament enacted legislation prohibiting future issues of bank notes in all colonies and ordered notes retired at the end of their term of issue. The British government acted on sound monetary policy, for the colonies early discovered the ease with which a paper currency could be used to create money where there was nothing to back it up. By 1764, £100 sterling was worth £190 of New York "paper" sterling, £200 in Maryland currency, about £1,000 in North Carolina paper money, and an astonishing £1,100 in Massachusetts Bay Colony currency.

In banning colonial coinage production and systematically destroying the issuance of a paper substitute, Parliament may have wished to force the colonies to rely on coin from Britain and foreign monies, thereby ensuring continued loyalty to England. To be sure, it severely limited the colonists' economic freedom, and when the Continental Congress met at Philadelphia in 1774, it could only recommend

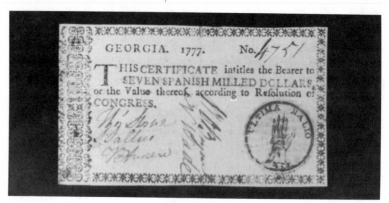

Colonial paper money was overinflated and generally issued without gold or silver backing. Dr. Radford Stearns collection.

and cajole—it could not tax, because there was no money.

Congress solved this problem in fairly short order by issuing bills of credit, but even this decision was not without controversy. Gouverneur Morris of New York laid before the Congress a report from the Committee on the Expediency of a Continental Paper Currency, which proposed that each colony should "strike for itself the sum apportioned by the Continental Congress," or that the Continental Congress itself should do all the printing and assign to each colony a proportionate part. The latter alternative was chosen because of "the advantage of higher and more universal credit." In late June 1775, the Continental Congress approved emission of "a sum not exceeding two millions of Spanish milled dollars . . . in bills of Credit," all to be used "for the defense of America." The Congress decided to produce 49,000 bills of each denomination from $1 to $8 and 12,000 $20 bills. Within five months, this sum was expanded among twelve colonies (Georgia excepted) to $3 million. The distribution of this sum is revealing about the population of early America. As the chart below demonstrates, the most populous colonies, which received the greatest allocation of currency, were Virginia, Massachusetts, and Pennsylvania, while New York, Connecticut, and North and South Carolina were of approximately equal size.

One of the first of the continental paper money issues. Dr. Radford Stearns collection.

DISTRIBUTION OF FIRST CONTINENTAL CURRENCY ISSUE (1775)

Colony	Amount	Percentage
New Hampshire	$ 124,000	4.1
Massachusetts	434,000	14.5
Rhode Island	71,960	2.3
Connecticut	248,140	8.2
New York	248,140	8.2
New Jersey	161,290	5.3
Pennsylvania	372,210	12.4
Delaware	37,220	1.2
Maryland	310,175	10.3
Virginia	496,278	16.5
North Carolina	248,140	8.2
South Carolina	248,140	8.2
Totals: Twelve colonies, $3,000,000		100.0

Note: Figures may not add, due to rounding; percentages independently calculated. Source: *Journal of the Continental Congress*, Vol. 2, pp. 221-23 (1775).

Issuing bills of credit without backing would have been foolhardy, as the Continental Congress recognized. An important part of the plan called for the colonies to back the issue, and by a resolution dated the day after Christmas 1775, the Congress resolved that "the 13 United Colonies be pledged for the redemption of the bills of credit so directed to be emitted," though the means was left up to them. Among the printers of these early issues was one Benjamin Franklin, who had learned the trade as a boy and was now among the foremost craftsmen in America.

In issuing the currency that was to finance the defense of the colonies, the Continental Congress promised redemption in Spanish milled dollars, which circulated widely at the time and continued to do so until well into the middle

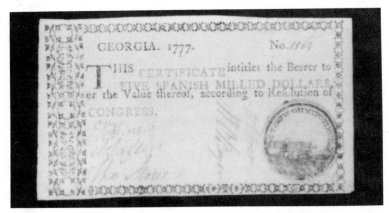

Paper money was supposed to be convertible into milled dollars — but more often than not there was no redemption possible, and the worth of the paper dollar shrank. Dr. Radford Stearns collection.

of the next century. Yet since there was no real money backing up the promise, the pledge was an empty one, and the state legislatures were left to their own devices to persuade their citizens to accept the credit emissions. In Pennsylvania, the Committee of Safety passed a resolution with precise penalties for failure to accept the paper continental dollar: "Forfeit of goods offered for sale or bargained for or debt contracted—and pay a fine of five pounds to the State" for a first offense.

War Issues

As the war prospects became poorer for the Americans and the Treasury grew ever barer, Congress provided more empty pledges in the form of paper bills of credit and continental currency. But there was no coin to redeem the money with; and by early 1778, after the disastrous winter at Valley Forge, the continental paper dollar was worth barely 16 cents in coin. Then, as American fortunes fared better after the victory at Saratoga and the French alliance with the American cause (ratified by Congress in May 1778), the paper's worth rose to 25 cents in coin.

New bills of credit were issued by Congress in attempts to compensate for depreciation, but as long as there was no backing for the paper, it was doomed to fail. By the end of the war, notes were circulating at a rate varying between 500 and 1,000 to the Spanish milled dollar; Congress itself ended the charade on May 31, 1781, when it declared continental currency no longer legal tender.

Largely owing to the unhappy experience with paper money in the colonial period and during the Revolutionary War, the federal constitution adopted in 1789 specifically prohibited issuing bills of credit. The money immortalized in the phrase "not worth a continental" nearly ruined any chance for issuance of paper money by the government of the United States, which stayed away from like issues until the second great conflict to enmesh the American nation—the Civil War.

The experience of the young United States of America was repeated elsewhere, especially in Europe, which used paper currency to expand the money supply without increased precious metal backing. England was a notable exception, however. From the mid-1600s, private industry, principally through goldsmiths who accepted deposits and issued certificates in exchange, took the initiative in issuing paper legal tender. The Bank of England later began to do the same. Less happy developments occurred in France, where John Law, a Scotsman, created what amounted to a French central bank. He then proceeded to overinflate the paper currency that it issued by having little precious metal backing, and permitted the bubble to burst by failing to redeem through a scandalous investment in the Louisiana Territory. Until the mid-nineteenth century, such was the fate of most government-sponsored enterprises in paper money.

Broken Bank Notes

West of the Pecos, and in much of the American nation, the constitutional prohibition of federally issued paper money left private enterprise to fill in. Hundreds of wildcat

Private bank note of the period issued by the Second Bank of the United States.

banks were created, many with their own fanciful currency issues on fine engraved paper secured against counterfeiters and embellished with colorful designs. Many of these banks entirely lacked deposits. Others simply overinflated; when payment in coin was demanded, they closed their doors and the notes became "broken" and worthless. Today, many of these issues are prized by collectors who avidly seek out paper money for an unusual name, design, or even vignette. Some of the issuers, however, had solid financial reputation and integrity; the Second Bank of the United States was one example, since a significant portion of its deposits consisted of government securities and coin of the realm. But even in this instance, the end of the Bank's federal charter during the term of President Andrew Jackson profoundly affected the value of the bank notes that it issued.

Return to Paper Currency

The federal government returned to paper currency during the Civil War. Despite the constitutional objections of some officials, including Treasury Secretary Salmon P. Chase, who conceived the plan, the government actually had little choice. Whereas the federal budget in the 1840s had averaged $32 million a year, and in the 1850s $60 million, the costs of the Civil War were astronomical—$2 million per day, an average expenditure of $684 million per year. At the suggestion of Secretary Chase, President Abraham Lincoln called for an extraordinary session of Congress on the Fourth of July 1861. Government coffers were virtually empty, and according to Chase's estimates, continuation of the war would cost $318 million that year. To finance the war, Chase called upon Congress to authorize government borrowing in a unique manner—by issuing noninterest-bearing notes payable upon demand, interest-bearing notes, and long-term bonds. Congressional debate was voluminous, and there is little doubt that members of the House and Senate had no idea they were creating the basis for modern American finance. Their concern was simply to win a war.

Demand notes for 1861—today prized collectors' items, worth many times their issue price—were issued in fifteen different types, each payable where U.S. supply of specie, or coin, was maintained. More money was needed, however, and the executive branch led by Chase again went to Congress, this time asking for $150 million in U.S. notes ($60 million of which were to be legal tender). The legislation almost never made it to the floor, for the House Committee on Ways and Means was deadlocked. Nevertheless, it was obvious that the Union itself was at stake, and so the committee permitted the measure to go to the floor of the House for a direct vote, where it passed handily, 93 to 59.

Yet even Chase remained doubtful. Besides having what he called "a great aversion to making anything but coin a legal tender in payment of debts," he feared that coin itself would soon be withdrawn from circulation by a suspicious populace, and it was. In one of the more telling ironies of the period, the portrait of Salmon P. Chase appeared on the dollar bill, making him one of the best-known persons in the nation through a medium he deplored.

As more and more money was required, the fear grew that the Supreme Court would invalidate the legal tender acts. Chief Justice Roger Taney, whom President Jackson had appointed as a reward for faithful service in destroying the Second Bank of the United States, was a confirmed Southerner, loyal to the Confederate cause even as he

Abraham Lincoln, President during the Civil War, was faced with the delicate political dilemma of how to maintain the legal status of currency and the constitutionality of the Emancipation Proclamation simultaneously.

headed the judiciary of the Union. Pending cases in the lower courts argued that the government's legal tender provisions were unconstitutional, and, were the Supreme Court to sustain such a proposition, the federal government's ability to continue financing the war would be seriously jeopardized. When Taney died in 1864, Lincoln had to choose a successor. Congressman George S. Boutwell, later Secretary of the Treasury, confided in his diary one of the reasons Lincoln decided to name Chase to the high-court position: "We want a man who will sustain the Legal Tender Act and the Proclamation of Emancipation."

Unconstitutional Issues

When it finally came to the Supreme Court to make a rule on the legal tender question in *Hepburn* vs. *Griswold* in February 1870, Chief Justice Chase declared the legal tender currency legislation he had helped to create unconstitutional. Yet paper money continued—and politics was a reason for it. Following the decision in *Hepburn* vs. *Griswold,* two vacancies in the Supreme Court were filled by nominees of President Grant, all of whom favored the legal tender currency. After their confirmation, a move was made to reargue in the Supreme Court; Chase's decision was reversed by a 5 to 4 vote, and on May 1, 1871, paper currency was permitted to continue.

Post–Civil War Issues

Although private currency issues were ended by a tax on bank notes not printed and issued by the government, a national currency issue by local banks was permissible based upon deposits, which in turn formed reserves for the currency. After the Civil War, thousands of national banks were created all over the land, and most issued their own paper money in the manner permitted by law. There were also several different types of government-issued currency backed by gold, silver, or both. The problem, at least at the

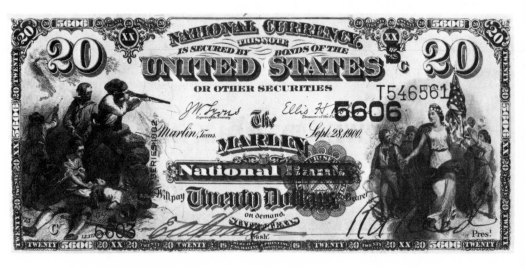

An example of national currency.

"Money standard" of mid-nineteenth century that was both distinctive and different.

start, was that the greenback's purchasing power was not equal to that of its metallic counterpart. For a time there was actually a three-tiered system under which the gold dollar, the silver dollar, and the paper dollar all had different purchasing powers. This confusion in part led to three major banking panics before 1900 and forced the government to achieve stability through parity—issuing notes convertible directly into coin, in addition to being legal tender in themselves.

If the economics of the period seem confusing, they were. Imagine trying to make purchases where "discounts" for the use of paper money had to be calculated and gold coin was preferred to silver or paper fiat money. The varieties of notes continued to grow, however. Redeemable coin notes were issued in 1890 by the Treasury Department to pay for silver bullion purchased to turn into dollar coinage; gold certificates were also issued, with comparable redemption privileges. During the Civil War and until 1875 there was even fractional paper currency (issued in denominations under $1) to replace change that had been withdrawn from circulation.

With certain exceptions, all of these notes are today highly collectable. Most contain unusual designs, often in exquisite colors, originally conceived to confuse counterfeiters as much as anything else. Since all but the fractional

Treasury coin note, series of 1890.

currency issues continue to be legal tender (and could be redeemed at face value if desired), for the most part the lower denominations are collected today. Some of the notes honor such famous Americans as the Union generals Philip H. Sheridan and George H. Thomas. Others depict great moments of American history: the discovery of America by Columbus, on the $5 note; De Soto's first visit to the Mississippi River, on the $10 note; the baptism of Pocahontas, on the reverse of the $20 note; the Pilgrims' embarkation, on the reverse of the $50 bill; the signing of the Declaration of Independence, on the $100 bill; the surrender of General Burgoyne to General Gates at Saratoga in 1777, on the $500 note; and Washington resigning his commission, on the reverse of the $1,000 bill. Other sketches on the faces of these notes depict General Winfield Scott entering Mexico City during the Mexican War, Commodore Perry at the Battle of Lake Erie during the War of 1812, and Washington crossing

American history engraved onto its currency — the reverse designs of some of the most beautiful issues of American currency ever produced (1865 to 1877). Shown here on the $50 note is the Pilgrims' embarkation, and on the $1 note their landing; De Soto's discovery of the Mississippi appeared on several notes.

The Bureau of Engraving and Printing, as depicted by their engraving artists.

the Delaware. Among silver certificate issues, the so-called Education series of 1896 deserves to be mentioned because its allegorical scenes are among the finest examples of printed and engraved art.

Each of these notes was printed by the Bureau of Engraving and Printing, a division of the Treasury located in Washington, D.C. The Bureau was founded in 1862, during the Civil War, to manufacture the paper money Congress had authorized. In the main Treasury building across the street from the White House, four women and two men separated the $1 and $2 U.S. notes printed for the government by private bank note companies. For helping to save the Union, each of the employees was paid $50 per month, presumably in specie, not paper. Through the years, the Bureau's ranks grew to more than 3,500 employees and produced billions upon billions of dollars worth of paper money each year—at a cost of $18 or less per 1,000 notes of any denomination and with a spoilage rate of less than 2 percent.

Until early in the twentieth century, the Bureau of Engraving and Printing primarily printed government greenbacks and national currency for private national banks. But this system of banking was strangling the national economy, so Congress set out to change the way in which the nation's money supply was created. Thomas W. Wilson, a history professor at Princeton University, wrote in 1897

Other examples of national currency that helped lead to the creation of a new "national bank," the Federal Reserve.

that "nothing but currency reform can touch the cause of the [monetary] discontent." Four years later, in his popular *History of the American People,* Wilson warned that a new national bank of the United States was necessary because the government truly needed a "fiscal agent" to facilitate commercial credit transactions.

Federal Reserve Notes

On March 4, 1913, Thomas Woodrow Wilson became President of the United States. From the start, he promised to devote "the utmost serious and immediate attention" to monetary reform. William Jennings Bryan, Wilson's choice for Secretary of State, proved to be an effective advocate before Congress in the cause of monetary reform. Even though he had run in support of bimetallism, he recognized the importance of a sound, centralized management in which the government, not the people, ran the national monetary system.

The Federal Reserve System changed American economic life by reorganizing the banking system and also the money circulated. Federal Reserve notes were soon produced at the Bureau of Engraving and Printing and became more and more widely used. Five dollar, $10, $20, $50, and $100 denominations were printed for the 1914 series, and by 1918 there were $500, $1,000, $5,000, and $10,000 notes. The highest piece of currency ever printed by the United States was a $100,000 federal note, bearing the portrait of the man who perhaps more than any other helped launch the organization that still controls American economic life, Woodrow Wilson.

Today the Federal Reserve silver and gold certificates are no longer printed; neither can be redeemed, though both may be used as legal tender. What are left are specimens for the collector: a sample of an issue, a note from a district with low printing figures, or perhaps even a particular serial number.

Collecting bank notes, unlike coins, is terribly exacting. Since figures are available for the number of specimens printed, and because each piece of currency bears a unique serial number, there can be quite a contest to acquire the lowest and best-printed number of an issue. Although it is incorrect to think of "000000001" as the first note of issue, many collectors nonetheless find it desirable. (Because of

Largest denomination ever printed — $100,000 — used only for intra-system transactions by the Federal Reserve.

the way the numbering machines at the Bureau of Engraving and Printing are set, the number works backward, commencing at 999999999 and ending at 000000001.)

As the cost of acquiring currency that is legal tender is so expensive, many collectors start with a modest collection of American currency issues—principally by types, unless they are fascinated by currency errors or serial numbers—and then branch out into foreign issues, especially those that are no longer legal tender. They may also look for those U.S. currencies that can no longer be redeemed, such as "broken" bank notes (notes issued by a bank that failed).

FOREIGN PAPER CURRENCY

Foreign currency is invariably more colorful than American. Since the U.S. defense against counterfeiting is to use sophisticated engraving techniques on a well-known design, multicolored designs are not compatible with the intaglio printing medium. Many of the most exquisite of these foreign notes, which seem to carry all the colors of the spectrum, are relatively modest in price; as with coins, their prices depend on availability and desirability to collectors.

Storage of paper money collections can be a problem, although a variety of covers available in most hobby stores can keep the bills crisp (the most desirable state of preservation). One danger to avoid is a plastic that is not inert, for the "bleeding" of this material will ruin most pieces of paper, which are highly absorbent. Most hobby stores stock special paper money holders or albums that resemble a photograph holder; each note is secured by a mount at the corner, which fixes but does not damage the bill.

Paper currency is relatively easy to display, based upon the thickness of the various notes. Two sheets of glass, obtainable at any hardware store, are an excellent means of mounting the pieces. These will leave the currency undamaged, while permitting ready examination of both sides. There are also a number of holders used in museums that are effective for display.

If there is anything that a paper money buff is pleased with, it is the acquisition and display of an uncut sheet of paper money. Typically, sheets are available in units of 32 characters, 16 characters, 8 notes, and 4 notes. The serial numbers are not consecutive, but rather have identical last digits because of the method of numbering.

During the 1930s and earlier, sheets were typically made available to collectors in limited quantities. Then, some thirty years ago, for security reasons the Bureau of Engraving and Printing ceased making sheets available to collectors, and a secondary market began to develop.

By the early 1980s, uncut sheets commanded a substantial and healthy premium among not only collectors of paper money, but all collectors interested in neatly showing off some or all of their collection.

Starting in 1978, the American Numismatic Association through its officers and legislative counsel began a campaign to have the Bureau of Engraving and Printing reissue the uncut sheets. After some cajoling, the Bureau agreed to try this on an experimental basis with $1 and $2 bills. The notes were made available over the counter, as well as by mail, and promptly proved to be a hit with vast segments of the population.

People who never collected coins, or paper money, seemed interested in having the uncut sheets, which the Bureau mounted in an attractive black display panel. Some collectors retained this, while others took the sheets to a conventional framer, asked to have a matte placed over the currency, and a glass frame added. (The cost of doing this, by the way, is substantial, since glass is usually sold by the square inch.)

A number of dens and offices began to sprout the uncut currency, and the Bureau of Engraving and Printing gave every sign of catering to the market. From the initial order, the Federal Reserve districts of each city were utilized. Orders may still be sent to the Bureau, Washington, D.C. 20220, for the $1 sheets based on the following schedule (which includes delivery by registered mail): 4 subject sheet, $9.50; 16 subject sheet, $28.00; 32 subject sheet, $47.00.

Collecting Medals and Tokens

THE ART OF THE MEDAL

Medals are moments in miniature frozen for all time. Made of precious metals, bronze, pewter, or even pressed into wood, medals date back to the golden age of Greece when skilled artisans painstakingly designed commemorative medallions to celebrate various events. Coins may be older than medals, but the results of coinage design competition are distinctly inferior to the earliest known examples of medallic art.

The first known commemorative medallions are believed to have been manufactured in Syracuse on the island of Sicily at the end of the fifth century B.C. Whereas early coinage is primitive, even crude, the earliest examples of medallic art show a refined, exacting, and almost precise understanding of the intricacies of detail and composition. For more than two millennia, craftsmen have been emulating and improving the techniques of the ancient Greeks.

These medallions were created by the artisans Phrygillos, Kimon, and Evaenetus, whose names survive in perpetuity on their creations. The Syracuse medallions actually had a legal tender value—10 Attic drachmae or 50 Sicilian silver litras—so in the conventional sense they are not medals. A medal by definition has a two-sided design, either im-

Early Greek medallic art includes these commemorative medallions of Syracuse, which show a highly refined, exacting technique.

101

pressed into or raised from a rounded or multisided surface, and it is not legal tender. Scholars, historians, and coin collectors have debated the status of the Syracuse medallions for more than four hundred years, many arguing with great fervor that because of the abnormal dimensions, extraordinary artistic designs, and nominal values of these pieces they could better be characterized as medallions than coins. To some degree, the circumstances under which these magnificent pieces were issued puts them outside the ordinary scope of coin of the realm. To commemorate the start of the New Games at Syracuse and the "Crowning Mercy" at Assinaios following the defeat of the Athenians, two main types were produced: a portrait of a nymph, Arethusa, with her hair in a beaded net; and another of the maiden goddess Persephone crowned with a barley spray. Each is so intricate that the pupils and irises of the eyes are visible, showing an almost microscopic fineness in composition. Unlike the coinage of the period, which was largely rough-hewn in appearance, these cast medallions had a wonderful precision.

The medallic portraiture perfected by the Greeks enjoyed mass popularity by the time Hellenistic culture was absorbed into the Roman Empire. Under the new order of the Empire, bronze medallions took on major importance and became popular commemorative cult pieces. It was common for prominent Roman senators and citizens to commission self-portraits on medals for distribution to mark significant events in their lives. At a time when the emperor still did not dare to place his own portrait on coin of the realm, medallic art allowed him to gratify his ego without risking the wrath of the Roman populace, who viewed portraiture coinage as an affront to the gods.

The bronze medallions bore highly stylized and idealized portraits of the emperors. For example, during the reign of the son of Marcus Aurelius, Commodus, who ruled from A.D. 180 to 192, the emperor was portrayed as Hercules, weary but resolute in his tasks. The reverse side of such a medallion, which was equivalent in value to the denarius, a monetary unit, usually depicted a deity of victory, a chari-

Example of Renaissance medallic art, produced some six hundred years ago. Note the intricate detail.

ot, or a similar image. Not until more than half a century after Commodus did the size and weight of the medallions differ from the monetary units. From that time the medal became an object of pure art—a vehicle that some of the most famous artists would use to create works in miniature.

Modern medallic art, according to scholars, was founded by Antonio di Puccio Pisano, known as Il Pisanello. Born in Pisa in 1395 and trained in Verona, Pisanello was a painter of portraits, frescoes, and animals. In 1438 he cast his first medal, 105 millimeters in diameter, of John VIII Palaeologus, emperor of Constantinople. Curators of the Samuel Kress Collection of Renaissance bronzes at the National Gallery of Art in Washington, D.C., and cataloguers of the

Molinari Collection of medals and plaquettes at Bowdoin College, Maine, agree that this piece, represented in each collection in a lead casting, marks the first medallic creation of the Renaissance.

Pisanello recreated the art of the medal as the Greeks had known it, with distinctive portraiture and design compositions that were original, realistic, yet imaginative. To this day, medallists and sculptors use this master's techniques and basic ideas as models. They have a vast array of medallions to be inspired by, for between 1438 and 1449 Pisanello produced numerous medals, ranging from powerful character portraits to themes of deep symbolism. Every medal is distinctively signed "Pisano the Painter," as if the grand creator of the modern medal wished to show that his medallic art was composed of brush strokes, though the medium is different from the fresco.

Pisanello's followers further developed his techniques and created their own distinctive methods of portraiture. His influence is present in nearly all medals produced in the century after his death by artists such as Jacopo Lixignolo, Bartolomeo Melioli, Gianfrancesco Enzola, Sperandio of Mantua, Camelio, Giovanni Maria Pomedelli, Caradosso, Cristofore di Geremia, and Niccolo di Forzore Spinelli (Fiorentino). Each artist had been trained as a goldsmith, coin engraver, and medallionist; during this period of the Renaissance the three trades often went hand in hand. Sperandio was probably the most prolific medallist, and from the number of important individuals who sat for portraits in bronze, it is clear he was held in high regard during his day.

In the post-Pisanello Renaissance period, perhaps the single most important force behind medallic art was the papacy. The mint at the Vatican was not only a major source of money, it was also home to a number of important me-

Early papal portrait medals. Pope Innocent XII appears on this medal, which commemorated his reign from 1691 to 1700.

Botticelli's portrait of a young man with medal, probably fifteenth century. According to Clive Stannard, chief of the Money & Medals Program of the Food & Agriculture Organization of the United Nations, the metallic object in the youth's hand is actually a coin bearing the portrait of Nero.

dallic artists, whose portraits of various popes helped their art to flourish and left a record of the period. With Pope Paul II, who commissioned a series of medallic portraits, an official series began under several different artists.

As with painting and other arts, medallists are generally attributed to various schools, places, or periods. For the collector, however, the most emphasis is placed upon the designer and on the individual beauty of the piece. Truly one of the most interesting indications of the popularity of medallic art during the Renaissance is a painting by Botticelli of a young man holding a casting of a medal honoring Cosimo de Medici, a piece believed created by Fiorentino.

In the following years, new medallic techniques were employed: casting gave way to striking, reliefs became slightly lower and detail less intricate. All the while, new

Early medallic tribute to New World discoveries.

schools and artists were emerging across Europe, and later in the United States. In the process, medallic commemoration achieved new significance as various governments commissioned presentation medallions.

Throughout American colonial history, European nations commemorated various events with medallic tribute. An early silver casting of 1556 refers to Philip II of Spain as "King of Spain and the New Western World." The voyage of Sir Francis Drake to the North and South American continents was commemorated in 1580 by a medal in imitation of ancient art, engraving and tracing the route of his ship. As our own Revolutionary War was being fought, representatives of American interests abroad, acting through Benjamin Franklin, ordered a series of medals celebrating victories of battles against the British. (These Franklin medallions were reissued in 1976 as a Bicentennial commemorative.)

Thomas Jefferson, then minister to France, became involved in issuing the fifteen commemorative medallions. In February 1789, Jefferson described each of the creations at length in his notes: there were medals honoring Washington and John Paul Jones, the great naval hero, the Battle of Saratoga, the evacuation of Boston, engagements at Stony Point, and the capture of Major André (which led to the discovery of Benedict Arnold as a traitor). Jefferson engaged the artists to execute the designs and personally hired a cabinetmaker to produce a box to hold the fifteen medals plus two others: a famous "Libertas Americana" medal, executed by Augustin Dupré and paid for by Benjamin Franklin as his personal tribute to American independence, and an equally famous depiction of Franklin by the same engraver.

Jefferson described the "Libertas Americana" coin and its symbolism in these words: "A head representing American Liberty; its tresses floating in the air. The cap of Liberty on the point of a spear. 4 July 1776 (The day on which the United States declared themselves independent)." The reverse of the medal, equally beautiful, is identified by Jefferson as "an infant Hercules, cradled in a buckler, and

Medallic art of Benedetto Pistrucci.

strangling the two serpents. A leopard comes to devour him; but Minerva interposes her shield (characterized by the fleurs-de-lis of France)."

Medallic manufacture at the U.S. Mint began in the mid-1790s and continues to this day. Many of the issues, ranging from peace medals for presentation to Indians to those honoring secretaries of the Treasury, directors of the Mint, Presidents, and special events commemorated by Congress, are known in their original form and in mint restrikes. The restrikes, which form the basis for the mint list, can be ordered by any individual by applying to the Philadelphia Mint. The cost varies depending on the size of the medal, but all of the many commemorative tributes done by the Mint over the past 180 or so years are available to the collector.

Some of the finest medals of the nineteenth century were created by an Italian gem engraver named Benedetto Pistrucci. His method of production was distinctive. First he made a model of a drawing draft in beeswax on a sheet of glass; then by skillful use of what resembled graph paper and a draft drawing, he was able to calculate precisely how each portion of the design would appear when fully reduced. The figures in Pistrucci medals are invariably exact, and his creations are thus highly prized by all medal collectors for their distinctive artistry.

Theodore Roosevelt inaugural medal created by Augustus Saint-Gaudens, 1904.

In America by 1870, the greatest artists in sculpture and portraiture had turned to the medal, not unlike their Roman predecessors, to create distinctive commemorations. Augustus Saint-Gaudens, James Earle Fraser, John Flanagan, Victor David Brenner, Bela Lyon Pratt, and others created magnificent medallions prized by today's collectors. Like other pieces of fine art, most of these medals have appreciated in value through the years.

Perhaps the greatest patron of these artists was President Theodore Roosevelt, who engaged the sculptors for medallic works and also to redesign American coinage. Brenner's medallic tributes to Lincoln, and most of Saint-Gaudens's medallions, owe their existence to "T.R."

Roosevelt also brought artistic value to the presidential inaugural medal. The tradition for such a medal actually began with William McKinley's second inauguration in 1901, but after his assassination and Roosevelt's assumption of the presidency, the 1904 election gave Roosevelt the opportunity to develop the modern medal fully. Without the President's knowledge, the inaugural planning committee authorized Joseph K. Davison's Sons of Philadelphia to strike what amounted to little more than a copy of the rendering done by the U.S. Mint in 1901 for its standard presidential series. The portrait of Roosevelt by Charles Barber is not especially imaginative or bold, but the likeness is striking and fully conveys "T.R.'s" energy. Yet the President did not like its realism. Instead, he invited Augustus Saint-Gaudens, then the foremost sculptor in America, to the White House and personally requested that he execute a special inaugural medallion.

Saint-Gaudens, though initially reluctant to undertake the work, collaborated with a young New York sculptor named Adolph Weinman, and together they created a magnificent rendering of Roosevelt in the classic style of the Greeks. Tiffany & Company was selected to produce the creation, which was cast with molten metal as the ancients had done, rather than struck on a press. T.R. was evidently pleased, for he wrote to Saint-Gaudens at his Vermont studio to thank him "for consenting to undertake the work."

In a handwritten comment, he declared: "I thank heaven we have at last some artistic work of permanent worth." And, in a postscript to the two-page letter, he added: "I don't want to slop over [this], but I feel just as if we had suddenly imported a little of Greece of the 5th or 4th century B.C. into America. . . ."

Since the time of Roosevelt, the inaugural medal tradition has grown. Some chief executives like Franklin D. Roosevelt have taken a personal interest in the medallions. FDR appeared as much interested in the arts as his cousin Teddy and took an active role in the design of his four inaugural medals, making suggestions about design to the sculptors and even sitting for them when required. Harry S. Truman, Dwight D. Eisenhower, John F. Kennedy, and Lyndon Johnson all posed for sculptors creating their inaugural tributes; aides to Richard Nixon termed a sitting "out of the question" and submitted photographs, as did Gerald R. Ford and Jimmy Carter.

Ronald Reagan understood the artistic process involving inaugural medals perhaps better than any other modern president. His medal is a front portrait rather than the three-quarters view or profile that is so typical. A full-facial portrait is difficult to execute because it requires extraordinarily high relief (the nose is substantially above the other features on the planchard) and because a front-on view does not allow for as much artistic freedom and interpretation as a side view does.

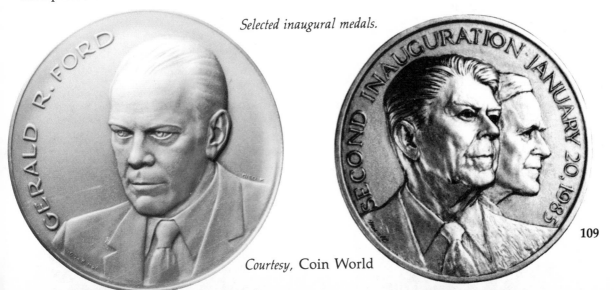

Selected inaugural medals.

Courtesy, Coin World

109

President-elect Reagan did something else to assist the sculptor that was extraordinary: he sat for a life mask. In this process the face of the model is swathed with Vaseline, after which a straw is placed in each nostril. Then plaster is dripped over the face, forming a cast that goes directly to the contours of the individual. A very lifelike result is apparent. The medal comes about as a result of this effort and is extraordinary in every artistic respect.

Despite the somewhat wooden designs of many of the presidential medals, collecting them has become a popular pastime, and for some a profitable one. The 1936 inaugural medal depicting FDR and his vice-president, John Nance Garner, initially sold for $2.50; today the asking price is in excess of $500. A bronze rendering of the Eisenhower inaugural medal from 1953, which originally cost $3 and sold 25,685 copies, now regularly changes hands for $75. Even the 1969 bronze rendering of Nixon, which cost $6, has an asking price of more than $20 today.

Presidential inaugural medals are not the only pieces that exonumists, as some medal collectors call themselves, desire to accumulate. A number of fine artists have created

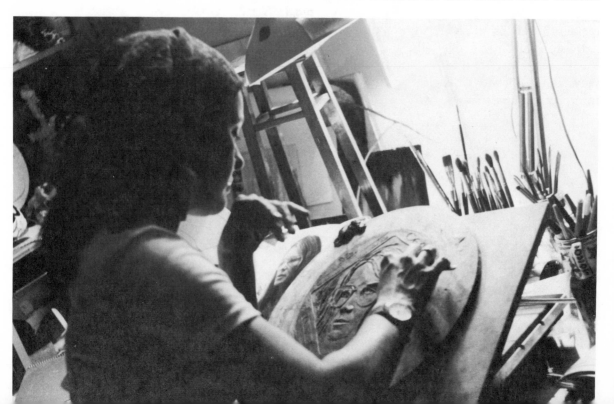

medals on a variety of subjects. Congress has authorized the U.S. Mint to strike national medals on subjects ranging from a celebration of the centennial of the San Francisco cable car to the 1972 Transportation Exposition in Washington, D.C. These national medals, which number in the hundreds since 1856, when a medal department was formally organized at the U.S. Mint, are highly collectable. So,

Sculptor Elizabeth Jones creating an art medal honoring American feminist Gloria Steinem as part of the "Ceres" medal program, sponsored by the United Nations Food & Agriculture Organization (FAO) in Rome. Monies derived from the sale of the medals are used to assist agricultural programs in developing countries. Jones works a Plasticine model to refine the portrait and interior design, creating the image that will be reduced in size on the finished medal. Then she wraps flexible plastic stripping gently around the model, takes bubble-free wet plaster, and spoons it into the basin created by the model at bottom and the stripping at the side. Once the plaster cures, it is refined and details are added. Later, a galvano is made to reduce the design to a die that produces the finished medal. Jones was appointed Chief Engraver in 1982 by President Reagan.

The finished product—FAO'S Gloria Steinem medal.

too, are the products of commercial producers. In the twentieth century there have been a number of private manufacturers of commercial medallic art, including Tiffany & Company of New York. Probably the foremost firm is Medallic Art Company, which has produced more presidential inaugural dies and medals than any other company. Yet despite the relative commercial success of the art medal and the artistic appeal of these large-size sculptures in metal (which can often be a full three inches in diameter), the popularity of modern medallics must take into account the Franklin Mint, which created the coin medal.

Some examples of the modern art medal.

113

The Franklin Mint's fifty-state Bicentennial tribute.

The U.S. Mint's national Bicentennial medal.

Coin medals differ from the art medal not so much in design or detail as in the extent to which the relief of the design is raised from the surface of the planchet. Whereas a fine art medal can require up to a dozen strikes of a multiton press to create the correct metal flow and impression, the coin medal can usually be brought up in a mere two strikes. Also, the art medal traditionally has been produced in a florentine or sandblasted finish, while the Franklin Mint has popularized the manufacture of proof-finish (mirrorlike surface) medals.

The Franklin Mint has offered series of medals on a specific theme, such as famous women, famous black Americans, or even antique cars. Precious metal has been used in virtually every instance, and some of the leading sculptors in the nation have been employed to lend respectability to its designs. They have created an audience for the art of the medal through their vigorous national advertising and direct-mail campaigns, and brought the medal beyond the hard and true coin collector. In the process, the entire method of collecting medals has been revolutionized, and it seems fair to say that the Franklin Mint has broadened the scope and interest of medallic art in America.

It would be a mistake, however, to associate modern medallic art exclusively with the Franklin Mint. Despite its introduction of the medal into the homes of millions of Americans, there are a number of artists whose serious work and study, as well as production methods, preclude the use of the basically low relief that characterizes Franklin Mint products.

This is not to denigrate the Franklin Mint, whose sculptors have consistently put out fine products, and whose archives show that virtually every major sculptor and medallist today has produced medals for this private mint. Their output includes two official presidential inaugural medals, in 1972 and again in 1976, and other commemorative pieces known the world over.

Nonetheless, other medals have been produced whose intent never was to capture the mass market. These are frequently oddly shaped, have a particularly high relief and an exquisite beauty that only the owner of fine art can truly appreciate. Some would term them art for the classes, not the masses.

In 1983, the American Medallic Sculpture Association was formed with an eye to enhancing man's immortality through the art medal. They successfully mounted an exhibition of thirty-nine major medallic artists at the American Numismatic Society in New York, the American Numismatic Association in Colorado Springs, Colorado, the U.S. Mint at San Francisco, and Georgetown University's Lauinger Library in Washington, D.C.

The U.S. Mint's national Bicentennial medal.

The Franklin Mint, largest private mint in the world.

TOKEN THOUGHTS

While medals generally are considered to be an exquisite art form, they have limited utility except in the sense of aesthetic appreciation. Not so with the other area of exonumia—tokens. Like coin of the realm, tokens are used in exchange transactions but lack the legal tender attributes of government-manufactured money because they are made by private manufacturers. Generally, a token carries on its face a message of some kind, though it can be blank and merely serve as a slug designed to activate some vending device. Common uses for tokens today are for payment of bus and subway fares, for use in vending machines in a particular location, and as advertising promotion for merchants. Regardless of their use, they are numerous and highly collectable.

Historically, tokens have played a more significant role than they do today. During the time of Andrew Jackson, the defeat of the charter of the Second Bank of the United States in 1833 brought tokens out in large numbers. The reason for the tokens was not advertising—though each contained political propaganda that seems amusing 150 years later—but economic preservation. The effect of Jackson's "killing of the Bank" caused virtually all gold, silver, and copper coinage to be hoarded by citizens who feared complete economic disaster. The deposits of the United States were withdrawn from the Bank, as they were needed for ordinary expenditures of government. Such funds as revenues were placed in state banks and within a subtreasury system. For its part, the Bank went down fighting, ruining the credit of the nation in the process and creating the Panic of 1837.

Jackson, to complete the destruction of the Bank, ordered that its currency notes be dishonored for public land and debt obligations, and the so-called Specie Circular of July 11, 1836, accomplished that goal. But since many other banks in the nation also held these bank notes, the urgent demand for gold and silver coin for all purchases created a coin shortage and panic. Suddenly, money was withdrawn

Early colonial tokens (coppers).

Examples of New York City transportation tokens struck through the years by the Roger Williams Mint, a private concern in Rhode Island.

Thomas Benton's currency was called a mint drop, and here the copper that circulated in place of withdrawn cents, nickels, and minor silver pieces is shown with a reverse similar to that of the large cent then circulating.

President Andrew Jackson succeeded in destroying the Second Bank of the United States by failing to renew its charter. When a massive depression wracked the nation as a result, hard-times tokens such as this one began to circulate, mocking "My substitute for the U.S. Bank."

from circulation as citizens tried to hoard cash. Even coppers were pulled out of circulation in the process. From this background, hard-time tokens were born.

Tokens began to circulate, almost as specie in themselves, with portraits of General Jackson, President Jackson, or, in some renderings, Emperor Jackson. Many were produced during the subsequent administration of Martin Van Buren, Jackson's chosen successor.

The themes are virtually all political, and most of the pieces are actually patterned after the design of coin of the realm. "Benton's Mint Drops," a popular motto on some of the tokens, mocked the advocacy of a gold and silver standard coupled with a federal paper currency. (Paper money would be issued above $20 denominations, but coin alone would be utilized for lower denominations under the Benton proposal.) Patriotic themes also were predominant. "Millions for Defense but Not One Cent for Tribute" was a frequent motto on these issues. Also appearing at the time was a now-famous antislavery token, with a kneeling slave in shackles beneath the motto: "Am I Not a Woman and a Sister?"

Caricatures of Presidents Jackson and Van Buren were also dominant elements. One typical design featured an angry Jackson, sword in hand, plumed in military uniform beneath the motto: "I Take the Responsibility"—a reference to his primary role in creating the situation that made the token coinage necessary.

One reverse utilizes the jackass, symbol of the Jackson party, and characterizes it as "Roman Firmness," further challenging the President with his "The Constitution as I Understand It" philosophy. A November 1837 piece makes no pretense of its origins; the motto says that the copper is a "Substitute for Shin Plasters."

Yet another token, with "Executive Experiment" as its motto, depicts the federal subtreasury in the form of a turtle. Some satirized Jackson's personality more directly, like the hard-times token that is labeled: "My substitute for the U.S. Bank." It features a bust of Jackson with the words: "MY experiment, MY currency, MY glory." The reverse tells the tale of what the financial panic was about: beneath a running hog labeled "My Third Heat" (a not-so-subtle reference to the three runs for the presidency made by Jackson), and a label of "MY victory" above "Down with the Bank," there is the inscription: "Perish Credit, Perish Commerce."

Other tokens mocked Jackson's receipt of an honorary law degree from Harvard Law School by placing the initials of the academic honor LL.D. onto a jackass. John Quincy Adams of Boston, a former President who had attended Harvard, refused even to attend the ceremony that honored Jackson, because he considered his education so low as to demean the degree and the university.

Between 1832 and 1844, these hard-times tokens circulated widely. Many are crudely struck, though today all are widely collected as beautiful examples of political art. Each carries with it a portion of American history—a unique, distinctive reminder of a different age.

Hard-times tokens remain relatively inexpensive, at least for most issues. Several guides to collecting them are available, the most important being the study Lyman Low did at the turn of the century. In that pamphlet, some 183 different tokens are catalogued, and while the listing is incomplete, it is invaluable to today's collector. (Numismatic publisher Sanford J. Durst has recently reprinted the Low listing, bringing down the price.) Other possible sources include the old *Coin Collector's Journal* of April 1938 and the *Standard Catalog* (Wayte Raymond) from 1941.

As the nation settled down after the twelve-year depression that caused the hard-times tokens to circulate, it soon verged on the Civil War, in which the problem of circulating currency began anew. Once again, specie, or coin of the realm, was withdrawn from circulation by a panicked public. Despite the government's increased coinage production efforts, coppers simply did not circulate. Civil War tokens swiftly emerged, most of which were issued by merchants in the form of "store cards," or tokens redeemable for merchandise. Today, thousands of types are known and have been catalogued in the several works that cover the field

Andrew Jackson's vice-president, Martin Van Buren, was just as opposed as Old Hickory to the continuation of the Bank of the United States. When Van Buren was elected to succeed Jackson, and hard times continued, he too was ridiculed with copper metallic currency.

Daniel Webster, a senator from New Hampshire, statesman, and orator, was mocked with this "credit currency" token, a reference to the fact that he was in the pay of the Bank of the United States, which issued credit funds.

When the federal government's food stamp program was created, the units were in dollars. Printed currency produced at the Bureau of Engraving and Printing in Washington could be used—but only in whole-dollar amounts. To avoid paying out cash for the difference between the price of an item and the nearest dollar equivalent, some stores produced tokens in minor amounts, redeemable only at that store for more food.

(see the Bibliography for a listing). Yet new pieces are still being discovered all the time, leaving the field wide open for the collector interested in acquiring tokens from a particular state, city, or country town.

No one volume exists of all the U.S. tokens ever struck; when the tokens of other countries are considered, the sheer number is overwhelming. Still, prices for most tokens are modest, and this does make them attractive to acquire. Since so many are uncatalogued, it is an area where the sophisticated token collector who learns to recognize rarity can readily pick up bargains by looking in "junk boxes" at antique fairs across the country.

For the really interested token collector, a national organization that has issued a bimonthly journal since 1964 can be of some assistance. The Token and Medal Society (TAMS) not only attempts to catalogue new issues but also to sponsor research into older token issues and to assist members in buying, selling, and trading their collections and finds.

A casino token in the amount of five dollars.

The History of American Coinage

The coins and the paper money of the United States alike constitute an important part of our national heritage. From the first silver pieces struck for Massachusetts Bay Colony to the earliest emissions of paper money in the various colonies, all the monies of America tell a fascinating tale of history, power, glory, and intrigue that is not readily divisible by colony or even by monetary type. No collection of American money is complete without both coins and paper currency, so any discussion of the history associated with them requires an examination of both.

COLONIAL MONEY

Prior to the Revolution, the money used throughout colonial America varied from region to region. On the eastern seaboard, the most common money was probably the Spanish real, or pillar dollar, which was frequently divided into eight pieces for smaller denominations—hence the term "pieces of eight." These interesting coins, the subject of chilling tales and romantic pirate lore, were struck throughout Spanish Latin America—in Bolivia, Chile, Colombia, Guatemala, Mexico, and Peru—and were widely circulated in the thirteen colonies and later in the early states. Although all other foreign legal tender was banned in the mid-nineteenth century, there is still an old law in the statute books that, if followed, would require the U.S. Treasury and Post Office to accept "the pieces commonly known as the quarter, eighth and sixteenth of the Spanish pillar dollar" at valuation rates of 20 cents, 10 cents, and 5 cents, respectively.

Although foreign money was far more visible at that time than domestic, numerous coin and paper issues were made within the individual colonies, and government-authorized bills of credit were also available. All these can be collected today. The first paper bill of credit originated in Massachusetts during King William's War in the last decade of the seventeenth century. Paper money issued before the Revolution served in several colonies, principally to finance military expeditions for the Crown. During Queen Anne's War in the early eighteenth century, paper money was issued in Connecticut, New Hampshire, New Jersey, New York, and Rhode Island. Farther south, the Carolinas issued paper currency when they began to defend their western frontier. In nearly every instance the experiment was a failure, as the paper money depreciated in value relative to the Spanish pillar dollar and British currency. Throughout the eighteenth century, the British Parliament passed various acts designed to limit or prevent further proliferation of paper currency in North America, calling for a rapid retirement of the circulating notes. Consequently, to the collector of today, they have become more valuable.

Early Problems

During and after the War for Independence, the various states and the confederated government issued several different types of paper money, all of which were backed solely by the integrity of the revolutionaries. Earlier paper money issues of the colonies usually had been backed by the power of the colonial governor to tax the population and thus pay off the face value of the notes. The states gave the federal government no taxing power, however, and ravaged by war, they barely managed financial survival. Predictably, the currency suffered.

As for the signers of the Declaration, their lives, fortunes, and sacred honor had been pledged to the Republic, but so far as the holders of continental currency were concerned, their words were worth only the paper they were printed on. The fortunes of many of the signatories were decimated by war, and their lives were constantly threatened. Consequently, the value of the currency they supported was sustained only by fiat, and it fluctuated constantly, acting as a bellwether of the fortunes of the young nation. By war's end, the economic devastation was so complete that $1 in coin or specie was worth $80 in continentals. Of the $240 million in bills of credit floated by Congress, $1 in specie was paid for each $100 in paper. Hence the phrase "not worth a continental," which is still used to denote a valueless currency.

Today, many people delight in acquiring the notes, basing a collection on the state of a bill's origin, unusual denominations that were issued, or on certain combinations of the hand-inscribed signatures found on each note.

If the continental currency was disappointing because the money was not worth the weight of the paper it was printed on, gold, silver, and copper coinage also had their problems. The metal content of coins in similar denominations varied widely and often did not correspond to fluctuating market prices of gold, silver, and copper. As a result, tables of foreign exchange were often required to determine the worth of a New England shilling in Virginia. When the gold-to-silver ratio changed, or copper became scarce, it was common for holders to melt existing coin for the bullion content. This problem continued throughout the first century of American independence, contributing to what was later called the "Crime of '73," and it had an economic impact that was felt in the twentieth century.

Bermuda "Hogge" Money and Other Coins

Fascinating stories are linked to the coins of the colonies and their dependencies. The earliest monies in British North America were probably used on Somers Islands, now

Hogge money of Bermuda, where the island was considered part of land owned by the Virginia Company.

known as Bermuda. The islands, today a British colony, were controlled by the Virginia Company at the start of the seventeenth century. Early explorers had named it the "isle of Devils" because its treacherous coral reefs had sent many Spanish and Portuguese vessels to watery graves. Sixteenth- and seventeenth-century voyagers who passed close by the island and survived told chilling tales of black creatures who inhabited it and made strange noises. These witches were actually wild boar, or "hogge." The swine, which had apparently survived a shipwreck, flourished in the balmy climate of the island, and their progeny saved the lives of generations of sailors who took refuge on the island following unfortunate brushes with the coral.

In the early 1600s, the British claimed Bermuda, which had then been renamed for Juan de Bermúdez, its earliest known explorer, and set about colonizing the island. One of the first tasks of the colonists was supplementing barter transactions with money. While the precise origin of the first coinage is unknown, most experts presume that the mints of England created the so-called hogge money, brass pieces depicting the life-saving boars on one side and the shipping vessels of the period on the other. The earliest American coins are quite rare, and nearly all in a poor state of preservation, principally because of the corrosive effect of the salt-water air on the copper. Naturally, they are sought by collectors of early Americana.

New England Monies

Although Bermuda lays claim to the earliest American coinage, the first monies produced in the continental United States came from New England. Wampum, or money made from seashells, formed the basis for the earliest monetary system of Massachusetts Bay Colony, supplemented by whatever foreign coins abounded, bills of credit, and, of course, barter. By 1640, the Massachusetts legislature stated that the legal exchange rate was four pieces of white wampum per penny, while the scarcer blue was good at two pieces per penny. As both types of wampum became more available, their value diminished. In October 1650, the legislature changed the conversion rate for white wampum to eight per penny, the black or blue to four. Around this time, an influx of counterfeit coins from abroad provoked the legislature to authorize its own mint and coinage, although the act was virtual treason (only in England and under the king's authority could coin be struck).

The earliest coins included the Pine Tree issues, in 3- and 6-penny denominations, together with the shillings, and all bore the date 1652. For more than thirty years, these coins were produced in New England and tacitly accepted by the Crown because so far as the surface impression could show, all were produced earlier. In the final years of the seventeenth century, the Pine Tree sixpence played an interesting role referred to in the Mother Goose nursery rhyme: "There was a crooked man, and he went a crooked mile/He found a crooked sixpence against a crooked stile." The crooked sixpence was a silver Pine Tree piece. If modern historians are correct, during the Salem witchcraft hysteria of 1692 these coins were bent for use as amulets to ward off such evil spirits as might be found lurking in the dark woods of Massachusetts.

History aside, the earliest monies of New England are much prized by today's collectors. In October 1970, one Pine Tree shilling in the collection of the Massachusetts Historical Society was put on public auction in New York. The coin was in extremely fine condition, showing just a bit of circulation and wear, and it was sold to Henry Allen for $130. When Allen's colonial collection was sold in February 1977, the coin brought $310.

Early colonial coins that are quite rare are priced accordingly. An undated New England shilling, produced around 1652 and preceding the Pine Tree money, is a good example. In 1957, at an auction held in conjunction with the annual convention of the American Numismatic Association, a specimen in very fine condition—meaning that it was worn from some circulation but still in a reasonably good state of preservation—sold for $700. Two decades later,

This undated New England shilling sold for $31,000 at a 1976 public auction sale.

1652 Pine Tree shilling.

when Stack's Coin Company auctioned the Laird U. Park Collection of Colonial Coinage, the identical specimen received a bid of $31,000 from an eager collector. For a rarity, such growth in value is not unusual, nor is it restricted to colonial monies.

Other Colonial Monies

Other colonies also struck coins and tokens. These include the shillings of Lord Baltimore in Maryland; private coinage from the same colony struck without government authority by Annapolis goldsmith John Chalmers; farthings and half pennies imported to New Jersey from Ireland by Mark Newby in the early 1680s; and patented coins of William Wood. Wood's money, known today as "Rosa Americana" issues, was first produced in 1722 with a royal patent for its composition—a combination of silver, copper, and zinc. Wood's issue was the first attempt to create a coin that could circulate in all the colonies at the same rate of exchange. Colonists as well as many English swiftly rejected the issues, which were based upon the weight of the pieces and the value of the metal. At that early stage in

Portrait of Lord Baltimore on one of Maryland's colonial coin issues.

"Rosa Americana" issues, by William Wood, were made of silver, copper, and zinc, and duly rejected by the colonists.

American monetary history, even the metal content of the copper half penny had to be true in order to get merchants and others to accept it.

THE FIRST AMERICAN MONEY

Coinage is a prerogative of sovereignty, and the Declaration of Independence marked the first efforts to create a coinage of the United States of America. In 1776, the first American dollar was struck. It bore the motto, "We are one," in English, and depicted interlocking rings with the names of the thirteen original colonies. However, this common coinage was generally a failure; the war totally disrupted finances and led to many different paper issues in odd-looking denominations. The reminder that we have of it today is the Latin motto still found on our national money: *E Pluribus Unum.*

The first continental currency issues were authorized by Congress on May 10, 1775. Each of these notes—printed in $1, $2, $3, $4, $5, $6, $7, $8, $20, and $30 denominations—purported to be redeemable in Spanish milled dollars (the whole of the piece of eight). Benjamin Franklin was intimately involved in this first issue. Like many of the founding fathers, Franklin was concerned with creating a solid

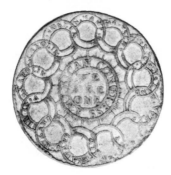

Continental dollar of 1776.

129

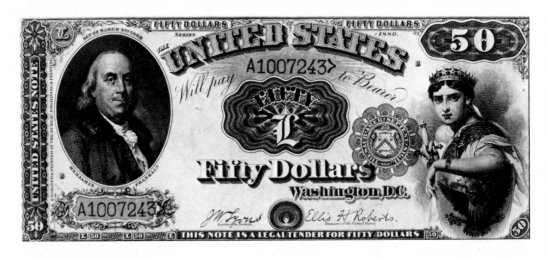

Dr. Benjamin Franklin.

*Patterns of the proposed Robert Morris coinage —
cent, quint, and mark.*

monetary system. Chief among the earliest concerns was the counterfeiting of paper currency. The British became quite expert at this and used it effectively as a form of economic warfare. By making a plaster cast of a tree leaf and then a leaden mold, Franklin created a distinctive design that was difficult to reproduce. As a professional printer, Franklin actually oversaw the printing, and many bills from Pennsylvania, New Jersey, and Delaware bear the legend: "Printed by B. Franklin."

With the defeat of Cornwallis at Yorktown in the fall of 1781, the Revolutionary War came to an end and a new era of American coinage began. The Articles of Confederation authorized Congress to create executive departments, including one dealing with finance. From Thomas Jefferson's account we learn that "as early as January 7, 1782 [Congress] had turned their attention to the monies current in the several states, and had directed the Financier, Robert Morris, to report to them a table of rates at which the foreign coins should be received at the treasury. . . ."

That same month, Morris began advocating "the necessity of establishing a standard of value . . . and of the adoption of a Money-Unit" called the quint, which could serve as a common denominator between the then-circulating foreign coins and domestic coppers in the several states. The common divisor of the various values was 18,720, but after the peculiar pence of South Carolina was eliminated, it became the more manageable figure of 1,440. The lowest unit of value was thus 1/1440, or a cent. Although pattern, or experimental, coins were struck for the cent, the quint, and the mark, equal to 1,000 cents, Congress failed to approve this novel idea. As Jefferson explained, "[T]he general views of the financier were sound, and the principle was ingenious on which he proposed to found his unit," namely, that it would enable each of the newly formed states to maintain a sense of currency independence while at the same time sharing in a national monetary system. But, said Jefferson, "it was too minute for ordinary use, too laborious for computation . . . entirely unmanageable for the common purposes of society. . . ."

Jefferson's "Notes on Coinage"

Jefferson himself was busy compiling what is known today as his "Notes on Coinage," first printed in the *Providence Gazette and Country Journal* on July 24, 1784, and widely circulated thereafter. He strongly favored the decimal coinage system that with some exceptions is still in use today. In fixing the unit of value, Jefferson asserted, "these circumstances are of principal importance. I. That it be of *convenient size* to be applied as a measure to the common money transactions of life. II. That its parts and multiples be in an easy proportion to each other. III. That the Unit and its parts or divisions be so nearly of the value of some of the known coins as they may be of easy adoption for the people."

Jefferson's proposal included a standard based on silver and gold, in a 15 to 1 ratio, and a decimal system with the cent equal to one-hundredth of a dollar, although in May 1785 he modified this by creating a smaller unit "of which 200 shall pass for one dollar." The half cent and the cent both would be produced in copper—though he later experimented with silver-plugged copper coins.

There was still no national mint, though several private facilities in northeastern states did produce coin at a profit. Jefferson recognized the need for a national mint, but from the start Congress balked at the cost, for the young nation was still deep in debt and a system of taxation was voluntary until adoption of the federated Constitution in 1789. Congress initially chose to authorize contract coinage to private manufacturers, as did the states, which had authority to approve coinage until 1789.

As it happened, the experiment with privately coined money worked reasonably well on a state-by-state level, and abysmally on a national level. The public did not need precious metal coins, but good coppers to make change that could be circulated throughout each region. Thousands of copper pieces were privately produced for Massachusetts, Connecticut, New York, New Jersey, and Vermont, in a variety of designs and denominations.

Collecting Early U.S. Coins

Most of today's collectors seeking to acquire these early American coppers collect more than one or two types. Because there was no mechanized process at the time to duplicate a design exactly, each die had to be cut by hand, so each type had many variations. Based upon their condition and the attractiveness of their design, these coins fetch relatively modest prices, given their age, but there are high-priced variations of the scarcer types. A 1787 New York copper with the state coat of arms on one side and an Indian with a tomahawk on the other sold for $21,000 at a 1976 public auction. On the other hand, more common varieties of coppers in good condition are within the means of the majority of collectors. An average price range for New Jersey and Connecticut coppers might be anywhere from $12 to $40, while some virtually uncirculated common pieces sell at four-digit figures. As with most coins, the prices have mounted steadily in recent years. A quarter of a century ago, records from public auction sales of these coins regularly showed that the specimens in better condition brought from $9 to $20. Today, diminishing supply, increased demand, and the general fascination of collectors and buffs of American history for these pieces, have driven prices to $500 a coin or higher.

The Fugio Cent

Coins known today as Fugio cents were the first national currency authorized by the Continental Congress, whose *Journal of Proceedings* tells of a special coinage contract given to James Jarvis of New Haven, Connecticut. On April 21, 1787, Jarvis was given permission to strike into coin some 300 tons of government copper, provided the United States received a 15-percent premium to be used to reduce the national debt. A specific design was mandated by resolution on July 6 of the same year: "13 circles linked together, a

Contract coinage thrived until 1789.

"We are one" on the Fugio cent depicted an idealized goal rather than a political fact.

small circle in the middle, with the words 'United States,' around it; and in the centre, the words 'We are one'; on the other side of the same piece the following device, viz: a dial with the hours expressed on the face of it; a meridian sun above, on one side of which is to be the word 'Fugio' and on the other the year in figures '1787'; below the dial the words 'Mind your Business.'" The design and wording allude to a saying in Franklin's *Poor Richard's Almanack;* the sundial represents time, and the word *fugio* is Latin for *flee,* implying that "time flies."

Jarvis had considerable trouble raising the capital to procure copper, and he ultimately defaulted on his contract. Unfortunately, though he produced half a million pieces with the Fugio design, they were lighter in weight than the federal standard. Based on their weight, the Fugios were valued at only about 63 per dollar. Under existing American law, Treasury officials were liable to the extent of their own fortunes for any losses, and sought to avert personal disaster by selling the Fugios in bulk to a New Yorker named Royal Flint.

$21,000 was bid for this piece of contract coinage.

135

The transaction was financed entirely on Flint's credit, because he hoped to make a killing by reselling the coins to merchants in need of change. The public in general was still in no mood for short-weighted coppers, however, and the coins were soon being discounted at the rate of 21 cents per 100 pieces. Flint, unable to make the payments required by the agreement with the Treasury Department, went to debtor's prison.

A NATIONAL MINT

The creation of a mint for the United States proved a severe struggle. Key members of Congress were opposed to the cost involved, and votes on the critical proposals for its establishment were close. One such vote was taken in early March of 1791; the proposal at hand called for a national mint, and stated that "the President of the United States [would] be . . . authorized to cause to be engaged such artists as shall be necessary to carry the . . . resolution [establishing a mint] into effect." It passed in the House by the small margin of 25 to 21.

Another proposal, which did not pass, would have called for the reverse side of all silver coins to contain "two hands united, and around the margin of the pieces as many circles linked together as there shall be States in the Union at the time of the coinage, each circle containing the initial letters of the name of its respective State." A further losing proposal for the copper coins called for their reverse to have a "representation of America, in the usual female figure of Justice holding balanced scales, with this inscription, 'To all their due.' "

Pattern coinage (1792).

One of the more interesting provisions of the legislation that was approved described in great detail the designs and devices to be depicted on the new coins:

> Upon one side of each of the said coins there shall be an impression or representation of the head of the President of the United States ... with an inscription which shall express the initial or first letter of his Christian or first name and his surname at length, the succession of the Presidency numerically, and the year of the coinage. . . .

The bill also required that an eagle be depicted on all silver and gold coins. This proposal did not pass, so a series of pattern coins—experimental issues produced for examination by the Senate and House—each carried Washington's profile facing left, his first initial, his last name, and his office (President) on the obverse, and an eagle on the reverse. Very few specimens were struck and only a small number are available to the collector. As with many coins, the value of these has changed dramatically through the years. A quarter century ago, prices ran to about $125. At the November 1976 auction of the River Oaks and Krugjohann Collection by Bowers & Ruddy Galleries, Los Angeles, a pristine example of a 1792 pattern half dollar with the Washington portrait by Peter Getz brought a bid of $5,000.

Despite Getz's fine die-cutting skills and obviously well-executed portrait of Washington, there was opposition to the coin in the House of Representatives. Representative John Page denounced the depiction of Washington by stating that "it had been a practice in Monarchies to exhibit the figures or heads of their Kings upon their coins," then adding, "I am certain it will be more agreeable to the citizens of the United States to see the head of Liberty on their coin than the heads of Presidents." Page prophetically noted that "however well pleased they might be with the head of the great man now their President, they may have no great reason to be pleased with some of his successors. . . ." It is indeed intriguing to wonder what Americans might think of Millard Fillmore half dollars, Chester A. Arthur dimes, and Warren Harding quarters—not to mention more recent recipients of the highest honor in American politics.

The House then voted to adopt the emblematic design of Liberty for American coinage, but the Senate rejected the idea. After several days of dispute, both chambers agreed on the emblem design, and President Washington signed the bill into law on April 2, 1792.

Hamilton's 1791 Mint Report

Alexander Hamilton, the first Secretary of the Treasury, summed up the government stand on the establishment of a mint in his *Report on the Subject of a Mint* in 1791. With some exceptions, Hamilton's ideas still govern the U.S. Mint to-

Alexander Hamilton on a modern medal.

day. He devoted much thought to the intricacies of a coinage system based on Jefferson's decimal model, though somewhat altered, as well as to the choosing of a gold-to-silver ratio of 1 to 15 for valuation purposes. He also explained at length the reasons for the various weights chosen for each of the denominations proposed. Jefferson, who apparently saw either the early drafts or a copy before its official release to Congress, wrote Hamilton on January 24, 1791, that he had read the *Report* "with a great deal of satisfaction," probably because it so closely paralleled his own thoughts. "I concur with you in thinking that the unit [of value] must stand on both [gold and silver] metals," he declared; but his preference was plainly toward making "the unit of money a part of the system of measures, weights and coins," which would have given legal tender to a coined ounce of silver.

Hamilton's *Report* contained a mere twenty-one sentences on the organization of the national mint, but the principles he set forth proved to be of lasting value. Although the original Mint Act of 1792 has been almost entirely rewritten, the daily functioning of the U.S. Mint at Philadelphia as described by Hamilton remains intact today. In charge is a director, who is assisted by an assayer, a chief coiner, an

The earliest coinage was struck in copper because the surety bond required for precious metal coinage could not be met.

engraver, and "as many clerks, workmen and servants" as are necessary, subject to presidential approval.

Gold, silver, and copper coins were authorized under the 1792 act. The gold pieces were an eagle $10, a half eagle $5, and a quarter eagle $2.50. The dollar, half dollar, quarter dollar, dime, half dime, cent, and half cent were struck in silver. Cents and half cents were produced in copper.

Production of the coins was to take place "from time to time" under the act. A death penalty was instituted for counterfeiting, to assure monetary integrity, and it was necessary to have an annual "assay," or trial, of the coins. At the annual trial, the Chief Justice of the Supreme Court, the Secretaries of State and the Treasury, and the Attorney General were required to appear with other officials to test the money produced at the U.S. Mint, and then make a report to the President and nation on its fiscal state and production accuracy.

Hamilton's gold to silver ratio of 1 to 15 was adopted in its entirety in the original Mint Act, and, within a very

John Ward Dunsmore's painting of the first assay, where Martha Washington personally examined coin made from her silver.

short period of time, it nearly drove the mint bankrupt. As to coining money, two methods were acceptable: the government itself could create coin from its own bullion; or individuals could deposit silver and gold bullion with the mint for free manufacture into coin of the realm. President Washington approved "procuring 15 tons of Copper, and proceedings to coin the Cents and half Cents of Copper,

The first Philadelphia Mint.

1792 Half disme; first pattern coin made from Martha Washington's flatware. Note the spelling of "dime," peculiar to the period.

The silver plug in this 1792 cent gives intrinsic worth to a small denomination.

and Dimes and half Dimes of Silver." There was no mention of where the silver bullion was to come from, but if tradition is correct, President and Mrs. Washington's silver-plate service was sent to the mint for melting and coining into 1,500 half dimes. A spot price for copper at the time was 16 cents per pound for 15 tons. Altogether, a sum of $10,000 was required to commence operation of the first national mint in Philadelphia.

Design Problems and the Lack of Metal

Problems of design continued to arise in spite of attempts by engravers to work up acceptable coin patterns. The earliest renderings of Liberty—a woman with flowing hair—appear crude by today's standards, but they accurately represent American art of the period. Except for the 1,500 half dimes, all coins were made in very limited quantities (less than a dozen pieces) some time after September 21, 1792, when English coining presses were installed. Of these early coins, only the silver 1792 half dime is really collectable in the general market today. The others are extremely scarce and highly sought after by serious collectors of Americana.

The 1792 cent, with a silver plug at its center, which was introduced as a pattern to give even the coppers a precious metal value, today is worth over $50,000, when it can be obtained. Recently one sold for $105,000. As for the silver half dime, somewhere between 1,500 and 2,000 specimens are believed to have been struck, and their price is frequently $1,000 or more. Twenty-five years ago, when there were fewer collectors and more of these coins available, an average price was about $150.

Early on, the Philadelphia Mint had problems securing sufficient metal for production. In late November 1792, Washington wrote to Hamilton to complain that "the late rise in the price of Copper and the difficulty of obtaining it render it improbable that the quantity authorized to be procured can be had unless some part of it be imported by

This 1796 dime, first year of issue, is worth upward of $7,000 in uncirculated condition. Even in circulated condition, it has a minimum worth of $500.

the United States," and he recommended that copper be actively sought from the markets abroad, especially from Sweden. Shortly thereafter, Congress was called on to keep the coin composition value in line with market prices by reducing the weight of the coppers more than 21 percent, to 208 grains (from the 264-grain coin authorized earlier) and also proportionally to reduce the copper composition of the half cent. The legislation was enacted into law on January 14, 1793. As a result, no coppers were produced at the 264-grain weight, and not until early 1793 were the old large coppers placed on the production rolls.

Total coinage for the year 1793 approximated 146,000 pieces, mostly comprising several different varieties of large cents, but including 35,000 smaller half cents with the attractive Liberty carrying a liberty pole and wearing a cap on

America's first gold coins.

The 1793 half cent.

her flowing hair. Today, the early 1793 cents and half cents are highly sought after collector prizes, although the prices are not beyond the range of most collectors, especially for the half cent.

A Liberty with flowing hair, classic Greek face, and bearing two distinctive symbols associated with democratic institutions is typical of the designs of the period. The cap atop her tresses is a throwback to ancient Rome, where the hat was a sign of the free man; the pole is of more recent origin—the French Revolution—again symbolic of freedom. These symbols were chosen because both represented new democratic systems, in which freedom and equality were the goals and aspirations of the people.

The early need to change the weight of the copper coinage should have served as a warning that the fixed system of composition and value for precious metals was in danger, but Congress ignored it. As it turned out, Hamilton's 1 to 15 ratio, while it may have approximated the values of gold and silver at the time of the drafting of the mint legislation, was way out of line with the world market price by the time the draft became law, and hopelessly outmoded by 1795, the year the mint began production of eagles, or $10 gold pieces, and $5 gold pieces, or half eagles. (The time lag resulted from the terms of the original Mint Act, which required a high surety bond from the officers in charge of coining as a check against their honesty. So long as they were unable to raise the bond, no silver or gold coin could be produced. Finally, desperate for coin, the legislators reduced the terms of the bond.)

By the middle of the decade, the silver-to-gold ratio had slipped to $15\frac{1}{2}$ to 1. As a result, American coins flowed abroad, where they were first exchanged for Spanish pieces of eight and then melted by bullion speculators who lapped up the difference in value, sometimes as high as 4 or 5 percent. Even though the mint was actively producing the early silver and gold coins of high denominations, few gold coins survived these grand melts. The situation became so bad that in 1804 the mint director, apparently with the approval of President Jefferson, suspended production of sil-

*As a result of the silver/gold ratio imbalance, President Jefferson sus-
pended production of silver dollars in 1804. This 1804 dollar, actually
manufactured in 1836, is worth more than $500,000 today.*

ver dollars and the $10 gold piece, on which a 40-cent profit
could be made if the exchange ratios were different
enough.

Part of the initial problem of American gold coinage was
the lack of a domestic supply of the metal. Some parts of
North America had been explored for gold by Spanish colonial interests centuries earlier, but for the most part, success was restricted to Mexico and South America. Then, in
1828, gold dust was discovered in Georgia, about sixty
miles north of Marthasville, and the first American gold
rush began. The rich ore of the Dahlonega region, as it is
known today, gave new impetus to precious metal coinage.
A short time later, gold was also discovered in North Carolina, near Charlotte.

The First Branch Mints

The nation's commercial expansion underscored the need
for more coin of the realm, which the Philadelphia Mint
was unable to supply. To remedy this problem, Congress

First mint - marked coin. The "O" stands for New Orleans, the mint that struck this 1838 - O half dollar.

authorized the first branch mints, at Charlotte, Dahlonega, and New Orleans in 1835. Soon the gold lodes of the regions were being coined into quarter eagles, half eagles, and $10 gold pieces, while at New Orleans the silver that flowed from Mexico and South America was recoined into American denominations.

Nothing in the branch mint act of 1835 expressly permitted the use of mint marks, but the Treasury Department and the U.S. Mint decided to use different symbols to differentiate the products of the several mints. In the periodic assays to determine the fineness of gold coin against the statutory requirements, the mint marks were distinguishing features. From this administrative convenience, today's collector has distinctive reminders of the early Georgia gold rush, as well as the silver money that slipped through gamblers' hands in the casinos of New Orleans.

THE DEVALUATION OF 1834 AND THE COINAGE ACT OF 1837

By the mid-1830s, it was apparent in Washington that the gold-to-silver ratio question was not going to resolve itself, and that the commercial needs of the growing nation required a circulating coin of the realm. Banks periodically sprang up, and many issued paper currency backed by their reserves. As they were unregulated, these wildcat banks more often than not defaulted on their obligations, leaving broken bank notes in their stead. While the issuers probably planned their bust in advance, they did so with a mind toward garnering the largest amount of cash in the shortest period of time. By printing bank notes with high-quality engraving and ponderous-sounding names, they suckered many depositors with colorful, if valueless, paper.

Devaluation

In 1834, admitting defeat to those who had been melting coin for the difference between its gold content and actual worth, the government devalued the dollar by 6.28 percent, altering the gold content of the coins to form a 16 to 1 silver-gold striking ratio. (It thus took sixteen silver dollars to equal one gold dollar.) The effect on gold coinage can most immediately be seen in the availability today of 1834 half eagles. Those manufactured prior to 1834 contain 0.2578 troy ounces of gold, weigh 8.75 grams, with a fineness of $0.916\frac{2}{3}$, and are valued in fine circulated condition at nearly $2,000 and at five times that price in uncirculated condition. The lesser-weight 1834 half eagles, which have an entirely different design, contain 0.241687 troy ounces of gold and weigh 8.36 grams, with a fineness of 0.8992. There are several different types of each of the coins, but the price spread for collectors seeking to purchase them is roughly one-tenth that of the undervalued, "heavy" 1834 coins.

For collectors today who study records of the period such as mint reports, the figures are deceptive. Production records show that the 1796 eagle has a known mintage of 4,146 specimens, which is high when contrasted to figures for the same $10 denomination in the 1860s and 1870s. Yet, when compared to some of these lower-mintage specimens of later date, the 1796 is a substantially rarer and more expensive coin. In the 1978 edition of *A Guide Book of United States Coins,* the valuation of the 1796 eagle is given as $15,000 in uncirculated condition and $3,600 in the circulated, very fine state of preservation. In 1863, just 1,248 eagles were produced at the Philadelphia Mint, yet in the same guidebook the uncirculated version is valued at $5,000 and a very fine specimen at $2,000. There are many other examples for pre-1834 gold coinage. In each instance the calculated policy of the United States, which at that time was to maintain the value of its gold dollar for trading purposes, created a coin rarity for future generations.

Worth considerably more as uncirculated than as circulated.

COMPARISON OF PRE-1834 EAGLES AND POST-1834 EAGLES (TYPICAL SPECIMENS)

Coin	Mintage	Valuation	
		Uncirculated	Very Fine
1796	4,146	$15,000	$3,600
1863	1,248	5,000	2,000

Note: Most pre-1834 coins, despite high mintages, were melted for their bullion content.

The Coinage Act of 1837

The Coinage Act of 1837 was the first major revision of the coinage laws since 1792. This act revised the minting and coinage laws, changing the composition of gold coins to the more convenient 0.900 fine, or pure, gold content, and reducing that of silver to a subsidiary status, except for the dollar coin, the production of which began again after a hiatus of thirty-six years. A new, sleek Liberty design now appeared on the coins, thanks to the creative talents of Christian Gobrecht. His seated Liberty, bearing a shield and

Christian Gobrecht's dollar design. This 1844 proof specimen sold in Bowers & Ruddy Galleries' Fairfield Collection auction in late 1977 for $2,750.

holding the liberty pole and Phrygian cap, became the dominant design on American silver coinage in the last half of the nineteenth century. To be sure, so prominent a design had its critics and still has even today. Cornelius Vermeule in his classic *Numismatic Art in America* comments: "Clutching her ridiculous little hat on a pole and a shield nestling in the drapery at her side, Liberty looks anxiously over her shoulder as if the horde of Indians were sprinting through the starry firmament toward her."

There are a number of major variations in the silver series of 1837 that many collectors seek today. Whenever a weight change took place, usually a reduction through the revaluation of silver, arrows were placed at either side of the date to let the users know of the alteration from the previous year's issue. This occurred again in 1853 and in 1873.

The arrows at the date reflect a weight change in the coin. "In God We Trust" was added to the 1864 coin.

THE CALIFORNIA GOLD RUSH

The California gold rush of 1848 was the most significant event in the numismatic history of the United States since the U.S. Mint was authorized in 1792. Within a short period of time, a $20 gold piece, or double eagle, had been authorized, and a $1 gold piece was created.

The vastness of California's gold was underrated by nearly all who were connected with it—the miners, the financiers, and the government. The burden of shipping bullion to the East became too much, and a series of local private mints and private assayers began operations. As gold was discovered in other western states, comparable situations resulted. Today, this territorial, or pioneer, gold is much prized by collectors of western Americana, as well as by numismatists. Designs for the coins were often crude, reflecting the difficulties of cutting a die in frontier mints. Nevertheless, the Mormon gold coinage of Utah bearing the all-seeing eye, the "slugs," or $50 gold pieces, of California, and the endless odd-denomination varieties of struck ingots with hallmarks of particular assayers have long fascinated collectors. Each piece has its own story to tell about issuance, design, and use. The tales could well fill a book, covering not only the numismatic aspects but also the lore of the West.

The first double eagle, dated 1849. This unique specimen is in the Smithsonian Institution's National Coin Collection.

Selected specimens of pioneer gold.

The Need for a Western Mint

Almost at the start of the gold rush, a U.S. Assay Office was set up in San Francisco, but it became apparent within a few years that coins, rather than bullion slugs, were desperately needed. At the time of the great gold rush, California had no standardized currency. American gold issues, French Louis d'ors, Dutch guilders, and Mexican reales circulated side by side. Such an arrangement suited a territory with a small population, but with a rapid increase (more than 100,000 traveled the continent to try their panning luck), it became totally inadequate. Shopkeepers measured gold dust on their scales, and in the case of the larger gold finds, territorial issues were produced for assayers, but a barter system was applied to most small transactions.

On July 3, 1852, Congress approved creation of a U.S. Mint at San Francisco, which was at work by April 1854. Minting, smelting, and assaying operations were all conducted in a tiny building sixty by sixty feet, as more than $4 million in gold coin was struck during the first nine months of operation. These coins, all bearing the San Francisco Mint mark—the letter "S"—contained the very same gold that was mined in that area. In 1855, the San Francisco Mint was also given dies cut in the East for subsidiary silver coinage. The introduction of coinage manufacturing gave the West an attribute of the more developed eastern society. Interestingly enough, it also created a major influence on coin design at Philadelphia, which almost immediately began to experiment with Indians in the role of Liberty.

Indian Designs

The appearance of the American Indian on American coins was virtually inevitable. The Indians by the mid-nineteenth century were slowly being dispossessed of their land and placed on reservations for their own "protection." Yet they had a culture hundreds of years old and a way of life that was conveyed most romantically to the curious

151

Idealistic and more realistic interpretations of native Americans as they appeared on American coins.

American public through pulp novels and journalism. In an age of excitement and exploration, the staid portraits of Liberty on coinage left a great deal to be desired. A seated Liberty, holding her cap and pole, simply no longer reflected the nation's inner and outer restlessness.

James B. Longacre's design of the Indian princess in fanciful headdress was made in this spirit, and the choice of subject was apparently deliberate. The first $1 gold pieces struck in 1849 bore the traditional Liberty found on other denominations. By 1854, however, with the creation of the San Francisco Mint, the design on the coin was changed to reflect Longacre's idealized Indian. The $3 gold piece, first coined in 1854, used the same design. Three years later, chief engraver Longacre designed the so-called Indian head cent, depicting Liberty in headdress.

For those who collect by topic, a type set of Indians on American coinage is truly challenging.

Indian head cent by James Longacre.

INDIAN HEAD COINS
(A TYPE SET)

	Years Minted
(1) gold dollar.	1854–56
(2) gold dollar.	1856–89
(3) $3 gold piece	1854–89
(4) $2.50 .	1908–29
(5) $5	1908–29
(6) $10	1907–33
(7) 5 cents	1913–38
(8) 50¢ Arkansas centennial .	1935–39
(9) Daniel Boone bicentennial	1934–39
(10) Oregon Trail	1926–39
(11) Rhode Island tercentennial	1936

Note: Various dates and mint marks were struck for all coins.

THE DEVELOPMENT
OF THE SMALL CENT

Problems with both the copper half cent and its large 1-cent counterpart had been brewing for most of the nineteenth century. The half cent was never a popular coin because of its small purchasing power, its bulky size relative to other denominations (it was just a millimeter smaller than the quarter), and because it was not legal tender for any debts.

The minting records for the half cent reveal that few were produced between 1793 and the late 1850s. Early on, in 1811, production was halted entirely for fourteen years due to lack of domestic interest and because the manufacture of more than 1 million pieces in 1809 proved sufficient for commercial and related uses (artisans and craftsmen sometimes melted the coins down for their metal content). Official mint records also show that between 1836 and 1849

Half cent of 1857, last year of issue.

no half cents were produced for circulation, but that small numbers were manufactured as proof specimens intended for collectors—an early recognition by mint officials of the small but growing number of coin collectors. All told, while more than 150 million large cents had been produced by the mid-1850s, fewer than 8 million half cents had been coined.

Large cents faced a problem similar to that of the smaller half cent. A bulky coin just 1 millimeter smaller than the half dollar, its exacting weight apparently was more useful to craftsmen in search of specific quantities of copper in melted form than as coin of the realm. Produced only at the Philadelphia Mint (which until the twentieth century was the only facility to produce minor coin denominations), the coin did not travel well across the expanding nation and

Light in weight, the silver 3-cent piece was a ready replacement for large old coppers.

perhaps contributed to the decision in 1851 to create a new 3-cent denomination. Initial efforts centered on the cent, though it was the silver 3-cent piece that first came into being. In 1850, the diemakers at the Philadelphia Mint began to produce a series of pattern "small" cents made of copper, copper-nickel, and billon (a silver-copper mixture). The distinguishing feature of these pattern pieces, many of which are scarce, though available to collectors today, is that they all have holes in their centers.

Pattern cent designs, circa 1850.

Throughout the rest of the decade, until enactment of the small cent legislation, the mint's engraving division was kept busy producing patterns for new small cents. Meanwhile, large cent production began to dwindle. By 1856, it was clear that the Treasury was ready to act, and legislation was introduced to create a 19-millimeter cent, containing a copper-nickel alloy and less than half the weight of the large copper. James B. Longacre prepared a mock-up of the proposed new design of a flying eagle and ordered several hundred specimens struck for examination by various members of Congress. As mint director James Ross Snowden explained to Treasury Secretary Guthrie, in a letter dated December 4, 1856: "It would probably aid us in our efforts to deliver the country from the present large and unsightly [cent] coin if a specimen [small cent] were furnished to each member of Congress." These 1856 flying eagle cents, a pattern of 1,000 pieces issued to convince Congress of the wisdom of the 88 percent copper, 12 percent nickel small cent, today are prized by collectors and generally sell for more than $1,000, depending on condition.

The 1856 flying eagle cent, actually a pattern rather than a coin.

The first official issues of the small cent, bearing the flying eagle obverse, followed passage of the act of February 21, 1857. Public reception was so enthusiastic that the mint was forced to limit the number of pieces each person could receive to $50 worth, in exchange for large coppers. A total of 17 million small cents was produced in 1857 and 24 million pieces in 1858. By 1860, after just four years of production, the Philadelphia Mint had produced more small cents than all the large cents manufactured between 1793 and

Public reception was so enthusiastic that conversion of large coppers into small cents had to be limited.

1837 and more than all the old copper coins produced from 1838 to 1857.

After only two years of regular use, the design of the small cent was changed to the famed Indian head cent, misnamed, since Longacre's sketches show that the subject he created was more Greco-Roman than native American. Mint director James Snowden, however, was unhappy about the reverse design and proposed that a shield be added to symbolize national unity, since the thirteen original colonies' stripes would be displayed. Longacre's cent was finally perfected and the design remained until 1909, when the first of a series of American portrait coins was introduced.

THE CURRENCIES OF THE CIVIL WAR

The demise of the large and half cents coincided with the difficult period in American economic history immediately preceding the Civil War. Curiously, the money of the nation played a role in that struggle. Gold discoveries in the South and trading in the port of New Orleans were largely responsible for the creation of several U.S. minting facilities in the southern half of the country. However, not only was minor coinage forbidden at these production outlets, but, except at New Orleans, so was subsidiary silver coinage. Gold coinage depended largely upon bullion available for deposit, which was minimal, so the amount of specie actually available at any one time was usually small.

One of the more interesting consequences was the rise of the bank note issued by a money depository with a paper obligation drawn on a portion of its actual reserves. In the antebellum period, these banks periodically sprang up, accepted deposits, issued paper currency, and inevitably folded, unable to meet their current obligations.

The Civil War brought great economic instability to both the Confederacy and the Union. Even in retrospect, it is hard to say which of the two sides suffered greater monetary troubles. Each was handicapped by a shortage of specie, and each chose to adopt a temporary money standard, which was probably illegal in the case of the Union (though the Supreme Court later ruled otherwise) but necessary for both sides to finance the war. If the hard times brought Union and Confederate states alike to the brink of economic ruin, for today's coin collectors the era is among the most colorful in the nation's history.

As coins of the government ceased to circulate, ingenious alternatives devised by the citizenry began to take their place; so, too, the paper money issues of both the Confederate states and the Union. All are highly sought after items today, although they were extremely undesirable at the time. Paper postage stamps encased in metal became accepted substitutes for coin of the realm, and later fractional currency issues were printed by the federal government in various denominations up to $1 to substitute for missing coin. Stores issued their own scrip or tokens, and the monetary system of the nation split into several tiers.

Examples of encased postal stamps that circulated in the Civil War period.

On the primary level was the gold and silver coin previously produced and the diminished wartime production based on deposits at the Philadelphia and San Francisco mints. This was followed by manufactured minor coinage, which was not legal tender because it was not made of precious metal, and then by fractional paper currency and larger denomination paper, which initially was payable upon demand together with interest. These official instruments aside, there were private issues of paper money by various state banks, encased postage stamps, so-called store cards or tokens issued by individual merchants, and sundry other methods used as a means of obtaining change until 1864, when Congress finally acted to prevent any further production of this private money. Nevertheless, more than 25 million pieces of scrip and token issues were created by hundreds and hundreds of different merchants across the nation. Today, those who acquire these pieces (many of which are still inexpensively priced) have a treasured reminder of very different times.

As the Confederacy prepared for secession from the Union in late 1860, times were perilous for federal facilities located below the Mason-Dixon line, such as the Dahlonega and New Orleans mints. On January 19, 1861, Georgia left the Union. In less than a month, three branch mints—Charlotte, Dahlonega, and New Orleans—found themselves behind "enemy" lines.

Charlotte closed quickly. New Orleans, for a time in 1861, served three masters—the Union, the State of Louisiana, and the Confederacy—and then closed from a shortage of bullion. Dahlonega also closed, but not before the superintendent tried to enlist his services with whichever side wished to continue paying him.

For its own part, the Confederacy was critically aware of the problem of maintaining a domestic money supply. The forty-second law passed by the Provisional Congress of the Confederate States of America regulated "foreign coins in the Confederate States," and an examination of the legislative history makes it quite clear that the only money referred to was money of the United States, which was to be used, as before, by the citizenry. By further stating that "all laws and parts of laws now in force for the regulation of the Mint and branch mints of the United States . . . are hereby declared to be in full force in relation to the Mints at New Orleans and Dahlonega," a number of gold pieces' were produced at those two sites for the Confederacy from dies previously shipped from the Philadelphia Mint for regular production. On May 14, 1861, the Confederate Congress nationalized federal properties, suspended all operations at Dahlonega in order to centralize at New Orleans, and refused to permit any change beyond allowing an assayer to utilize facilities for refining and examining local gold production.

Louisiana's mint continued to operate as a federal facility even after secession, though it was promptly seized by the state before the Confederate Congress took any action. Perhaps wisely, at least for the Confederacy, Louisiana officials ordered the continued striking of half dollars from existing dies and bullion supplies within the large vaults of the mint; more than 1 million specimens were manufactured. Once the Confederacy took over operations, even more were produced. All are identical to the 1861 half dollar issues manufactured under the federal aegis. Interestingly enough, these coins were so widely circulated that those preserved in their original mint state are worth perhaps ten to twelve times as much as even a minimally circulated counterpart.

The Confederate half dollar design.

The Confederacy also made a brief attempt to strike a Confederate 50-cent piece with the obverse of the U.S. issue (which bore the portrait of a seated Liberty surrounded by stars), and a new reverse with the seal of the Confederacy. Sabotage at the New Orleans Mint prevented the use of

One of a dozen original cents made for the Confederacy.

regular steam presses to coin these new 50-cent pieces, but a hand press produced four pattern pieces, which survive today.

When the Confederacy made its initial plans for secession before Abraham Lincoln became President, it seems that the entrepreneurial agents for the American Bank Note Company were engaged to manufacture a series of paper money notes for the Confederacy and that in Philadelphia Robert Lovett, Jr., a die-sinker, was requested to manufacture small-denomination coins for the proposed nation. American Bank Note handled the transaction through its New Orleans office, while Lovett began work through a jewelry firm located near the U.S. Mint at Philadelphia. When, on April 18, 1861, Abraham Lincoln—in office just forty-six days—forbade any trading with the Confederate states, Lovett feared arrest and ceased all work after manufacturing a dozen copper-nickel cents. Some two weeks later, Tracy R. Edson, the president of American Bank Note, reluctantly wrote a long and detailed letter to the company's New Orleans office in which he ordered all Confederate printing operations discontinued. The office was transformed into the Southern Bank Note Company and continued manufacture for the Confederacy until Union forces captured New Orleans in the spring of 1862. This forced the Confederacy to shift currency production to England, where sympathizers to the rebel cause manufactured currency and placed it on ships to run Lincoln's blockade.

Union Experiments with Paper Money

In the meantime, the war depleted the Union's coffers to an even greater extent than the fiat money of the various state banks.

The Constitution adopted in 1789 seemed to make clear that only gold and silver coin could pass as legal tender. The half cent, large cent, and small coppers circulated simply to produce change for the higher legal tender denominations. But with less and less money available, and with more and more expenses, the federal government opted to borrow public funds and issue paper redemption certificates. On July 17, 1861, Congress authorized manufacture of up to $250 million in currency, of which all bore interest at 6 percent except for $50 million worth in $10 to $50 denominations. The interest-bearing note was "a legal tender for all debts, public and private, except duties on imports and interest on the public debt, and is exchangeable for U.S. six-percent, twenty-year bonds, redeemable at the pleasure of the United States after five years." A second, noninterest-bearing type had similar restrictions but could be used to pay back loans of the United States. Demand notes themselves were convertible directly from "greenbacks," as they were widely called, into coin of the realm.

Initial terms of the legislation required that the first or second Comptroller of the Treasury and the Register of the Treasury sign all of the notes by hand after they were produced by a contract-printer in New York (the American Bank Note Company, which previously had been the Confederate source for paper money). The impracticability of this soon became obvious, and in less than three weeks, the law was changed to permit clerks instead of their superiors to sign by hand each of the notes. All told, a force of some seventy clerks was employed, each at a salary of $1,200 per year.

The government's experiment with paper currency was proving expensive indeed. Early in 1862 it was decided to standardize signatures and incorporate them directly into the plate-printing process. Within a short time, a Bureau of Engraving and Printing was established in the Treasury Department to manufacture currency. The printing department of the Treasury initially employed a manufacturing force consisting largely of women. Working in the attic of the building still located opposite the White House in Washington, more than seventy clerks did the printing, drying, and, later, laundering operations for previously used currency.

Five-cent note with portrait of Spencer M. Clark.

The Great "Portraiture" Scandal

In the latter part of 1863, a scandal erupted involving Spencer Morton Clark, first chief of the National Currency Bureau (as it was then known), and several higher-ups in the Treasury Department. Newspapers alluded to promiscuity and immorality on the part of the women clerks and their superiors. Treasury Secretary Chase ordered an investigation into what he thought were groundless charges and was surprised to read the report of a War Department detective named Lafayette Baker citing widespread corruption. Matters were not helped by the prominence of Clark's portrait on the 5-cent note in the second issue of fractional currency. *The New York Times* and other newspapers editorialized against this practice, and as a result, Congress passed a law effective to this day prohibiting any living person from being commemorated on the coins or currency of the nation. The immorality charges refused to die, however, and in May of 1864, James A. Garfield, later to become President, headed a blue-ribbon panel in the House of Representatives. Though the nine-member commission found no evidence of misconduct, the backlash was felt for years, at the instigation, some believed, of the bank-note companies, which wished to retain production rights for the currency.

The 2-Cent Piece

In 1864, a large part of the problem with small change and the pseudo-currency private issues was solved by in-

The first coin to bear the national motto, "In God We Trust."

troduction of a 2-cent denomination. By manufacturing nearly 20 million 2-cent pieces, the mint brought the number of low-denomination coins almost up to the public's needs; a nickel 3-cent piece authorized the following year completed the process.

The 2-cent piece, or tuppence, played an even more important role in the history of American coinage. Treasury Department archives reveal that a minister of the gospel from Ridleyville, Pennsylvania, the Reverend M. R. Watkinson, declared in a letter to Treasury Secretary Chase in mid-November 1861 that "the recognition of the Almighty God in some form in our coins" was an overlooked facet of our money, and that implementation of a motto such as "God, liberty, law" would "place us openly under the Divine protection we have personally claimed."

A week later, Chase wrote to James Pollock, director of the Philadelphia Mint, stating that "no nation can be strong except in the strength of God, or safe except in His defense," and adding: "The trust of our people in God should be declared on our national coins." Chase then ordered the director to "cause a device to be prepared without unnecessary delay with a motto expressing in the fewest and tersest words possible this national recognition."

Pollock examined the laws governing the mint and found

The 3 - cent (nickel composition) coin.

Salmon P. Chase, Secretary of the Treasury when legal tender currency notes were created, and Chief Justice of the Supreme Court when they were declared unconstitutional.

that the Coinage Act of 1837 prescribed certain devices and legends for American coinage. He concluded that no new mottoes could be added without congressional approval. Legislation came in 1864, creating a 2-cent piece with a design left up to the mint director and the Treasury Secretary. The preceding December, Chase had written to the mint director approving the mottoes for the new tuppence, "only suggesting that . . . it should be changed so as to read: 'In God We Trust.' " Subsequently, various coinage acts passed by Congress permitted the specific motto "In God We Trust" to be placed on national coinage. When President Theodore Roosevelt caused it to be removed from the double eagle and other coins, a public furor forced Congress to mandate that all precious metal coins struck after July 1, 1908, bear the motto. In 1955, Congress amended the law to require that the motto be placed on all American coins and currency.

THE LEGALIZATION OF PAPER MONEY

Production of paper money did not end with the Civil War, and before long it became apparent that the two-tiered money system was creating chaos. Greenbacks were "discounted" for specie. Frequently there was no convertibility at all. A constitutional challenge was mounted against the issuance of legal tender notes. If it had succeeded, our modern economic history, not to mention that of American coin collecting, would have changed dramatically.

Hepburn vs. *Griswold*

As it turned out, the legality of paper money issues was finally sustained by the Supreme Court in 1869 in one of the most dramatic events in American monetary history. At issue was the power of Congress to make paper money legal tender for all debts, public and private. Chase, who as Treasury Secretary had been a prime mover behind the fiat money to fight the war and pump money into otherwise empty coffers, sat as Chief Justice. To some there was no doubt where he stood on the issue. Congressman George S. Boutwell, who later would become Treasury head, confided in his diary one of the reasons Lincoln had nominated Chase to the Supreme Court: "We want a man who will sustain the Legal Tender Act and the proclamation of Emancipation."

Chase had been on the Court for four years when *Hepburn* vs. *Griswold* was called to the calendar. There had been other legal tender cases in the interim, but all had been dealt with procedurally to avoid any real conflict while the nation was still at war or in its immediate aftermath. In this instance, however, the court would not be able to duck the issue. The case was presented by Hepburn, an individual

Legal tender note bearing an engraved portrait of Lincoln.

who owned a promissory note dated 1860 and payable two years later. Griswold had made payment in U.S. Treasury notes rather than gold or silver. Ironically, Chase's portrait appeared on some of the very pieces of currency called into question. But the Chief Justice confounded everyone by declaring the legal tender acts unconstitutional, based on the apparent approval of gold and silver payments only. Even this was not the last word, for it was clear to the government that without the power of fiat money—currency built on the gold and silver coinage that the nation was founded on, but in the form of paper money and credit— economic recovery would be impossible. President Ulysses Grant nominated two strong advocates of the legal tender acts to sit on the Supreme Court, while a senior justice opposed to the legislation retired, and the government moved to reargue the case they had just lost. The new appointees held firm and, on May 1, 1871, by a vote of 5 to 4 with Chase in dissent, the Supreme Court reversed its earlier decision and gave life to legal tender notes and the paper money we collect and spend today.

The Carson City Mint

While the North and the South did battle, the West grew. In Nevada, a transplanted New Yorker named Abraham Curry purchased land near Virginia City (and the as-yet untapped Comstock Lode) for the sum of $500 and built a town to memorialize the great frontiersman Kit Carson. Carson City soon became the center of all mining activity in the region, and in 1862, Curry went to Washington to persuade Congress to authorize a branch mint in the growing community. A sum of $80,000 was appropriated to purchase the land, and on September 24, 1866, the cornerstone was laid. In the middle of construction, congressional funding ran out, and Curry was constrained to appeal to Washington for help. The lobbying effort proved successful, and the building of the mint at Carson City was rapidly approaching completion when the entire region surrounding Carson City was devastated by an earthquake three days after Christmas 1869. Most of the city lay in ruins—except for the fortresslike mint. While the citizens of Carson City

The U.S. Mint at Carson City, Nevada.

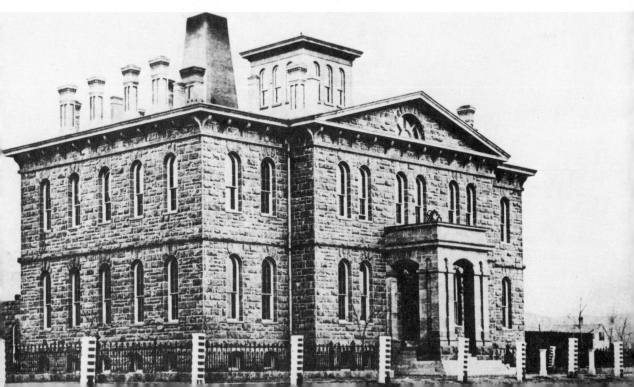

began to rebuild, the mint started operation eight days into the new year of 1870.

Production and manufacturing at the Carson City Mint, whose mint mark, "CC," was placed on all its coinage, was primitive even by standards of the day. As was the practice with the other branch mints, dies came from the main facility at Philadelphia and production presses were also shipped westward. The initial source for gold and silver coinage was the Comstock Lode site, just twenty-one miles from the new mint. A rail spur was built, and the Virginia and Truckee Railroad carted ore daily for refinement and coining. At that time, bullion was deemed more desirable than coin, and refining the ore into pure precious metals took time. Since the highest coin denomination was the double eagle, or $20 gold piece, the large quantities of metal

Carson City's famous mint mark, many times enlarged.

extracted from the ground required bullion brick production at the mint, if only for accounting and convenience.

Most of the coins produced at the Carson City Mint are scarce and highly collectable today. Nearly all the gold coins are heavily bagmarked and weakly struck, especially the large double eagles. Presses from the East were capable of exerting 150 tons of pressure, but often this was insufficient to bring up the metal on the coin into its proper pattern. As the struck coins came off the presses, they clanged together, becoming nicked and scratched before entering circulation. Consequently, collectors pay a high premium for uncirculated coins from the Carson City Mint and also for those that appear relatively unflawed by the production process itself. In some instances, such as the 1870 double eagle from the Carson Mint, there is no truly uncirculated coin known; nonetheless, the almost uncirculated specimens of the 1870-CC double eagle command an asking price above $10,000.

The 1870 - CC double eagle, valued in excess of $30,000.

Probably the rarest coin from this mint is a 20-cent piece, coined to augment the quarter as a sort of "short double bit." The mint at Carson City manufactured some 10,000 pieces of the coin, yet only about a dozen are known to exist today. A letter of March 1877 from director of the mint Henry R. Linderman to Superintendent James Crawford at Carson City offers a plausible explanation for the rarity. Linderman had a fairly keen grasp of congressional sentiment, and by 1877 there was substantial opposition to the continued use of the 20-cent denomination, which most legislators believed wasted the mint's time and the public's

Some 10,000 of these 1876 - CC 20 - cent pieces were coined; all but about a dozen were melted, giving the surviving specimens a value in excess of $40,000.

money. With the decision to eliminate the denomination all but certain (Congress did not actually pass the law ending production until 1878, but during the last two years, only proof specimens were made for collectors), Linderman issued what amounted to a recall order for the issues struck during the previous year. "You are hereby authorized and directed to melt all 20 cent pieces you have on hand," he wrote Crawford, who presumably complied. Some specimens were saved, however, and these rarities command prices as high as $60,000 at public auction.

The Comstock Lode and the "Crime of '73"

While the Carson City Mint churned out its coins, the event of real import for numismatists was occurring some twenty-one miles away at the Comstock Lode at Virginia City. The abundance produced there was already proving a threat to the balance of gold and silver in the nation's money supply. Even though paper money was soon to be legalized by Supreme Court decision, the populace preferred metallic money. Although the true value of silver to gold decreased as more of it was extracted from the mines of Nevada and elsewhere, a silver dollar produced by the government was nonetheless supposed to have a value identical to its gold counterpart.

Henry Linderman, as director of the U.S. Mint, recognized the impending problem, and in his annual report to the Treasury Secretary for 1867 he predicted that with the completion of the transcontinental rail link (which occurred two years later, in 1869), American bullion extraction would increase "to an extent hitherto unknown," and that the price of silver would plummet in the process. The railroad was essential to transport the metal eastward, and then to Europe—cutting a journey of three months or more by sea to several days.

To compound the problem, free coinage of silver was permitted immediately after the Civil War. Any individual could deposit silver bullion with a U.S. mint and for a minimal service charge convert the bullion into coin of the realm. As long as the price of silver was approximately equal to the amount of precious metal in the coin, free coinage posed no threat. In 1870, however, production of silver increased by nearly 5 million troy ounces over the previous year's yield. And by 1872, production had nearly doubled from the 1870 figure.

When Linderman and John Jay Knox, comptroller of the currency, first suggested a massive overhaul of the minting and coinage laws in 1870, it is doubtful whether demonetization of silver was uppermost in their minds. In January 1870, draft legislation was written in the Treasury Department under the aegis of Knox and Linderman, and in February 1873, coinage legislation was finally passed for enactment into law on April 1, an event called the "Crime of '73." But there really was no "crime," at least in the truly criminal sense of the word. Perhaps there was some surreptitious action on the part of government officials who misled Congress for the better public good by merely commenting on the merits of the legislation as it pertained to revising the minting and coinage law. Some commentators in the years immediately following passage of the Coinage Act of 1873 surely thought so, and indeed, some writers in the twentieth century are sure of it. But the record tends to show otherwise.

The "Crime of '73" and the demonetization of silver was

The year 1873 was the last year of issue for these coins; Congress refused to authorize continued striking of them.

a major campaign issue in every presidential election between 1873 and 1900. Presidential debates were held on whether or not a crime had indeed been committed and whether the free coinage of silver again ought to be permitted. The great orator William Jennings Bryan's most famous speech, warning against crucifying "mankind upon a cross of gold," was directed specifically to the silver coinage issue.

THE COINAGE ACT OF 1873

For its part, Congress gave ample debate over five separate sessions. Yet the basic issues that were debated by the senators and representatives had very little to do with the prices of silver and gold. Rather, they concentrated on the new functions of the mint and on the denominations that were either being eliminated (such as the 2-cent piece) or the weight changes that were being made on other pieces. Within the Treasury, Linderman and Knox solicited the views of virtually every past and present mint official to ask how the mint could be improved. Elsewhere, debate over who should handle the engraving and production of coin and medal operations brought various factions within and outside the mint to heated verbal encounters. Yet, in the end, the dominant memories revolve around the obscure provisions that enumerate the coin of the realm and make no mention of the silver dollar. So, too, by omission rather than express provision, the coinage of silver into domestic money was eliminated, with one important exception: a trade dollar, or special coin designed for use in international trade, was authorized for manufacture in the United States and use abroad under a system whereby the mint could set a charge for undertaking the coinage of the piece.

In 1873, Congress created a trade dollar with limited legal tender status; production ceased a dozen years later. This uncirculated specimen recently sold at public auction for $3,000.

This coin was unique in America. *The New York Times* of April 24, 1873, reported: "Great expectations . . . entertained of the trade dollar as a means of creating a home demand for . . . bullion and keeping gold in the country." But those goals proved idealistic. The price of silver continued to decline and by 1886 had dropped below $1 per ounce (so that the average dollar in silver coinage actually contained a bare 77 cents worth of silver); even the heavy trade dollar lost favor abroad.

Passage of the Coinage Act of 1873 came on February 12

of that year—and none too soon. The price of silver, which had averaged approximately $1.29 per ounce or more in every year since 1833, began to drop in value. By 1874, because of the rising mining operations in the West, which by then were nearly tripling the production levels of 1867, the price of silver declined to an average of $1.27 an ounce. And by 1876, the price had dropped to $1.15 an ounce. The intrinsic worth of the money produced by the U.S. Mint was no longer equal to its face value. If the silver coinage was to be accepted by the people as legal tender, they would be doing so purely out of faith in their government.

For today's collector, these dramatic times are represented by a number of different coins. Foremost is the trade dollar itself, widely considered to be one of the more attractive coins produced by the Philadelphia Mint. Its 1½-inch diameter (38.1 mm.) gave William Barber, of the mint's engraving staff, space to create a masterpiece of design. Mintage figures for the coins never were especially high (out of twenty-six different dates and mint marks, seventeen had under 1 million pieces produced), and, given attrition on a natural basis, melting both at home and abroad, and like factors that cause price appreciation, nearly every one of the trade dollars has a keen value to collectors. Those in superior condition are especially prized, and it is not unusual today to see an uncirculated trade dollar sell in the four-figure price range.

As late as 1949, some trade dollars were still reportedly circulating in the Orient, and in that same year R. S. Yeoman's *A Guide Book of United States Coins* listed average values for the coins in average condition (fine) as somewhere between double face value and $6. Today, of course, the coins have a substantial collector's premium, and prices of $75 and above for the same average circulated (fine condition) trade dollar are not uncommon.

A circulated trade dollar with "chop marks" symbolizing its acceptance by an Oriental merchant.

Weight reduction was signified by arrows at the date.

Other coins of the period include the so-called arrows-at-date coinage, produced by the Philadelphia Mint in 1873 and 1874. During the latter half of the nineteenth century, the mint noted changes in the weight of coinage with arrowheads on either side of the date on the obverse. Because the method of testing whether a coin was counterfeit or true was to weigh it, these arrows notified the user that there had been a government alteration of the standard previously used.

In 1853, the arrows signified a weight reduction; two decades later, they indicated an increase of silver in the coinage. Because of a peculiarity in the die-cutting process by which the date was placed on working production dies, some of the early issues of the year have a "closed 3" on the date—so noticeable that in January 1873, mint director James Pollock requested that his chief coiner, A. Loudon

A major variety found on coinage — collectors focus on the open or closed "3" in the date 1873.

Snowden, prepare "an entire new set of figures avoiding the defects of those now in use."

Consequently, collecting the date 1873 alone has proved to be a popular pastime. The types and varieties are:

1873 COIN TYPES

(1) Cent   (7) Dime   (13) Quarter Eagle ($2.50)
(2) 2¢   (8) Quarter   (14) $3
(3) 3¢ Nickel   (9) Half Dollar   (15) Half Eagle ($5)
(4) 3¢ Silver   (10) Silver Dollar   (16) Eagle ($10)
(5) Nickel   (11) Trade Dollar   (17) Double Eagle ($20)
(6) Half Dime   (12) Gold Dollar

NOTE: In addition to above regular types, arrowheads appear at the side of the dates on dimes, quarters, and half dollars.

This small yet challenging collection is not without its compensation to the holder.

PRICE RISE OF 1873 COINS

Type	Date	Auction Sale	Price
1873 $3 gold (proof)	May 1965	Metropolitan N.Y. Numismatic Convention (Stack's)	$ 2,600
	Oct. 1967	Charles Jay (Stack's)	2,900
	Oct. 1974	Paxman (Bowers & Ruddy)	21,000
1873 3¢ nickel	1949 (Guidebook of U.S. Coins)		
proof			8
uncirculated			2.25
proof	1979 (Guidebook		200
uncirculated	of U.S. Coins)		100
proof	1983 (Guidebook		650
uncirculated	of U.S. Coins)		165

This proof 1873 $3 gold piece sold for $2,600 at a 1965 public auction, and in 1974 for $21,000.

The Coinage Act of 1873 marked the beginning, rather than the end, of the battle to keep silver in American coinage. There were numerous legislative attempts to cope with the silver interests as the price of the metal dropped. Western mineowners demanded a resumption of the free coinage of silver. Internal economic troubles produced calls for domestic inflation as a cureall for the high debt of farmers, and indeed the nation itself. In September 1873, a banking panic gripped the financial community. On Sunday, September 21, 1873, President Grant and members of his cabinet met secretly in New York with representatives of the Stock Exchange at Wall Street to alleviate the financial pressure. The Wall Streeters sought a reissuance of greenbacks to artificially inflate the money supply and so counteract economic contraction. Grant and William A. Richardson, the new Treasury Secretary, offered numerous alternatives, one of which included use of greenbacks in government possession for the purchase of bonds from the exchange. Ultimately, some $26 million in greenbacks previously retired were reissued. And yet the feeling of Congress was that this was insufficient, especially since the coin of the realm, or specie, was still not convertible. For its part, Congress was not willing to stand by and permit the economic situation to affect voters; so several so-called inflation bills were introduced, coupled later with the 1875 Resumption Act, which called for resumption of specie no later than January 1, 1879.

THE NINETEENTH-CENTURY SILVER DOLLAR AND THE "STELLA"

For today's collector, the silver politics of the last quarter of the nineteenth century have little import except for one

A product of the Bland-Allison Act, passed over the veto of President Hayes.

factor. The Bland-Allison Act of 1878, passed over the veto of President Hayes, not only returned the silver dollar to mint production rolls but also directed that at least $2 million in silver be purchased on the open market and turned into coin. The coinage of the silver dollar was intended to be symbolic; but unlike prior issues, there was no "free coinage." In this instance, the price difference in value between the bullion content and the nominal, or face, value of the coin was to go to the Treasury, rather than to any private individual.

These silver dollars, or cartwheels, have only recently been examined fully. For many years, the coins—most of which never circulated except in the western states—gathered dust in the Treasury Department's Washington vaults, at other governmental facilities that stored coins, or in the cash drawers of private financial institutions. Before the early 1960s, it was possible to go to any bank and request a silver dollar as change; many were still in virtually uncirculated condition. The Treasury Department annually released bags of the coins at Christmas time, exchanging one silver dollar for each silver certificate note presented by the bearer.

While silver dollar mintage statistics are fairly exact, the number of pieces that has survived is uncertain. Many of the pieces produced were melted or recoined by the mint, which, in compliance with the Pittman Act of 1918, melted more than 270 million coins. Then the exact number retained by the Treasury remained unknown for many years. Finally, before the price of silver drove the coins out of circulation, a significant quantity was available to eager collectors.

As long as the Treasury retained its hoard of the coins, collectors were wary of approaching the denomination. If the Treasury were suddenly to release a bag or more of one date and mint mark, the market would be upset, as in fact happened with the 1903 dollar minted at New Orleans. Mint records show that 4 million pieces were produced, yet the coin was not available to collectors in any significant quantity. By 1962, the price of the coin had climbed to $1,500, and there was every indication that it would continue upward. At Christmas time, however, the Treasury yielded an entire bag of the piece, and overnight the price dropped to one-hundredth of its previous value. Similar events occurred after the inventory of the Treasury Department vaults in 1963, when some 3 million rare Carson City silver dollars were discovered. In this instance, however, the government was wiser and marketed the coins to collectors. After several years of effort, about 2 million pieces were sold for some $55 million; the balance remained in

Left: One of many bags of silver dollars found in Treasury Department vaults in Washington as a result of a 1964 audit.

Below: This 1903-O silver dollar was valued at $1,500 until the Treasury Department released a hoard in 1963; the price plummeted to $15 overnight, but today the value has again begun to rise.

Treasury vaults awaiting destruction or release, pending a new appreciation of value. In 1980, they were finally sold.

At the time of the Coinage Act of 1873, coin collecting as a hobby was in its infancy. Perhaps fewer than a thousand individuals pursued coin of the realm, and those who did inevitably began by collecting foreign coinage, which had circulated in the nation until just before the start of the Civil War. With the aid of reference books and periodicals such as the *American Journal of Numismatics,* however, domestic coinage, especially from the colonial period, became col-

An early member's medal of what today is called the American Numismatic Society.

181

lectable, and groups of collectors were meeting periodically and forming clubs. But while coin collecting per se was in its infancy, the sophistication of the collector surely was not. In this period and in the dozen years following, a number of specimen coins were produced at the mint as proofs only—specifically intended for collectors.

At the mint, coins were usually weighed by potential users, who promptly placed their own mark, or "chop," on the coin—a hallmark containing a Chinese character that at once told the weight and purity. These various chops, each highly individualized, are well worth collecting.

Like many other pattern coins, the $4 gold piece issue, nicknamed the Stella because of the star on the reverse side, has a fascinating history. This coin symbolizes a battle that took place during the last quarter of the nineteenth century, and well into the twentieth, to create a coinage that could win international acceptability without conversion into differing currency units. The Stella had its metal content in gold, silver, and base metals stamped into it in metric figures (precursor of another effort by Congress a full century later that was rejected as impractical). In an attempt to persuade the members of the House and Senate to report the denomination favorably, the mint director or-

A pattern coin of $4 denomination — the gold "Stella," a true metric coin. This specimen is valued at more than $40,000, an excellent return on a coin purchased for the cost of its gold content in the year of issue.

dered that a series of pattern pieces be made for distribution; members merely paid the cost of the precious metal and received a coin whose value today is in excess of $60,000. (A year after the 1879 flowing-haired pattern, twenty-five different pieces of two distinctive varieties, with coiled and flowing hair, were produced by the Philadelphia Mint from 1880 dies; their value today is above $80,000 for the flowing-hair type and six figures for the coiled hair.)

If few can afford the Stella, other coins that Congress rejected are more readily affordable and equally full of history and potential in value. The half dime departed as the nickel interests of Joseph Wharton provided that a larger 5-cent coin would be the only unit of that denomination. The 2-cent piece also came to an end, after just a decade, as did the silver 3-cent piece, though a nickel counterpart continued until it was realized in 1889 that Americans did not like to use the number 3 in daily economic transactions.

THE SAN FRANCISCO MINT

America of the 1870s was a growing nation—an economic dynamo. Just as the Stella patterns first produced in 1879 were emblematic of the new internationalist outlook, the transcontinental rail link in 1869 marked the beginning of internal movement. More and more citizens journeyed westward, and it became obvious that a money supply centralized at Philadelphia with a small branch mint at San Francisco would not be sufficient to meet the ordinary needs of commerce. The Carson City Mint in Nevada was at best an interim solution to cope with the silver and gold of the Comstock Lode. The operations of the U.S. Branch Mint in San Francisco were conducted in a building originally sixty by forty feet, subsequently remodeled into a sixty-foot-square facility. By late 1868 it was apparent that, with the new demand, the facility would soon be unable to undertake assay and coin production work simultaneously.

The Old Granite Lady at San Francisco, built more than a century ago and today preserved as a museum.

The Old Granite Lady

San Francisco's second mint, known today as the Old Granite Lady, opened for business in the summer of 1874 at the corner of Fifth and Mission streets.

Serving as a mint until 1937, the Old Granite Lady, with its pillared, Greek Revival architecture withstood the San Francisco earthquake of 1906 but nearly fell to land speculators who hoped to turn it into a high-rise or parking lot—the fate of the first mint in San Francisco. In the end, thanks to the White House and the director of the U.S. Mint in San Francisco, the Old Granite Lady survived and is now completely restored as a museum of American coinage, the City of San Francisco, and of western history. The exhibits include many coin rarities produced within its very structure.

"S" Coins

Through the years, the coins from the San Francisco Mint have acquired a mystique among many coin collectors, in part because of the generally lower number of mintages there than at either the parent mint at Philadelphia or the other branch mint at Denver. It also derives from the several truly key rarities, each identifiable by the famed "S" mint mark, that have emerged from its coining room. In 1870, just two specimens of a $3 gold piece were produced with the San Francisco mint mark; one piece was reportedly placed in the cornerstone of the Old Granite Lady, though this has never been accurately confirmed. The second specimen, which traveled via a number of collectors to the late Louis Eliasberg of Baltimore, is now valued at well over $100,000. Close behind the $3 gold piece is an 1894 dime. For reasons that are still unclear, it was decided to produce no dimes for circulation that year at the San Francisco minting facility. Friends of Superintendent John Dagget persuaded him to produce a small quantity as souvenirs, and some twenty-four specimens were struck. Fourteen of

This dime, given as a birthday present to Hallie Dagget in 1894, is worth more than $100,000 today.

these were subsequently melted down; from the rest, little Hallie Dagget, the superintendent's daughter, received three dimes as a birthday present and was told to save them until she grew up.

Hallie spent one of the dimes, dated 1894-S, almost immediately on an ice cream dish; the remaining two specimens, however, she put away until 1954, when they were sold privately. Today, the pieces sell at close to $100,000 each, adding all the while to the intrigue of acquiring coinage of the San Francisco Mint.

Even in the 1950s the San Francisco Mint made news. As an economy measure, the mint was closed in 1955. Almost immediately the coinage still in circulation with the "S" mint mark became scarce and began to increase in value. After the coin shortage of the mid-1960s forced the reopening of the San Francisco Mint under the demoted status of an Assay Office, with the unusual power to strike coin, it was almost anticlimactic when the decision was made to continue minting operations on the west coast.

Even more surprising was the decision to begin striking proof coinages with the San Francisco mint mark. Branch mint proofs had been struck through the years (the 1894-S dime is one such specimen), but for the most part proofs

In 1955, production at the San Francisco Mint temporarily ceased — and in collectors' eyes, this enhanced the value of all the "S" coins.

Proof 1969-S cent, struck especially for collectors.

were reserved for Philadelphia. In 1968, however, San Francisco took the honors and in the process created an entirely new type of American coin—the proof legal tender specimen produced from a mint and never intended for circulation. Through 1970, cents and nickels were still being regularly produced at San Francisco both as specimen (proof) pieces and for circulation; and until the end of 1974, cents continued to be manufactured with the familiar "S" mint mark. When mint officials perceived that the coins were being collected faster than they were being produced, they opted to strike San Francisco coinage without a mint mark except for pieces in specimen sets. Because of the generally low mintages, some of these pieces (especially the lower denominations) have had a phenomenal increase in value, based on original cost and subsequent price quotations. The 1975-S proof cent, of which 2.9 million pieces were produced, currently sells for more than $15, while the entire proof set (cent through dollar) cost a mere $8 to purchase from the mint. (The cent is a popular denomination, 1975 was the first year of "noncirculating legal tender" issuance, and fewer specimens are available than are desired.)

ADDITIONAL MINT FACILITIES

From the earliest times, the locations of mints in the United States were based upon the commercial needs of the economy. The Civil War disrupted the use of the several southern facilities, and in 1873 the coinage legislation enacted by Congress retained only the parent mint at Philadelphia, together with branches at San Francisco and Carson City. Within five years, however, it was apparent that additional facilities were needed, and a number of cities placed bids with the national legislature for the honor of hosting a mint. Among them were Cincinnati; Springfield, Illinois; Kansas City; Charlotte; Quincy, Illinois; Indianapolis; St. Louis; Louisville; Athens, Georgia; Omaha; Atlanta; Denver; Rock Island, Illinois; New Orleans; and Salt Lake City. After a lengthy series of hearings by the

Committee on Coinage, Weights and Measures, it was decided to reactivate the closed New Orleans Mint, expand the Philadelphia Mint, and, a dozen years later, to change the status of Denver from an assaying facility to a full-fledged branch mint.

The 1892-O Half Dollar

For today's collector, the reopening of the New Orleans Mint in 1879 proved to be a momentous event. Although the facility ultimately closed in 1909, its last thirty years gave us a rich collecting heritage. The majority of issues do not qualify as genuine rarities unavailable to the majority of collectors; yet even coins sold at moderate prices have shown a strong tendency to increase in value. The 1892 half dollar from the New Orleans Mint (usually referred to as an 1892-O half) is a good example. Mintage figures show that some 390,000 pieces were produced for the first year of issue of the Barber design series (a matronly bust portrait of Liberty facing right). In 1954, an uncirculated specimen was auctioned by Stack's as part of the Anderson DuPont Collection for $32.50. Just three years later, at the sale of the Empire Collection, a comparable (but not identical) specimen sold to a bid of $55. When the Samuel Wolfson Collection was placed on the auction block in May 1963, yet

The 1892-O half dollar, whose value has steadily increased through the years, now sells for about $600 in choice uncirculated condition. Photo by Carol Herman, courtesy of New England Rare Coin Galleries.

another coin of the same date, mint mark, and condition realized $82.50; and six years later, the R. L. Miles, Jr., specimen brought a winning bid of $105. Representative prices since then have been $290 at the October 1973 auction of the George F. Scanlon Collection and $430 at the May 1977 sale of the Getty Collection by Bowers & Ruddy. The total growth over the entire period amounts to more than 1,200 percent. From 1973 to 1977, the coin appreciated 48 percent, or 12 percent per annum.

Resumption of manufacturing operations at the New Orleans Mint was as much a function of silver politics as anything else, since the basic manufacturing function there was producing subsidiary coinage (though some gold pieces were manufactured in the latter years of operation). Incredible as it may seem to today's generation, brought up on paper money as the basis of a monetary system, the late nineteenth and early twentieth centuries were dominated by proponents of the gold standard and those of free silver—inevitably at loggerheads. Today it is hard to see what all the hoopla was about, but when Bryan gave his dramatic "cross of gold" speech, he captured the popular imagination, if not the votes, of the American people.

THE GOLD STANDARD AND NATIONAL BANK NOTES

Bryan's quixotic battle is nowhere recorded in coin, but hundreds of so-called Bryan dollars were produced and widely circulated in the Midwest and West. These "dollars"—some satirizing Bryan, others praising his goals—are

"Bryan dollars" were popular items near the turn of the twentieth century.

Designs on U.S. coins at the turn of the century.

highly prized by collectors today and, in a sense, bridge the bimetallism of the nation's early history and the adoption of the gold standard made official by Congress in 1900. So does paper money produced by the government during the same period. National bank notes, which formed an important part of the national currency supply, were gradually augmented by silver certificates (payable upon demand in silver dollars struck by the Treasury), gold certificates (proof of a deposit of gold coin in the Treasury, for which the notes were redeemable), and the Treasury, or coin, notes issued by the Treasury after passage of the Legal Tender Act of 1890, for payment for all silver bullion purchased, but redeemable in either silver or gold at the option of the Treasury Secretary.

All these pieces of paper money remain legal tender to this very day, though the government is no longer required to pay out either gold or silver coin to redeem them. It is unfortunate that federal law prohibits reproduction of any of these notes in full color, for they are among the most beautiful pieces of art ever designed. Vivid colors, radiant bursts of engraving, and intricate designs characterize these distinctive notes, and it is not at all unusual for a single specimen in crisp, uncirculated condition to sell for $1,000 or more above its face value.

America adopted the gold standard in 1900. Between 1904 and 1916, American coinage changed so completely that today's collectors, and even art critics, look back upon the period with little less than awe. During this era, the Federal Reserve System was formed, and the whole system of coinage and currency distribution changed dramatically. New designs were found for every circulating denomination, cent through double eagle, and a commemorative $50 gold piece was created. To collect a type set of coins produced during this period is indeed a massive task, for it includes not only the old Barber-designed Liberty heads on the dime, quarter, and half dollar, but also the new designs of sculptors completely independent of the mint. Most of these coins are among the more valuable issues of the twentieth century and have a price progression record that seems promising for the future.

THEODORE ROOSEVELT AND TWENTIETH-CENTURY COIN DESIGN

President Theodore Roosevelt, perhaps more than any other person, is responsible for today's coin design. During his term of office, Roosevelt befriended a number of artists, some of whom complained of the poor quality of American coinage. The President therefore commissioned Augustus Saint-Gaudens, the sculptor, to create new designs for the double eagle and eagle, and Bela Lyon Pratt to redesign the quarter eagle. Neither of the designers, of course, was employed by the mint, and, much to the consternation of the

Augustus Saint-Gaudens designed this double eagle.

engraver, Charles Barber, Roosevelt was actively interested in promoting their designs. The correspondence between Saint-Gaudens and Roosevelt, some of which was published in *The Century Magazine* more than half a century ago, yields a delicious chunk of the vitality of "T.R." and the zest for life he thought should be reflected in the national coinage. Despite some contemporary criticism, the Saint-Gaudens coins are among the most beautiful ever produced, and Pratt's incused design displays bold initiative.

Calling the Saint-Gaudens design "my pet baby," Roosevelt battled mint officials at every step. Charles Barber, jealous of his prerogatives as designer, threw roadblock after roadblock in the way of the designs for the double eagle, which, while smaller than the silver dollar, nonetheless proved difficult for the 172-ton presses of the Philadelphia Mint to strike. Saint-Gaudens's initial designs called for an extraordinarily high relief, which was later modified when it was discovered that nine blows from the press were needed to bring up the metal flow and the coin design fully.

The Ultra-High-Relief $20 Piece

From the very first trial strikes, however, comes one of the most interesting numismatic rarities of the twentieth century: the "ultra-high-relief" 1907 $20 gold piece. Identical in design to the regular issue, the principal difference between these early issues and the regular circulation strikes (bearing the roman numeral later changed to arabic numerals) is in the height or depth of the piece. Regular

America's most beautiful coin, an Augustus Saint - Gaudens design for a 1907 $20 gold piece, made at the specific request of President Teddy Roosevelt.

double eagles have a relief of approximately 2½ millimeters, which means that the design rises that height from the flan, or planchet, of the coin. A higher relief struck early in the production cycle has a depth of 3 millimeters. And the first fourteen coins struck and presented to Theodore Roosevelt, who gave them to friends as souvenirs, are 4 millimeters high. Through the years, several of the ultra-high-relief specimens have crept into the market, usually by private treaty (an agreement between two parties). In December 1944, when the J. F. Bell Collection was sold at public auction, a specimen yielded a price of $2,800. Another specimen, in the auction sale of the Jerome Kern Collection by B. Max Mehl in 1950, brought $3,800. The last private auction sale record for the coin was in 1974, when Stack's sold a specimen. From the bidding by mail before the sale, the cataloguers estimated a final price in the neighborhood of $125,000 to $150,000—itself remarkable, since up to May 1974 no American gold coin had ever sold for a six-figure price. Bidding commenced at $110,000 and began to climb rapidly. Within minutes, it reached $200,000, and as the auctioneer's hammer clanged down for the third time, collectors, investors, and dealers in the room all broke into applause. Few doubted that when the specimen was again sold it would command an even higher price. In 1979, Donald Kagin purchased the Capitol Coin Company specimen at auction for $225,000.

The 1909-S V.D.B.

While Charles Barber served as chief engraver of the Philadelphia Mint, no outside artist's work was safe. Victor David Brenner, commissioned by President Roosevelt to create a Lincoln design for either the cent or the nickel, incurred the chief engraver's wrath when his models prominently displayed his own name on the reverse. Brenner agreed to modify this to include only his initials and to place them more discreetly on the reverse. But Barber was not mollified, and when President Taft asked for a minor alteration, Barber took the opportunity to urge removal of the initials. The dispute over Brenner's initials created a numismatic rarity: the 1909 Lincoln cent, with initials, produced at the San Francisco Mint. The 1909-S V.D.B., like its counterpart at Philadelphia (the 1909 V.D.B.), still is a key piece in the Lincoln series. Barber won the dispute, but after his death in 1917 the initials were restored—this time to Lincoln's shoulder (and since 1918 they have been present on the coin).

Models for the Lincoln cent.

Dabbling in coin design was one of Roosevelt's pastimes. In 1908 he created a furor by ordering removal of the motto "In God We Trust" from the double eagle and eagle on the grounds that mere mention of the deity was sacrilege. Congress responded by mandating "that the motto 'In God We

"IN GOD WE TRUST" was inscribed on the double eagle by order of Congress in 1908.

Trust' heretofore inscribed on certain denominations of the gold and silver coins of the United States of America shall hereafter be inscribed upon all such gold and silver coins. . . ." Despite Roosevelt's displeasure, the motto was added anew to all eagles and double eagles manufactured after July 1, 1908, when the congressional mandate became effective. The later 1908 issues carry the motto, while the early ones do not. The San Francisco Mint, however, began operations later than usual that year and struck no coins without the motto. Of the motto pieces, the San Francisco strikings, by far the lowest mintages, are also the rarest. A choice uncirculated specimen of the 1908-S double eagle could easily cost more than $3,000.

The Buffalo Nickel

James Earle Fraser's Indian and Bison (also known as the Buffalo nickel).

In 1913, the nickel was redesigned. Barber prepared patterns with a portrait of George Washington, but the designs were stiff and reveal perhaps why his earlier inventions had been discarded. Instead, Treasury Secretary Franklin Mac-Veagh selected artist James Earle Fraser (best known for his statue "End of the Trail"), who created one of the most expressive issues ever coined by the U.S. Mint. The so-called Buffalo nickel (the beast depicted on the reverse is actually a bison) bears a composite portrait of three American Indian chieftains, while the reverse shows a bison modeled after Black Diamond, who was once housed in New York's Central Park Zoo. Fraser created a vivid and graceful portrait of a 1,550-pound animal on a coin just 21.2 millimeters in diameter.

Upon its introduction in 1913, the design proved so popular that many people wanted to know who had served as the models for the Indian chiefs. As tradition has it, the three models were Iron Tail, a Sioux chief; Two Moons, a Cheyenne chieftain; and John Big Tree, an Iroquois who lived to be over a hundred years old and in the mid-1960s received considerable attention in both the numismatic press and national news media. Clearly the distinctive origins of this design captured the popular imagination of the American public.

Liberty Designs

In 1916 the dime, quarter, and half dollar, all bearing the identical Barber design, were replaced with distinctive designs, all executed by sculptors outside the government: the

Mercury dime, Liberty standing quarter, and walking Liberty half dollar, first issued in 1916.

A more modest Liberty, the result of an act of Congress.

winged Mercury and walking Liberty of Adolph Weinman and the standing Liberty of Hermon MacNeil. The style of American coinage had evolved from the Indian head cent, which had portrayed a white princess with an Indian head-dress, to the genuine American Indian on the obverse of the new nickel. An individual had been portrayed on a coin for the first time with the Lincoln cent. The plump, matronly Liberty depicted on the nickel was replaced, as was Barber's Liberty, by a god (Mercury) on the dime, a goddesslike Liberty on the 50-cent piece, and a virtual "flapper" on the quarter dollar. A near-scandal erupted when it was discovered that the breast and thigh of Liberty on the quarter were partially exposed. Despite public uproar, there was little the mint could do. Back in 1890, to prevent constant changing of coin designs, Congress had legislated that once a coin design was created, it was to remain on the coin for no less than twenty-five years, the only change being the annual date of coinage. Yet Congress (and the nation) chafed, and, in some of the most humorous (and certainly the least direct) debate ever heard in Congress, the decision was made by legislation to amend the design on the coin. Both versions of the standing Liberty quarter are highly collectable; the rarest date in the series is the first year of issue, 1916, in which the full glory of the American Liberty figure is on display.

In a major change about this time, the Treasury Department approved coinage of a $50 piece commemorating the Panama-Pacific Exhibition staged at San Francisco in 1915.

PANAMA-PACIFIC INTERNATIONAL EXPOSITION
1915 - SAN FRANCISCO - U. S. A.
COMMEMORATIVE COINS

AUTHORIZED BY ACT OF CONGRESS   STRUCK AT SAN FRANCISCO MINT

ONE DOLLAR GOLD—Designs by Charles Keck
Issue limited to 25,000 pieces.

OBVERSE: Head representing Labor through whose efforts the Panama Canal became a reality. UNITED STATES OF ✳ AMERICA ✳ 1915
REVERSE: Two dolphins indicating the meeting of the two oceans. ONE DOLLAR ✳ PANAMA-PACIFIC EXPOSITION ✳ SAN FRANCISCO.

QUINTUPLE EAGLE ($50) GOLD
ROUND AND OCTAGONAL
DESIGNS BY ROBERT AITKEN

The first Fifty Dollar Gold Pieces to be issued under the authority of the United States. Total issue limited to 3,000 pieces.

The motives used in these designs were selected by the sculptor because of their simple dignity and far-reaching significance, as well as for their decorative pattern.

QUARTER EAGLE ($2½) GOLD—Designs by Charles E. Barber
Issue limited to 10,000 pieces.

OBVERSE: Columbia seated on the mythical Sea Horse, Columbia with the Caduceus, the emblem of trade and commerce, inviting the nations of the world to use the new way from Ocean to Ocean. PANAMA-PACIFIC EXPOSITION ✳ 1915
REVERSE: American Eagle on a standard bearing the motto E PLURIBUS UNUM ✳ UNITED STATES OF AMERICA ✳ 2½ DOL.

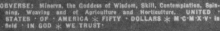

HALF DOLLAR SILVER
DESIGNS BY CHARLES E. BARBER
Issue limited to 200,000 pieces.

OBVERSE: Columbia scattering flowers; attendant with cornucopia, to signify the boundless resources of the West. Background, Golden Gate illumined by the rays of the setting sun. PANAMA-PACIFIC EXPOSITION ✳ 1915
REVERSE: Shield of the United States surmounted by American Eagle and supported on the one side by a branch of oak, emblem of strength and stability, and on the other side by the olive branch of peace. UNITED STATES OF AMERICA ✳ HALF DOLLAR ✳ IN GOD WE TRUST

OBVERSE: Minerva, the Goddess of Wisdom, Skill, Contemplation, Spinning, Weaving and of Agriculture and Horticulture. UNITED · STATES · OF · AMERICA ✳ FIFTY · DOLLARS ✳ M·C·M·X·V· in field · IN GOD ✳ WE TRUST
REVERSE: Owl, sacred to Minerva, the accepted symbol of Wisdom, perched upon a branch of western pine. · PANAMA-PACIFIC · EXPOSITION ✳ SAN FRANCISCO · In field · E ✳ PLURIBUS ✳ UNUM · The Designer's initials, R. A.
Dolphins, suggesting as they encircle the central field, uninterrupted water route made possible by the Panama Canal, occupy the angles of the octagonal coin.

An original Panama-Pacific commemorative set.

The coin is the largest denomination ever produced in quantity by the San Francisco Mint. Two distinctive varieties of these large units were produced—one round, the other octagonal. These were in turn marketed with a quarter eagle, a gold dollar, and a silver 50-cent piece. That $104 combination now sells for more than $30,000.

In 1921, with the institution of the Peace dollar to commemorate the end of World War I, the redesign of all American coinage was complete. Yet, except for the Lincoln cent, these designs were to be short-lived; most barely met the statutory minimum of twenty-five years, and in the case of the quarter, a special act of Congress was required to change the design in honor of the bicentenary of George Washington's birth in 1932.

"An End to War for All Time" was the subject of this "Peace" dollar, struck from 1921 to 1935, and again with a 1964 date.

The Washington Quarter

Washington's quarter was intended, initially, as a one-year commemorative to honor our first President. It proved to be so popular with the public that the design was retained for regular use. The legislation required the design to be modeled after the famed bust by Houdon, termed by most critics the finest contemporary portrayal of Washington, probably because it was created from a life mask cast in 1785 at Mount Vernon. In the heated competition for the honor of designing the new coin, the Washington Bicentennial Commission, the Treasury Department, and the

Federal Commission on the Fine Arts opted for the models of Laura Gardin Fraser, wife of the sculptor of the Buffalo nickel. But as fate would have it, outgoing Treasury Secretary Andrew W. Mellon preferred the model designs of John Flanagan, and as a result his creation has been found on the face of the Washington quarter since 1932.

THE DEPRESSION

The year following production of the first Washington quarter was one of the worst of the Depression. Franklin D. Roosevelt took office on March 4, 1933, with one-quarter of the nation's work force unemployed. At the federal minting facilities, presses were virtually at a standstill from the nearly total lack of demand for coin of the realm. Production finally began again, but at a fraction of the levels reached immediately after World War I. The Philadelphia Mint manufactured 14.3 million cents, in contrast to 392 million pieces in 1919; Denver produced a bare 6 million pieces, compared with some 57 million fifteen years earlier. To keep busy and justify its continuation, the San Francisco Mint struck 1.7 million half dollars but no minor or subsidiary coinage of silver dollars. Production of silver dollars had already been suspended in 1928, while the quarter eagle, whose manufacture was ended by Congress in 1929, at the beginning of the Depression, became a savings coin of the few who could accumulate money. Curiously, however, both eagles and double eagles were manufactured at the Philadelphia Mint, presumably from the melting and subsequent recoining of gold coin contained in government vaults, rather than from fresh deposits. But in this year that the mints nearly closed for lack of production, an interesting story emerged—the story of the 1933 double eagle, a coin it is still illegal to own.

An "illegal" coin, the 1933 double eagle was once in the collection of King Farouk. A specimen is in the Smithsonian collection and, some believe, others are in private hands.

When the pieces were produced at the mint is not difficult to ascertain, but the reason for their production is. Presumably the purpose was to keep operations relatively busy, thereby justifying the continuation of salaries. And so, on March 15, 1933, production began. Some 445,500 pieces were coined through May 19. In the middle of the production run (which was not halted), President Roosevelt issued Executive Order 6102, which required that all gold coin in the hands of the American people (except for those pieces that were "rare and unusual coin") be turned in and redeemed for paper money. More than $1.5 billion in gold coin would be confiscated and paid for in paper equivalent.

Roosevelt's scheme was daring, and to some extent it worked. By seizing most of the nation's gold, it was possible for him to manipulate the money supply and expand the currency at will—accomplishing what the Civil War theorists had only suggested on paper. Philadelphia reserved twenty-nine specimens for testing at the annual assay meeting in February 1934, and two specimens went to the Smithsonian Institution's national coin collection, which had formerly been kept by the mint itself. Remaining specimens awaited a directive from the Treasury Secretary, Henry Morgenthau, since circulation was impossible under the terms of the presidential decree. Three days after Christmas 1933, Secretary Morgenthau gave final orders to melt the coins. The eagles on hand were also melted down, though some had previously been placed formally into circulation. But since none of the double eagles dated 1933 had ever been placed into circulation, the government assumed that none existed, except for the two pieces in the Smithsonian collection.

It remains unclear to this day how the double eagle specimens left the Philadelphia Mint. Possibly when the assay commission met to test the coins on St. Valentine's Day, 1934, double eagles from another year were substituted. Or it is possible that a substitution took place from among the nearly half million pieces struck at the mint and later melted by weight (not individual count). In any case, it is clear that several specimens did escape, for before long, price quotations began to appear in several numismatic publications offering to purchase or sell the coin. It is known that J. F. Bell, the collector, managed to purchase one of the pieces, and that some time before the auction of his massive collection of gold coins in 1944, he sold it to L. G. Barnard of Tennessee. The parties and the sale are so well known because the federal government interrupted the transaction following its transfer to Barnard and seized the coin.

Extensive litigation ensued in federal court, with the result that the government was held entitled to seize the coin without compensating the holder, notwithstanding that he was a bona-fide collector, that the coin was purchased in good faith, and that it was valuable. Another 1933 double eagle surfaced in 1954, when King Farouk of Egypt had his coin collection sold by Sotheby's following his overthrow. The American government again intervened, and the piece was withdrawn from auction, its whereabouts unknown. Most experts believe there are other specimens floating around, waiting not only to be found but also to be vindicated in ownership by the change in the law in 1974 that permitted private ownership of gold again after a forty-year hiatus.

Fort Knox

With all the gold from the melted coin, the federal government obviously needed a suitable place of storage. In 1935, the rugged Maldraugh Ridge at the Fort Knox military reservation in the foothills around Louisville, Kentucky, was selected as the site for a vault to hold bullion, gold coin, and other rarities. Design specifications were rigid, requiring concrete walls 2 feet thick, some 750 tons of reinforced steel, and 4,200 cubic yards of concrete. The building's actual dimensions were surprisingly small—just 105 by 121 feet, and rising just 42 feet above the ground. The vault, a bare 40 by 64 feet, could nonetheless hold more than 12 billion ounces of gold.

Fort Knox, America's gold storehouse.

Transport of the gold bullion—nearly all from melted coin previously circulated before the facility was completed—took place on Sunday, January 18, 1935. Forty armored trucks laden with 480 boxes weighing 500 pounds each took 120 tons of gold to Pennsylvania Station, located fifty blocks to the north of the New York Assay Office. The shipments then had to brave the elements, including a major flood in the Ohio River Valley, before their arrival at Fort Knox. *The New York Times* editorialized against the move, wondering whether it was necessary, and fearing that some foreign nation (in a "Wellsian fantasy") might land foreign troops at the depository "and remove our gold reserve, leaving our paper money with no gold backing whatsoever."

West Point

At almost the same time, a depository for silver metal bullion was built at West Point, New York, on four acres of land just five hundred feet from the Old North Gate of the West Point Military Reservation. The silver vaults are considerably larger than their counterparts at Fort Knox, with a capacity for seventy tons of silver.

While the original purpose of the West Point depository was to hold silver bullion, it has had a number of other important functions, as far as coin collectors are concerned, since it opened on May 15, 1937, as a branch of the New York Assay Office. In the late 1960s and early 1970s, more than 2.9 million rare silver dollars were stored there. Previously held in Treasury Department vaults in Washington, these were the rare Carson City cartwheels that the government sold between 1972 and 1975 in a massive marketing campaign that raised more than $55 million in revenue and marked the formal entry of the federal government into the marketing and merchandising of rare coins. Then, in 1974, with the nation's money supply on the verge of a crisis from the shortage of 1-cent coins, West Point became an auxiliary mint. More than 1 billion pennies per year were produced at the West Point "Mint," which for technical and legal reasons was declared to be an adjunct of the Philadelphia Mint rather than of the Assay Office in New York City. When the Bicentennial coinage production rush started in 1975, West Point began to manufacture quarter dollars on a trial basis; and in 1977, it installed special presses to test new production methods. Even while minting, the West Point "Mint" continues to store silver bullion.

The Jefferson Nickel

A few months after the West Point depository opened for business, the Treasury Department decided to replace the Buffalo nickel, which had completed the minimum statutory life of twenty-five years in early 1938. The sec-

Original and amended design by Felix Schlag of the Jefferson nickel.

tion on printing and sculpture of the division of procurement within the Treasury sponsored a national design competition "for a new five cent coin to be known as the 'Jefferson Nickel.'" A portrait of Jefferson had to appear on the obverse of the coin, together with the inscriptions required by law. On the reverse was to be a rendering of Monticello, the beloved home of the third American President. (Photographs of Monticello from both a front and side view were available to competing artists.) The total of 390 entries received was not remarkable in the light of the prize money offered—$1,000—at a time when the average weekly wage for those Americans fortunate enough to be employed was $22.07.

Ironically, the winning entry by Felix Schlag—featuring an almost direct copy of the Houdon bust of Jefferson at the Boston Museum of Fine Arts and bearing a three-quarter view of Monticello both striking and daring—was not used, although Schlag won the prize money offered, and his initials were placed on the obverse nearly thirty years after its initial issue. Instead of Schlag's graceful view of Monticello, a more traditional, straight-on rendering was substituted at the insistence of the federal Commission on the Fine Arts.

Next to the Lincoln head cent, which dates back to 1909, the Jefferson nickel, which celebrated its fortieth anniversary in 1978, is the oldest continually circulating coin with the same obverse design. Through the years, of course, some aspects have changed, much to the delight of collectors. During the war years, for example, the composition of the nickel changed from 75 percent copper and 25 percent nickel to a trinary alloy of 56 percent copper, 35 percent sil-

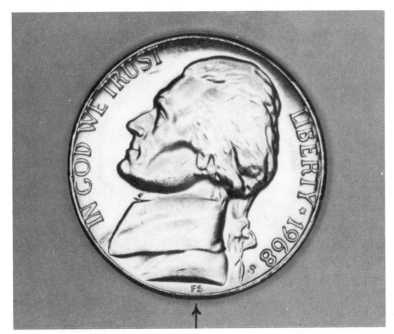

"FS" initials were added in 1966 in recognition of Felix Schlag's artistic accomplishment.

ver, and 9 percent manganese, principally because of the scarcity of nickel, a critical war material, and the need for copper.

For the Jefferson nickel, however, the war years proved significant in two ways: not only was a precious metal, silver, first added to minor coinage, but for the only time a mint mark was placed on a coin to signify its origin at the Philadelphia Mint. On all the war nickels, as they are called, the reverse side bears a mint mark above the dome of Monticello: the S for San Francisco, the D for Denver,

"War nickels" were struck from 1942 to 1945. They were the only American coins to bear a mint mark symbolizing Philadelphia until 1979, when it was added to the dollar, and 1980, when it was added to all coins except the cent. All coins now bear their mint mark to show origin.

and the P for the parent facility at Philadelphia. The large mint marks were designed readily to identify the nickels containing silver.

WORLD WAR II COINAGE

All coins from the years of World War II are highly collectable today. If uncirculated, they have an interesting history that is recalled in few history books but portrayed vividly in Treasury Department documents and the annals of Congress. After the attack on Pearl Harbor, a nation that had been at peace since 1918 was suddenly required to mobilize for war. Shortages arose at local markets. Beef, sugar, and other items both imported and produced domestically were available for nonmilitary needs in only limited quantities. Ration coupons (today also highly collectable) were required to make purchases. In every sector of the economy, materials were declared to be of critical importance for victory in Europe and Asia.

Coinage was affected early, since copper and nickel were both critical war materials used in munitions. The War Powers Act of 1942, which was ultimately to govern the nation's economic life for the duration of the conflict, also dealt with changes required in the monetary system. First came removal of nickel from the 5-cent pieces, resulting in

Pattern in plastic for a 1942 cent, which might have been used if petroleum (from which plastic is derived) had not become a critical war material.

a saving of some 870,000 pounds of metal—enough, according to debate in the *Congressional Record,* to supply the armor for 1,000 heavy tanks. The proposal to reduce the nickel content, alter the copper content, and perhaps add another metal, such as silver, came from Donald M. Nelson, head of the War Production Board. The use of silver proved ingenious, for at a mere 50 cents an ounce it required little capital expenditure and government supplies were well stocked.

The legislation passed Congress and was enacted just 110 days after Pearl Harbor. Nickel was thereafter eliminated entirely from the 5-cent piece; but the problem of critical war materials was not yet solved. Copper was now needed, and the basic unit of the American monetary system, the cent, was threatened. Production of pennies finally was halted by the mint to save copper, which made up some 95 percent of the alloy in the coin. Congress again took the initiative, passing legislation late in the year that produced a steel cent for 1943 (and, in 1944, a bronze cent made of spent shell casings), and nearly brought about the reissue of a 3-cent piece.

The coins produced during this period are a valuable reminder alike of the history of wartime coinage and of how even large mintage pieces can climb in value. Today, the 1942-P nickel, with a mintage in excess of 57 million pieces, sells for more than $10.

Late in 1941, as Pearl Harbor brought the war dramatically to the United States, the mint engravers were on the verge of manufacturing dies for the next year's coinage. Some of the dime dies for 1941 were inadvertently reengraved with a 1942 date. Ultimately, the error was discovered in production, and the 1942-over-1941 dimes are now highly prized.

A 1942-over-1941 dime, probably reengraved by the mint because of the military emergency and manpower shortage.

Franklin Delano Roosevelt was the first individual in the United States to be honored by act of Congress with a coin commemorating him. It was issued less than a year after his death.

At war's end, the mint was soon able to continue the design changes begun a few years before the world conflict. The death of Franklin Delano Roosevelt provided a convenient excuse to change the design of the dime, and chief engraver John Sinnock patterned a bust of Roosevelt after a sculpture done by Selma Burke, a black sculptor who won a design competition for a huge three- by two-foot profile of the President for the Recorder of Deeds building in Washington. In 1948, the half dollar was added to the list, with a bust of Benjamin Franklin modeled after another Houdon sculpture. The reverse shows a rendering of the Liberty Bell, located just a few blocks from the Philadelphia Mint studio where Sinnock worked. The reverse also bears an eagle immediately to the right of the bell—and therein lies a fascinating story.

The Coinage Act of 1873, governing the laws for mint operation, states that on the reverse of the quarter, half dollar, and dollar, an eagle or a representation of an eagle must appear. Until the issue of Bicentennial commemoratives in 1975 and 1976, the Franklin half dollar nearly became the only subsidiary coin above the dime denomination without an eagle engraved into the working dies. Mrs. Nellie Tayloe Ross, director of the Philadelphia Mint from 1933 to 1953, explained what happened at a meeting of the Franklin Institute in Philadelphia on April 29, 1948. Sinnock's design, following Mrs. Ross's instructions, featured the Liberty Bell on the theory that "the eagle was supposed to represent strength and freedom and that the Liberty Bell would suffice as a representation thereof." Preparations were made without an eagle until the untimely death of the chief engraver in 1947. Apparently having second thoughts (as she later said: "What could be a representation of an eagle but an eagle itself?"), Mrs. Ross ordered a minor design

Franklin half dollar, struck 1948–63.

change—the skillful addition of the small eagle by the new chief engraver, Gilroy Roberts.

For the most part, both the Roosevelt dime and the Franklin half dollar are not rarities today, though they are usually considered obligatory items in a general collection of American coins. To be sure, some pieces in each series have gained in value over the years, and few doubt that when silver was withdrawn from coinage in 1965 and many silver pieces melted, the scarcity of issues still circulating increased. But it remains for future generations to determine the real worth of some of these "common" coins.

THE 1950s

The year 1950 marked a resurgence in coin collecting, and because so much of what happened then affects the way coins are collected today, it is worth some comment. In that year proof coinage, suspended during World War II, was resumed, but in a substantially different form. Whereas up to this time individual coins from proof or specimen strikings had been available from the mint at Philadelphia, now only sets of the coins would be sold. Thus, while pre-1942 proof production figures differ for each denomination, all the post-1950 figures are identical. The number of sets ordered provides some measure of the interest of collectors across the country. In 1950, for example, there were 51,386 orders against a high of 21,120 sets produced in 1942; and since then, the demand has grown to such a phenomenal level that in 1964 a total of 3.9 million sets was produced by the mint.

In the same year the proof sets were introduced, the mint temporarily halted the manufacture of uncirculated sets containing a specimen of each coin produced at every mint during the year. Collectors who nevertheless sought to acquire one coin of each denomination from every mint found the task difficult, for the Denver Mint manufactured

A scarce nickel, with just 2.6 million made, the 1950-D is a semi-key date in the Jefferson nickel series.

just 2.6 million nickels that year. Today, an uncirculated example of the 1950-D nickel sells for over $10.

For whatever reason, the fifties may be characterized as economically tranquil. Compared to the prewar and immediate postwar periods, plus World War II itself, the fifties had little need for new coinage. By 1955 it was apparent that there was no necessity for more than a main mint and a branch mint in the western United States. It was decided to close the San Francisco Mint; the government would save several hundred thousand dollars by doing so, and—the theory went—the only people to miss the facility would be coin collectors. So the mint was decommissioned and made into an assay office, with the same status as the New York facility but an even more skeletal staff.

That same year the diemakers at Philadelphia made one of the more interesting blunders in modern coinage history. In the process of producing the dies for the 1-cent coin, the working die was hubbed twice, or created by a transfer from positive to negative image so that the lettering and date were not properly aligned. The result is a very obvious doubling of the letters and year of production. Precisely how many of the 1955 double-die cents were produced cannot even be guessed at today, but estimates considered reliable place the number at substantially fewer than 20,000 pieces. Some of the run no doubt was melted by the mint after the error was discovered. But unlike the 1933 double eagle, which was never formally released from the mint, the

The 1955 double-die cent.

1955 double-die cent was placed in circulation. From these 1-cent pieces, many collectors have found a keystone to their Lincoln cent book. Today, an uncirculated specimen of the 1955 double die, with no signs of having gone beyond the original bag it was shipped in from the mint, can carry an asking price of over $1,000.

THE 1960s

While the end of the San Francisco Mint put a premium on many of the coins carrying the "S" mint mark, the closing also helped to precipitate the shortage of coin that gripped the economy in the early sixties. As the economic expansion of that decade began, the need for new coin arose and existing facilities were unable to satisfy it. For coin collectors, the decade of the sixties was both a triumph and a tragedy. The year 1960 saw an unparalleled interest in numismatics and marked the commencement of a weekly newspaper, *Coin World*, which covered the news of the field. Coin collecting was transformed from the hobby of kings and presidents into an investment for millions of people. Again, proof set purchases provide a useful measuring device. In 1959, when a new reverse was added to the Lincoln cent to celebrate the sesquicentennial of his birth, 1.1 million sets were bought; the following year, the number grew by nearly half a million, to 1.6 million sets. The 1961 orders

Lincoln Memorial cent with the artist's sketch of design.

totaled slightly more than 3 million. At the same time, however, the coins in circulation were no longer reaching those who needed them most: merchants and consumers. Shortages began to crop up in the lower denominations as well as in the higher subsidiary issues, and the price of silver, after a period of low demand, started to creep ominously upward. As the price neared $1.29 an ounce—the level at which the silver content in coins exceeded face value—silver coinage began to disappear from circulation.

The Kennedy Half Dollar

After the assassination of President John F. Kennedy on November 22, 1963, one of the first pieces of legislation Congress passed under Lyndon Johnson was to replace the Benjamin Franklin half dollar with a suitable commemoration of the late President. The coin itself was not a commemorative issue, because it was intended for circulation, but popular misconceptions deemed its issue otherwise.

The goal of the White House and the Treasury Depart-

Kennedy half dollar.

ment was to issue a new coin on January 2, 1964—a seemingly impossible task given the regular schedule of mint operations. Normally, a design must be sketched, approved, sculpted, refined, made into plaster, converted into a copper galvano, or larger master sculpture, reduced in size, and made into a trial die. Then this die undergoes a series of trial strikes until every aspect of the pattern is correctly reproduced. The process takes months, yet President Johnson had ordered immediate production no later than the first working day of the new year. The solution was to use the portrait of Kennedy that had appeared on the mint medal commemorating his presidency, with the presidential seal on the reverse. Gilroy Roberts, as chief engraver of the mint, had executed the portrait, and his chief assistant, Frank Gasparro, had done the reverse. By modifying the original models, the mint shaved months to weeks and met the target date for proof coinage, though minor production problems prevented the actual circulation strikes from being manufactured until the last week of January.

However, despite massive efforts that produced more than 400 million pieces in 1964, the coin did not achieve wide circulation. Collectors hoarded the coins, as did those who wanted a souvenir of the late President. In addition, legislation that removed silver from most circulating coinage retained a nominal amount in the 50-cent piece and produced hoarding when the price of silver made the base metal content of these coins exceed face value.

The Philadelphia Mint.

The introduction of the Kennedy half dollar in 1964 probably sealed the fate of the 50-cent piece as a noncirculating denomination, as the Treasury Department recognized thirteen years later in proposing the coin's abolition. Had production of the Franklin half dollar continued, its composition would have changed with the other coinage the following year and the unit might have survived in circulation. But so long as the Kennedy 50-cent piece was produced, it was taken out of circulation by collectors, thereby fueling demand for a coin that never actually circulated. While the mint was manufacturing these vanishing Kennedy half dollars, there was increased demand for other coins as well. Concern mounted within the Treasury Department and in Congress over the U.S. Mint's inability to produce sufficient coin of the realm, and also over the withdrawal of vast quantities of coin from circulation. Past patterns of production and use indicated that there probably were enough coins in circulation and in noncirculating hoards to cover the cent and nickel, but it was equally clear that the shortage of silver would not permit any dimes, quarters, and half dollars to come out of hiding.

Kennedy mint medal.

The Treasury finally took steps to combat a coin shortage. It suggested that inasmuch as coin collectors were perceived to be a dominant cause of the shortage, mint marks should be deleted from all coins, making available fewer coins for collectors to acquire. This was coupled with a proposal to freeze the date on all coins and to produce them in vast quantities. Congress, perhaps hoping the coin shortage would ultimately just go away, complied with appropriate legislation.

The Coinage Act of 1965

The coin shortage persisted, and within a matter of months it was necessary for President Lyndon Johnson to put forth a comprehensive proposal that the whole of American coinage be transformed overnight from a system based on precious metal to a system in which the coins were backed only by the integrity of the government and legal tender statutes. The Coinage Act of 1965 created a cupro-nickel-clad coinage, made in three layers bonded together by a chemical process. Since copper formed the center layer and the striking process resulted in a flow of metal, all the clad coinage produced since 1965 has a narrow copper, orange-colored rim.

Provisions of the coinage legislation applied only to the dime and the quarter, not to the half dollar or the dollar coin. In the case of the half dollar, the decision was made to retain some silver but to manufacture a clad consistency through a skillful blending of the precious metal with both the copper core and the outer layer of copper and nickel.

The late Representative Wright Patman, chairman of the House Committee on Banking and Currency, chats with Representative Leonor K. Sullivan, chairman of the Subcommittee on Consumer Affairs of the House Banking Committee (dealing with coinage), and the author at a 1973 hearing on Capitol Hill. John Jay Pittman, then president of the American Numismatic Association, looks on (left).

The reason given at the time for retaining silver was to maintain some prestige in American coinage in a single circulating denomination. There was opposition to this in the House of Representatives, particularly by Representative Wright Patman, who chaired the House Committee on Banking and Currency. But President Johnson used his political muscle to enforce the passage of the provision, with little inkling that within five years this last element of silver would disappear from circulating domestic coinage.

The fate of the silver dollar is an interesting one. Because of the date freeze in effect in early 1965, all coins manufactured by the mint still bore a 1964 date. Pressured by western silver and mining interests, President Johnson by executive order directed that the Treasury Department commence striking silver dollars again, after a hiatus of some thirty years. Operations began almost immediately, using the dies for the Peace dollar created in 1921 and last circulated in 1935. Several hundred thousand pieces were manufactured at the Denver Mint when Congressman Silvio Conte of Massachusetts, a ranking minority member of the House Banking Committee, learned of the development. He was furious that at a time of national coin shortage, when every available mint press should be used to produce regular coin, the President had ordered manufacture of up to 45 million silver dollars that would circulate only in a few western states.

Word was sent to the White House that if production was not curtailed, the Coinage Act of 1965, then being considered, would be scuttled. Within a few days, hearings were held on Capitol Hill, and various mint officials testified before the House Banking Committee in one of the most interesting cover-ups in modern numismatic history. First, they denied that the coins had ever been produced. Then they said that some trial strikes had been produced but never for circulation. Finally, they indicated that even these trial strikes (which in fact numbered several hundred thousand pieces) had all been destroyed. Each statement was untrue, though it was accurate to say that the overwhelming majority of the 1964 Peace dollars produced by

Artist's rendering of 1964 Peace dollar, struck in May 1965. Courtesy Krause Publications.

the mint were melted. But the statements evidently proved satisfactory to the members of the House of Representatives who heard them, for no mention is made of the silver dollars thereafter in the legislative debates surrounding the Coinage Act of 1965.

Yet coins like the 1964 Peace dollar simply do not stay forever in the shadows. As in the case of the 1933 double eagle, some have surmised that similar silver dollars of older vintage, yet identical weight, were substituted at the mint. This theory holds that since the mint destroyed the sample production run solely by weight—without an individual check being made on each coin and its date—a substitution of older dollars was readily made for several new specimens, which were surreptitiously removed from the mint. Given past occurrences at the mints, such a possibility is not entirely unlikely. In addition, since at least two specimens were kept in the Washington laboratories of the U.S. Mint as production samples, until they were destroyed in 1970 when their existence was first questioned, many people believe that there are 1964 Peace dollars to be found and collected. In the early 1970s, an enterprising coin dealer placed an advertisement in *The Numismatist,* in which he offered to purchase a 1964 Peace dollar for $3,000. Immediately, the Treasury Department issued a press release stating that first, no such coins existed; second, if any did, they were the property of the U.S. government; and third, any found outside government hands would be seized without compensation to the owner. For a coin that did not exist, this declaration raised the issue of a massive cover-up. In any event, the publicity successfully removed any possibility that a specimen might turn up in the near future.

For coin collectors, the period between 1964 and 1968 was a trying one. Even though the date freeze was ended, mint marks were kept off the coinage by a law Congress passed to limit their use. Next, proof set production, which had been growing annually from 1950 to 1964, was suspended during 1965 and again for the following two years. A disastrous experiment with "Special Mint Sets" ensued, under which the Bureau of the Mint attempted to substitute choice uncirculated specimens for proof pieces. The Bureau's selection was not welcomed by the purchasers of that time, or by collectors today, most of whom virtually ignore the issues. But in 1968, when the deep thaw ended, the price for resumption was that mint officials had to go to Capitol Hill and, at formal hearings, admit that coin collectors were not really responsible for the coin shortage, and that the use of mint marks (which was resumed) was a useful distinguishing device needed for production purposes. Proof coin production also began anew. The San Francisco Assay Office was allowed once again to issue coin, and all proof and lower denomination coins were manufactured there instead of at Philadelphia.

Reintroduction of the "S" mint mark for circulating cents, nickels, and proof coinage was a boon to coin collecting, though within a few years the demand for the San Francisco pieces caused the Treasury Department to once again remove the mint marks. Nonetheless, the production of cents, nickels, and proof strikes at San Francisco and clad coinage at Philadelphia and Denver proved sufficient to produce collectables, not to mention coin of the realm. For a time, the absence of marks suggested that in the future collectors would need to obtain one coin per year from each denomination. Yet the San Francisco Mint has itself created another item for collectors, for by 1975 it was producing no coins for circulation. The noncirculating legal tender proof coinage produced by the San Francisco Mint is now collectable in its own right, and because of the small number of pieces available, it is apparent that some of the coins that have already appreciated substantially in value will continue to do so.

In 1969, the Treasury Department recommended that the 40-percent-silver half dollar be made identical in clad consistency with the other cupro-nickel pieces authorized by the 1965 coinage legislation. Representative Florence Dwyer recommended that the dollar coin be regularly produced for the first time since 1935, and with a dual commemoration in the design. Dwight D. Eisenhower, thirty-fourth President of the United States and commander of American forces in Europe during World War II, was to be honored with a portrait on the obverse, and the lunar landing of July 20, 1969, was ordered commemorated on the reverse side.

Draft legislation was submitted by the Treasury Department in what was then known as the Coinage Act of 1969, and each house of Congress promptly began its own consideration. The Senate gave the legislative proposal a rougher going at first. Western mining interests apparently tried to authorize a silver dollar as opposed to a cupro-nickel-clad coin. Mint director Mary Brooks approved a compromise offer of 150 million silver Eisenhower dollars, which would be sold to collectors but would not circulate. But she apparently neglected to confer with the House leadership, in particular, Representative Wright Patman, who refused under any circumstances to back a second measure authorizing a silver-clad coin, even if it was only intended for collectors.

When the legislation was introduced in October 1969 and hearings held, mint officials all anticipated prompt enactment into law. Nonetheless, when it came time to produce the 1970 proof sets and 1970 mint sets containing uncirculated examples of each of the denominations manu-

Man's landing on the moon in 1969 prompted a numismatic commemoration. NASA photo.

Galvano of Eisenhower dollar design as seen in early 1971. Mamie Eisenhower, at right, with Julie Nixon Eisenhower, David Eisenhower, Mary Brooks, director of the U.S. Mint, and an aide, views the galvano with the 1970 date. First year of coinage was actually 1971.

factured, they decided (probably to give coin collectors a bonus) to include the silver version of the half dollar as both a 1970-S proof piece and a 1970-D uncirculated specimen. As it turned out, the mint was acutely embarrassed

In 1970, the only half dollars struck were part of proof sets and mint sets — the first "collector only" coins produced by the U.S. Mint.

when Congress refused to consider the legislation at all, largely because Representative Patman would not budge on the issue of the silver dollar. Lacking legislative authority to produce a cupro-nickel half dollar, and unable to issue the half dollar as a silver coin because of the rise in its intrinsic value, mint officials awaited passage of the legislation, all the while producing proof and uncirculated silver versions for collectors. The logjam was not broken until December 30, 1970, when President Nixon signed the coinage legislation into law. As it turns out, the 1970-D uncirculated half dollar shows a mintage figure of just 2.1 million pieces, while the proof specimens record a mintage of 2.6 million. Today, the value of the coins continues to rise steadily, and in future years, few doubt that this will be one of the scarcer pieces from the seventies.

COINAGE OF THE SEVENTIES AND BEYOND

American coinage of the 1970s marks a new era in collection. In several instances, this decade has shown the wisdom of examining pocket change to find coins of value. In 1972, for example, a die was accidentally doubled, and a

The 1972 double-die cent, found in circulation and now valued at $200.

1972 double-die cent was created. Through careful examination of different types of Eisenhower dollars that the mint has produced, many collectors have found a number of varieties that are only collectable from pieces in circulation. Yet it must also be noted that at a time when more and more coins are being manufactured by the mint, fewer and fewer apparently are staying in circulation—perhaps a sign of the monetary needs of the economy.

The 1-Cent Piece

In 1973, the problems that had affected the higher denominations during the 1960s began to plague the 1-cent piece. The price of copper rose to such heights that the Treasury Department feared face value of the coin would soon be dwarfed by the value of its metal content. As a result, the Treasury began to examine other alternatives to the 1-cent piece. While the initial consideration centered on an aluminum substitute (which Congress specifically disapproved of after viewing pattern samples or trial strikes), the examination was ultimately broadened to encompass every possibility for the cent, including reissue of a 2-cent piece after a hiatus of more than a century. By the end of the inquiry, the Treasury Department decided it was time to reexamine the nation's coinage completely and contracted with a private consulting firm.

The recommendations of Research Triangle Institute, a North Carolina consulting firm, were startling: elimination of the cent; introduction of a 2-cent substitute; a change in the composition of the nickel to approximate that of the cupro-nickel-clad coinage; reduction in size of the dollar coin; and elimination of the 50-cent piece. Then Congress itself began to study American coinage laws, with the ultimate goal of thorough revision.

Commemorating the Bicentennial

While the study was in process, the United States celebrated the Bicentennial of its independence, and departing from tradition, the Treasury backed a move to issue commemorative coinage for the event. Commemorative issues have a long and checkered history in the United States, dating back to 1892 and continuing at sporadic intervals through 1954. But since the mid-1930s, the Treasury Department has steadfastly opposed them on the grounds that they interfered with the operations of the mint, created havoc with the domestic coinage regularly circulating, and in general disrupted the smooth flow of circulation so necessary to the national economy. The Bicentennial coinage was not at first enthusiastically received by the Treasury Department. But in March 1973, after three years of intense internal debate centered on possible disruption of the circulating coinage system, the Treasury proposed a limited commemoration in the form of two circulating legal tender coins—the 50-cent piece and the dollar—and waited for Congress to respond to their draft legislation.

Recognizing that the fears of the Treasury might be justified, at least in part, Congress nonetheless wanted a coin chosen for the commemoration that would appeal to the people. The quarter dollar, based upon the recommendation of the current president of the American Numismatic Association, John Jay Pittman, was decided on. In the Senate, the silver interests once again threatened to sandbag the proposal unless amendments were made, and in a series of stunning legislative maneuvers not only succeeded in adding a provision resulting in the manufacture of 45 million silver-clad Bicentennial pieces (15 million quarters, halves, and dollars) but nearly caused a gold Bicentennial piece to be issued as well.

To give its staff enough time to produce the coins, the mint succeeded in obtaining from Congress the equivalent of a date freeze, but with a twist; instead of 1974 coins with old designs, the Bicentennial coinage, with its distinctive reverse designs and dual 1776–1976 date, would be produced beginning in 1975. No other quarters, half dollars, or dollars would be manufactured in those years.

As for the designs for the new coinage, the mint opted for yet another national design competition open to all

Americans. Nearly five hundred entries were received, and a dozen were chosen by a blue-ribbon panel for the finals. Members of both houses of Congress and the Treasury Secretary selected the winning designs, which immortalized the work of Jack L. Ahr on the quarter dollar, Seth G. Huntington on the half dollar, and Dennis R. Williams on the dollar. The production of coins from these designs was not without difficulties. Huntington and Williams had never

America's Bicentennial commemorative coins were authorized by Congress after an epic struggle to win the Treasury Department over to accepting commemorative coin issues. A national design contest was held, some 500 entries received, and a dozen finalists chosen before the three winning entries were picked. In the end, immortality in metal was achieved by Jack L. Ahr, for his colonial drummer boy quarter; Seth Huntington, for his Independence Hall half dollar; and Dennis R. Williams, for his Liberty Bell design superimposed on the lunar surface. Other commemorative coins on pages 228 through 230 were struck by the mint in 1975 and 1976.

229

Above: *Plaster models of the semifinal designs were required before fi-nal versions were chosen for the Bicentennial coinage. Here, U.S. Mint director Mary Brooks, with Robert Weinman (left), president of the National Sculpture Society, examines some of the designs received. Larry Stevens photo for the U.S. Mint.*

previously executed a sculpture of the sort required to pro-duce a coin. And in the case of Ahr, a professional illustra-tor, his fine drawing was difficult to translate into plaster and metal. With the assistance of the chief engraver, Frank Gasparro, final changes were made in the plasters, which were then turned into coins for proof production in silver-clad material as well as cupro-nickel-clad metal for a regu-lar circulation run.

Dennis R. Williams (left), eighteen-year-old coin designer, with presidential counselor Anne Armstrong, who holds the galvano he created for the Bicentennial commemoration. Bicentennial administrator John Warner (now senator from Virginia) looks on.

Pattern coins for small-size dollar struck in 1977 with a 1759 date.

The year 1977 brought a reversion to the designs previously employed on the reverse of the quarter, half, and dollar, and also the possibility of a change in the size and design of the unit of value in the American monetary system. As part of the proposed change, the Treasury Department produced a series of pattern coins of varying shape and design, all of which were possible samples for a small-sized dollar. Most interesting among these was the multi-sided dollar coinage, bearing the portrait of Martha Washington on one side and the Washington family home at Mount Vernon on the reverse. The same basic design had been used in preparation of the 1965 copper-clad strikings, but for the first time a multiple-sided coin was suggested, though ultimately discarded because it was considered incompatible with automated merchandising machinery. Finally, chief engraver Gasparro put together a mock-up design for what he thought a small-sized dollar should look like and went so far as to create a plaster for it. This interesting piece of sculpture, which the chief engraver personally views as his crowning artistic achievement in his long career with the U.S. Mint, features on the obverse an attractive Liberty with flowing hair, a liberty pole, and liberty cap—a throwback to the nation's earliest coinages. The reverse pictures a soaring eagle. Throughout 1978, Congress was giving careful examination to the small-sized dollar proposal, as well as to other ideas to alter the familiar con-

Frank Gasparro working on model for a proposed small-size dollar.

tent and denominations of American coinage. For political reasons, Congress voted to scrap the Liberty design and to substitute a portrait of Susan B. Anthony, the nineteenth-century suffragette, for the mini-dollar. In October 1978, President Carter gave his approval to the Anthony mini-dollar by signing the bill into law.

Studying the history of American coinage enables you as collector and investor to choose a cohesive and logical system of accumulating pieces that will form the basis of a fine collection. From the lessons of history and from current events that suggest changes in various coin designs or denominations, it is possible to deduce what modern pieces are on the verge of being collectable and potentially valuable.

From every period in our history, coins reveal the economics and politics of the nation; in different designs, we can see the impact changing times have had on society as a whole. War and peace alike are reflected in coins, from a militant heraldic eagle of our early years to a Peace dollar of a half century ago. American coinage honors the newest scientific triumphs, such as man's first landing on the moon. These coins are a fascinating reflection of the achievements of the American people.

NEW COINS FOR THE EIGHTIES

Major changes in American coinage for the 1980s were first forecast by Research Triangle Institute, in its classic 1976 study examining critical alternatives for the American monetary system. Outgoing Treasury Secretary William Simon, in his "State of the Coinage—1977" address, issued during the closing days of the Ford administration, advocated change, principally in the form of a small-size dollar and elimination of the 1-cent piece. Mention was also given for the first time to the reinstitution of commemorative coinage, both as a revenue enhancement device for the federal government and as a means of broadening the U.S. Mint product line to collectors.

In making any decision to reissue commemorative coinage, the battle of the late 1930s cannot be easily forgotten. Existing practices at that time allowed the mint to continue to strike commemoratives of older designs simply by changing the date and the mint mark until the maximum amount allowed by the enabling statute was reached. Limited issues intended primarily for collectors (who themselves intended to resell at a profit) were common. Combined with a series of marketing abuses principally related to small production runs which private marketers bought out and hoarded until a high price was reached, this eventually caused a furor within the Treasury Department. Finally, hearings were held before the House Banking Committee, and the Cochran Report, written in large measure by a young collector named Harry X Boosel, was instrumental in amending the law to prevent the abuses of the past. Ironically, four decades later, Boosel had retired and was an elected governor of the American Numismatic Association. He was among many who were to advocate reissuance of commemorative coins.

Perhaps the biggest obstacle to the reissue of commemorative coinage was the Treasury Department's long-standing opposition to any deviation from the existing coin of the realm. Of the dozen or so commemorative coin bills that passed both houses of Congress between 1939 and 1954, most were vetoed by the President in a strong message. The message recalled the abuses of the past, cited a threat to counterfeiting, and alleged that confusion with the national coinage would result from commemorative issues.

Only the Iowa State Centennial and commemoratives honoring Booker T. Washington and George Washington Carver were successful in those years, while other events of truly national significance were relegated to national medals.

As any marketer knows, an art medal is beautiful, has a distinctive aesthetic feel, and is outsold by legal tender coins by a 10 to 1 margin.

In the final analysis, it was the Bicentennial coinage issues that helped turn the Treasury around. The quarter dollar circulated without any hindrance to the system, there was no appreciable increase in counterfeiting, and sales (while not as optimistic as planned by Congress), aggregated over 7 million sets of silver-clad coinage. For its part, Congress also began to turn around and take up a renewed interest in coinage legislation in general, and commemorative coins in particular. A series of events brought this out.

First, the House Judiciary Committee (an unlikely source since most coin matters have been handled by the House Banking Committee) dealt with a proposed recodification of the Minting and Coinage Law for the first time since 1873. While none of the changes were supposed to be substantive, a number of changes crept in.

Representative Doug Barnard (D-Ga.), then a ranking minority member on a House coinage subcommittee, suggested a commemorative half dollar honoring the bi-sesquicentennial of George Washington's birth. In 1791, it was Washington whose effigy was proposed on a series of presidential coins in the House of Representatives; while he declined the honor, a number of patterns exist that are still widely collected, ranging from "Washington as Emperor" to "Washington as Citizen." Pattern coins made in the middle of the nineteenth century also exist with the Washington portrait.

Washington as emperor in this early 1783 design.

In 1900, the first commemorative dollar coin was a distinctive tribute to Washington and the Marquis de Lafayette, while the coinage commemorating the sesquicentennial of American Independence in 1926 featured a portrait of Washington and the incumbent President, Calvin Coolidge. A mere six years later, of course, in honor of the Bicentennial of Washington's birth, the Houdon portrait of Washington was rendered in metal by John Sinnock, and the Washington quarter design (still in use) was born.

At hearings held before the House Coinage Subcommittee chaired by Representative Frank Annunzio (D-Ill.), Treasury caught all of the witnesses from the coin industry flat-footed. Most had expected Treasury opposition based upon the party line of years past; instead, U.S. Treasurer Angela M. (Bay) Buchanan, who had taken over supervisory control of the mint as a result of a bureaucratic reorganization, came out in favor of such a commemorative coin. Swift passage followed, and the new chief engraver, Elizabeth Jones, rendered an equestrian portrait of Washington that marked the first commemorative coin issue in twenty-eight years.

In the interim, the decision was made to eliminate copper in the 1-cent coin. This was necessitated by rising copper prices that, a decade earlier, had caused aluminum cent patterns to be produced. The result of all this was a zinc cent that was plated to 3/10,000's of an inch copper. Each of these new coins is about 14 percent lighter, yet the population as a whole does not seem to take any particular notice, perhaps because the coin (despite its excessive production) is not that widely used. In fact, the most recent surveys by the U.S. Mint and the Federal Reserve suggest that the 1-cent piece has an attrition rate of nearly 40 percent. Most people seem to believe that the coin's demise is ultimately inescapable, if only someone will brave the political consequences. Just as England's halfpenny died out in 1984 after a lifetime of 705 years, it seems apparent that the American cent will share that fate.

U.S. Olympic Coins

Issuance of Olympic commemorative coins honoring the quadrennial games held in Los Angeles in 1984 proved to be a political imbroglio in addition to a civics lesson on how a bill can become law. For the first time, really since the nineteenth century, coinage matters spilled over onto the front pages of the daily newspapers; even *The Wall Street Journal* devoted a lead story on its first page to the controversy, and thereafter closely followed the developments and ultimate resolution.

Conceptually, the idea for Olympic commemorative coinage dates back to the ancient Greeks and their distinctive numismatic tributes to victors in the ancient Games. In 1952, the Helsinki Games saw the introduction of the first modern Olympic commemorative coin, the Finnish 500 Markka, and later an increasing number of nations issued a variety of coins. By 1980, the Moscow Games saw forty-five different commemorative coins produced for the Games in a variety of metals that range from copper nickel, gold, and silver to rarefied platinum, which admittedly had a long ancient history in czarist coinage. The reason, increasingly, that vast numbers of commemorative types are utilized has to do with intricacies of marketing; to sell a single piece, by direct mail, is prohibitive. The longer the series, the more the costs can be amortized. Hence a significant number of pieces must appear as part of an ongoing program before the private marketer can make a profit.

The impetus for the 1984 Olympic coin program came from the U.S. Olympic Committee and the Los Angeles Olympic Organizing Committee. Both perceived, early on, that this was a revenue-producing device which could significantly assist American Olympic athletes while at the same time raising funds to help stage the Olympics. (In the United States, as opposed to many other countries, the Games are a private concern.)

The entire California congressional delegation, both House and Senate, agreed to sponsor a coinage bill, which was introduced in May 1981 to the plaudits of collectors and apparent skepticism on the part of the Treasury Department. The bill called for twenty-nine coins to be produced, one piece less than had been called for in the thirty-coin Canadian series of 1976, and many coins fewer than the forty-five-coin Soviet program of the previous Olympic Games.

To collectors, initially, it seemed almost like a dream come true—a commemorative coinage tree or even a fountain spewing commemorative coins.

Behind the congressional bill and both the U.S. Olympic Committee and the Los Angeles Olympic Organizing Committee was a consortium formed by Occidental Petroleum and Lazard Frères, the investment bankers, at first blush an unlikely combination to be involved in selling American Olympic coins. But it was Occidental and Lazard who put together the 1980 Olympic coin program, and made out quite successfully in the process.

Hearings were held in the Senate, and quite promptly the bill was unanimously passed. The problem, however, arose in the House of Representatives, for Representative Frank

Annunzio, chairman of the House Coinage Subcommittee, took a dislike to the bill and promptly became its enemy.

Annunzio's position as chairman of the Consumer Affairs and Coinage Subcommittee of the House Banking Committee is not normally a position of power; it is an ordinary subcommittee chairmanship, and in itself would probably not have been sufficient to sway the majority of members. This seems particularly true in light of the decision by Representative Fernand G. St. Germain (D-R.I.), chairman of the entire House Banking Committee, to become a key sponsor of the bill.

Nonetheless, Annunzio also held rank as a leading Democrat on the House Administration Committee, an internal organization which delegates parking spaces, office space, and even telephone numbers to members. In the ultimate battle that emerged, apparently every type of horse trade was utilized as Annunzio and St. Germain lobbied their fellow members for votes.

Each month that went by lessened the likelihood that the original program could be implemented, based simply on time considerations. A twenty-nine-coin program would, of necessity, involve twenty-nine different dies and an incredible amount of mintwork. As Annunzio dragged the program onward, the prospective marketers also seemed less willing to stick with a $30 million guarantee to the U.S. Olympic Committee, against royalties that they predicted could go as high as $100 million in the event of a sellout.

Ultimately, the Lazard and Occidental marketing organizations withdrew their offer, and Annunzio moved the bill forward. A final bid was made by the private marketing consortium, only to see the proposal voted down in Annunzio's subcommittee. The scene then shifted to the full House Banking Committee, where St. Germain cracked the whip and favorably reported the measure to the full floor of the House, utilizing a reduced number of coins, but a private marketing arrangement that likely would have featured Lazard Frères and Occidental Petroleum handling the bulk of the sales.

The drama now promised to focus on the floor of the

House itself, where a final vote would be set between the multi-coin proposal of St. Germain and the three-coin offer of Annunzio that was being given as an alternative.

Under House procedure, however, no measure may merely be debated without consent of the House itself; a "rule" is required, determining the scope of the debate and the manner in which voting can take place. The House Rules Committee is where this decision is made, and at a hearing, little noticed at the time, Annunzio successfully obtained a rule that would allow for the bill to be both debated, amended, and a substitute offered in its place.

In the twentieth century no full committee chairman bringing a bill to the floor of the House had been defeated, and for good reason; all were sensible politicians and knew how to count the votes beforehand.

In this case, St. Germain never stood a chance. He carried a cadre of eighty-seven supporters, but the rest voted with Annunzio. Annunzio had framed the vote in such a way as to allow the members not to vote against Olympic coinage, but rather for Olympic coinage—in Annunzio's image, not the ideas of St. Germain.

Against this melodrama, the nation greeted the three Olympic coins that emerged with a giant yawn. Annunzio's version called for 52 million pieces to be produced—2 million gold coins—and 50 million silver dollars, but lacked the imagination and the marketing plan ultimately to sell out the series.

One result for this is that the U.S. Mint was forced to come up with additional marketing plans within the scope of the two silver dollars (each .900 fine, in the traditional manner) and the $10 gold piece, also struck to traditional specification.

To assist in selling the gold, not only was it struck at the

Plaster of the first U.S. Olympic commemorative. The obverse by Elizabeth Jones is after Myron throwing the discus (a classical sculpture), and the trade-marked Olympic rings below the star symbolize the Los Angeles Games of 1984. The reverse, by Jones and John Mercanti of the Philadelphia Mint, shows a strong eagle.

West Point bullion depository, but a "W" mint mark (the first ever to appear on any American coin) was instituted. P, D, and S versions were also added. To assist in selling the silver dollars, uncirculated and proof versions were made, in both years of issue, and a variety created by using three mint marks: a "P" for Philadelphia, a "D" for Denver, and an "S" for San Francisco.

After more than a year of sales, the aggregate figures were less than those predicted by the Lazard-Occidental group at Senate hearings which sought to clarify whether the government or private enterprise could better sell the coins. Nonetheless, as far as commemorative coins go, the series appears to have been a success, with tens of millions of dollars worth of sales. What remains to be seen, however, is how this will translate into future commemorative programs, for already there are proposals to honor the Boy Scouts of America, the centennial of the Statue of Liberty, and other worthwhile projects seeking to dip into the federal gold mine of seigniorage.

In the 1980s, there has also been, increasingly, talk of change within the coinage system. The recodification of the minting and coinage laws gives credence to this possibility. The Lincoln cent, after all, saw seventy-five years of service in 1984; the Jefferson nickel has been issued since 1938, and the Washington quarter since 1932. Even the Roosevelt dime, first issued in 1946, is no longer a young coin with four decades of service. The relative new boy on the block is the Kennedy half dollar, first issued in 1964, but that, like the Susan B. Anthony dollar, no longer really circulates. The half dollar is still produced, however, unlike the Anthony dollar, of which 400 million examples continue to reside in government vaults.

These new commemorative coins for General Washington and the Olympics go hand in hand with the other American issues—the failures like the Anthony and Eisenhower dollars, and the successes like the Lincoln cent. Each has virtues that are evident to any foreigner who sees American coinage, as indeed they are to any American who takes the time to know our currency.

Sources for Information and Research

For the enthusiast, there are a number of periodicals and publications on coins, tokens, medals, and paper money from the United States and abroad. Most of the publications contain both articles and advertisements; some also have regular listings of price trends for various series (a good way to keep track of the ups and downs of coin values). Publications range from weekly newspapers with coin hobby news and advertisements from collectors and dealers around the country to annual scholarly tomes of more limited scope and subject matter. In between are quarterly journals and monthly magazines, some of which are sold on newsstands in cities across the nation.

The following is an annotated list of various publications of interest to the enthusiast, with a description of the contents, listings of regular features where applicable, and related items that may be useful to a potential subscriber.

PERIODICALS AND PUBLICATIONS

Weekly Publications

Coin World, Box 150, Sidney, Ohio 45367.

This publication has the largest circulation of any, covering the entire field of numismatics. The size of the paper is eighty pages or more each week, and it contains advertisements from dozens of dealers plus a classified section (currently averaging twenty pages a week) with hundreds of offerings from collectors and dealers alike. The format of the paper is that of a tabloid newspaper, with lead news stories of concern to collectors toward the front. Regular columnists include Q. David Bowers ("Numismatic Depth Study"), who for the last fifteen years has examined at length various historical and investment aspects of collecting, much as a major dealer would view them; Col. Bill Murray ("New-Mismatist"), a column intended primarily for the beginning collector; A. George Mallis ("Coinversationally Speaking"); David L. Ganz ("Backgrounder"); and others. In addition, there is a special "Coin World International" section pertaining to foreign and ancient coinage, as well as news from abroad and feature stories on other items. There is also a weekly pullout section called "Trends," which examines over two-week periods the prices of every U.S. coin in every generally collected condition, and keeps readers up to date on the value of their collections. Similar studies appear periodically for Canadian, Mexican, and other coinages. *Coin World* is available in many coin shops, and most collectors subscribe on an annual basis.

Numismatic News Weekly, Krause Publications, Iola, Wisconsin 54945.

In 1952, only two publications dealt with coins on a regular basis: *The Numismatist,* monthly journal of the American Numismatic Association (see below), and *Numismatic Scrapbook,* which has since merged with *Coin World.* In that year, Chester L. Krause began to publish *Numismatic News* as a monthly newspaper for coin collectors, carrying advertisements and news of interest to collectors. The publication now appears weekly and averages about thirty-six pages per issue. It too covers the entire field, though with more emphasis on American coinage than foreign. Columnists include Ed Reiter, formerly editor of the paper and a respected hobby journalist; Alan Herbert ("Odd Corner"), who has dealt with mint errors and similar items appealing to the specialist; Clifford Mishler ("Circulation Finds"), discussing which coins have been found in pocket change over the course of time; and others. There are approximately eight pages of classified ads each week. Regular readers' reports of circulation finds are invited and printed.

World Coin News, Krause Publications, Iola, Wisconsin 54945.

World Coin News pertains only to foreign coins—no American news coverage or advertising is included. For those who collect foreign issues, ranging anywhere from nearby Canada and Bermuda to faraway China, this weekly is the newspaper to read. Feature stories, regular columnists, and a small classified advertisement section afford maximum coverage in most of the areas of interest to American collectors in the foreign numismatics. Reports on the latest new foreign issues are included and later updated into the *Standard Catalog of World Coins,* published annually by Krause Publications.

Monthly Publications

COINage Magazine, Behn-Miller Publications, 17337 Ventura Blvd., Encino, California 91436.

This is a slick monthly magazine, with lots of color and newsy stories about coins, tokens, medals, and paper money. It averages more than 105 pages, including both advertisements and articles, plus regular columns covering a variety of fields. For collectors of ancient pieces, Joel Malter's "Classical Coinage" has been a steady feature for years. To those interested in collecting the errors produced and distributed unintentionally by the U.S. Mint, Don Wallace's "In Error" gives regular coverage. A steady view of the numismatic marketplace (examining sales, trades, and purchases in which collectors and investors are interested) is found in

David L. Ganz's "Coin Market Insider's Report." *COINage* is the number one monthly, with more than 160,000 readers per issue.

Coins Magazine, Krause Publications, Iola, Wisconsin 54945.

A monthly magazine with departments in the manner of some news weeklies ("Coins Commentary," "World Coin News," "U.S. Numisnews" are standard features), *Coins* covers much the same material as the weekly publications and other periodicals in the Krause chain. Columns include Walter Breen's "Bristles and Barbs," covering the world of numismatics; Carl Allenbaugh's "Expertease," examining humorous sidelights of coin collecting; Arlie Slabaugh's "Tokens and Medal Carnival," covering medallic art and peripheral interests; William Rodgers's "Personalities on Ancients," studying a different ancient coin each month; and Donn Pearlman, examining latest developments in the coin market. Each in the coin market. Each issue averages 105 pages, including advertising.

Bank Note Reporter, Box 9, Camden, South Carolina 29020.

Published monthly in newspaper form for collectors of paper money, this periodical contains regular columnists, news stories, and full coverage of the interesting world of "rag picking," as the paper money buffs call it. It is definitely a publication for the specialist in the field.

The Numismatist, American Numismatic Association, Box 2366, Colorado Springs, Colorado 80901.

The oldest continually circulating periodical on coins in the United States, this contains 220 pages per month of octavo-size (6" x 9") pages. Approximately one-third of each issue consists of news and articles covering the entire field of world numismatics. Regular columns include a discussion of counterfeiting as a contemporary problem; book reviews and library news (both of these mention the latest additions to the ANA's extensive library, which may be borrowed by mail); museum notes (on the accessions to the organization's cabinet); and other association news. In more than ninety years of regular monthly publication, the thousands of articles that have appeared in *The Numismatist* have proved remarkably beneficial to the collecting community at large, for the journal goes out of its way to explore many interesting areas of collecting that might otherwise be untouched. *The Numismatist* is sent free to dues-paying members of the ANA. Private subscriptions for nonmembers are available.

Error Trends Coin Magazine, Box 158, Oceanside, New York 11572.

For the collector of the "fido," or mint error, this is the definitive magazine in the field. Devoted exclusively to error collection, its causes, and related items, this newsy monthly has everything you need. Sample copies on application to the publisher.

Bimonthly and Quarterly Publications

Coin Prices, Krause Publications, Iola, Wisconsin 54945.
Issued bimonthly. Lists in comprehensive fashion the valuations of all U.S. coins in a variety of conditions. Also contains advertisements in a special section and usually at least one story pertaining to coin investment.

NASC Quarterly, published by the Numismatic Association of Southern California, Box 2377, Sepulveda, California 91343.
Quarterly journal of the association, with articles by members and some advertisements. Copy available free upon application.

Calcoin News, published by the California State Numismatic Association, 611 North Banna Avenue, Covina, California 91724.
Quarterly journal of the association, with articles by members and some advertisements. Copy available free on application.

NI Bulletin (publication of Numismatics International), Box 30013, Dallas, Texas 75230.
Monthly journal of the international field with advertisements so geared. Copy available on application. (Incorporates the Organization of International Numismatists, with which it merged.)

TAMS Journal, P.O. Box 375, Bryans Road, Maryland 20616.
Collectors of tokens and medals will be interested in this bimonthly journal published by the Token and Medal Society (TAMS), an organization of collectors of this interesting branch of numismatics. Included in each issue is a mixture of articles ranging from current medallic issues of a private, commercial mint to tokens used in musical machines.

Museum Notes, published by the American Numismatic Society, 156th Street & Broadway, New York, N.Y. 10032.
An annual publication of the American Numismatic Society, reporting on research at the society's museum located in New York City. Some of the articles are scholarly and pertain to ancient coinage; others discuss more recent coins. All are interesting to the student or collector in specialized fields. Some back issues are available from the society.

Other Periodicals

Numismatic Literature, published by the American Numismatic Society, 156th Street & Broadway, New York, N.Y. 10032.

This semiannual compilation, an annotated bibliography of current literature, covers the world. Publications from more than two dozen countries are examined and abstracts prepared. Magazines surveyed include standard numismatic publications, as well as other magazines of more peripheral interest, such as archaeological journals. For interested research institutions, the entire 100-volume series, issued since 1947, is available from the ANS. The periodical is free to all members, and nonmembers can subscribe.

Newsletters

There are many newsletters that service the coin field, ranging from weekly market updates to those whose focus is on particular areas of collecting. They are far too numerous to mention in full, but ten of the most interesting ones are:

1. **Coin Dealer Newsletter,** P.O. Box 11099, Torrance, Calif. 90510.

Weekly publication no serious investor can do without. Known as the "Grey Sheet" for the color of its printing stock, it prices coins that are traded regularly. Weekly. $60 per year.

2. **Ludwig Silver Dollar Report,** Box 6282, Toledo, Ohio 43614. Monthly. $35 per year.

3. **Swiatek Numismatic Report,** P.O. Box 218, Manhasset, New York 11030.

Focus mostly on commemorative coinages by a master in the field. Monthly. $60 per year.

4. **Rosen Numismatic Advisory,** Box 231, East Meadow, New York 11554. $60 per year. Monthly.

5. **David Hall's Coin Market Report,** Box 8521, Newport Beach, California 92658. Monthly. $97 per year.

6. **Fortune Teller,** Box 36, Midland Park, New Jersey 07432. Monthly. $42 per year.

Les Fox's journal of opinion makes compelling reading.

7. **Jeffcoat Report,** Iola, Wisconsin 54945. Monthly. $48 per year.

Critical commentary on the coin market by former editor of *Numismatic News.*

8. **Rare Coin Investor Newsletter,** Box 324, Lawrence, New York 11559. Monthly. $60 per year.

Joe Abiuso's digest of other newsletters. Quite interesting.

9. **Blanchard's Market Alert,** 4425 W. Napoleon Ave., Metairie, Louisiana 70001. Monthly. $60 per year.

"Hard money" views on coins.

10. **Private Coin Collector,** Box 62, Oxford, Massachusetts 01510. Monthly. $45 per year.

No advertisements. Good analysis of the marketplace.

Museums

Collectors at any stage inevitably visit museums. The beginner goes to see the major rarities and the extensive preparations for the display of rare and unusual coins. The more experienced collector usually wishes to study a particular type, or even a single specimen, which might throw a clue on an item of mystery.

Most museums with cabinets of coins permit people to study them outside the display cases. The American Numismatic Society in New York will open up its cabinets to anyone wishing to do scholarly work or even to examine particular coins to enhance his or her collecting knowledge. In almost every instance it is wise to get in touch with the museum curator in advance.

The following is a listing by state of major museums that maintain a particular coin exhibit or cabinet that might be of interest to collectors. The annotations are intended to describe in skeletal fashion only the museums and their holdings available for study.

All of the museums included in this list have free admission; most are open weekdays and Saturday. There are a number of other museums of a more commercial nature, and also some that charge admission. It is easy to locate these with a Yellow Pages directory. A fairly definitive listing of museums of all kinds with numismatic exhibits may be found in the current edition of the *Coin World Almanac*.

California

Old Mint Museum. San Francisco. Fifth & Mission Streets.

The former U.S. Mint contains displays of rare coins and gold from pioneer days. Offices have been restored to look as they did when the mint opened in 1870. Coin displays are impressive and varied, and include some of California's numismatic history.

Bank of California Money Museum. San Francisco. 400 California Street.
Monies of the American West, including pioneer and territorial gold.

Colorado

American Numismatic Association Museum. Colorado Springs. 818 N. Cascade Ave.

Extraordinarily wide scope. Major museum for coins, medals, tokens, and paper money. Modern medallic art exhibition hall. Special fourteenth-century coining press demonstration model; other unique items.

Denver Mint. Denver. 320 West Colfax Ave.
The U.S. Mint, Denver Branch, has its own special collection on display.

Connecticut

Yale University Library. New Haven.
Major collection of ancients and colonials.

Connecticut State Library Museum. Hartford. 231 Capitol Avenue.
Major collection of rare coins, including fine sampling of colonial issues.

Delaware

Delaware State Museum. Dover. 316 S. Governors' Avenue.
Coins not regularly on display, but fine numismatic selection in the collection.

Washington, D.C.

Smithsonian Institution. 14th Street & Constitution Ave., N.W.
The national coin collection. Includes the Chase Manhattan Bank Money Museum. The fabulous Lilly Collection of gold coins and other items are on constant display. Related materials.

Treasury Museum. Treasury Building, 15th & Pennsylvania Ave., N.W.
Memorabilia, coins, medals, and the like in a government museum run by the U.S. Mint.

National Gallery of Art, Constitution Ave. at 8th St., N.W.
Samuel Kress Collection of Renaissance bronzes.

Georgia

Atlanta Museum. Atlanta. 537 Peachtree St., N.W.

Dahlonega Court House. Dahlonega. Courthouse Square.
Monies from the old Dahlonega Mint and related memorabilia.

Illinois

World Heritage Museum. Champaign-Urbana (University of Illinois). 484 Lincoln Hall.
Extraordinary collection of coins, medals, and primitive currencies.

Indiana

Indiana University Fine Arts Museum. Bloomington. Fine Arts Building.
Specializes in ancient coins.

Louisiana

New Orleans Mint. New Orleans. French Quarter.
A restoration and conversion to a museum with coin display has been completed.

Maryland

Museum of U.S. Naval Academy. Annapolis.
Mostly naval medals (nearly 3,000).

Massachusetts

Boston Museum of Fine Arts. Boston. 465 Huntington Ave.
Magnificent collection, especially of ancient coins.

Harvard Museum of Fine Arts. Harvard University, Cambridge.
Magnificent collection in all fields.

Michigan

Detroit Money Museum. Detroit. National Bank of Detroit. 200 Renaissance.
Excellent collection in all fields; widely diversified, with fine displays.

Missouri

Truman Library. Independence.
Coins, tokens, medals, and paper money associated with the former President.

Washington University Library. St. Louis.
Roman and Greek coinages.

Nebraska

Omaha Public Library. Omaha.
Home of the Byron Reed Collection, including many rare coinages.

New Hampshire

Dartmouth College Museum. Hanover.
Displays of coins. Collection available for viewing by appointment.

New Jersey

The Newark Museum. 49 Washington Street.
Extensive collection, including New Jersey colonials, and more comprehensive items.

Princeton Art Museum. Princeton University.
Greek and Roman coinages.

New York

American Numismatic Society. 156th Street & Broadway, New York City.
Most extensive collection of any museum in the world.

Jewish Museum. 92nd Street & 5th Avenue, New York City.
Coins, tokens, medals, and currency relating to Jewish history and culture.

North Carolina

Charlotte Mint Museum. Charlotte. 501 Hempstead Place.
Coins and related memorabilia from the old mint.

Duke Museum. Durham.
Fine collection, part of the overall curatorial interest in ancient art.

Ohio

Cleveland Museum of Art. Cleveland. 11150 East Blvd.

Miami University Library. Oxford. Special collections room.
Roman and Greek coins. Magnificent collection of ancient and modern coins.

Pennsylvania

Franklin Mint Museum. Franklin Center.
Most extensive museum of medallic art in the world.

Philadelphia Mint. Independence Mall, first and second floors.
Mint museum of assorted items from the collection, the rest of which is now in Washington. Occasional fine collections on loan.

Carnegie Museum. Pittsburgh. 4400 Forbes Avenue.
Extensive collection of coins, tokens, medals, and paper money.

Texas

Museum of Natural History. Houston.
Monies of Texas.

Coin Clubs and Meetings

Meeting with fellow collectors is just plain fun. You have the opportunity to swap coins—and tall stories about "the one that got away." There are also the fraternal spirit of numismatics and the educational aspect of learning what others have successfully researched.

Many communities have coin clubs with regular meeting dates. There are also some county-wide organizations, state and regional groups, and, of course, national associations.

If you don't know where your local coin club is or how to contact it, you can write to the American Numismatic Association, the largest educational nonprofit organization of coin collectors in the world. This group, chartered by the Congress of the United States, is headquartered on the campus of Colorado State College and maintains an extensive list of coin clubs across the nation. For the cost of a self-addressed, stamped envelope, they will be happy to advise you of the nearest coin club to you, as well as its meeting nights and the name and address of the club secretary. Write for information to:

American Numismatic Association

Post Office Box 2366

Colorado Springs, Colo. 80901

Bibliography

BOOKS AND CATALOGUES ON COINAGE AND CURRENCY

This is an obviously broad classification. It has been divided for the researcher's convenience into several different areas, which take into account subject matter and time frame.

General

Bowers, Q. David. **Adventures with Rare Coins.** 1979.
History, investment, and fascinating tales by a major dealer in the field.

Brown, Frances. **Coins Have Tales to Tell: The Story of American Coins.** 1966. ANA Library No. GA40 B7.
Vignettes about distinctive coins.

Doty, Richard. **Coins of the World.** 1978.
An excellent paperback by the American Numismatic Society's associate curator.

———. **Money of the World.** 1979.
Survey of money in history, with exquisite photography.

Evans, George. **Illustrated History of the U.S. Mint.** 1886–1893. ANA Library No. GA80 E9.
Fascinating book sold to tourists at the Philadelphia Mint during the years of publication. Gives the history of the mint and of various coin rarities.

Hepburn, A. Barton. **History of Coinage and Currency in the United States.** 1903. ANA Library No. WB30 H4.
A major study on coinage and currency, written with the aim of promoting currency reform. Quite a bit of the background material is useful to the collector studying the period from the Revolution to the beginning of the 1900s.

Reed, Mort. **Encyclopedia of U.S. Coins.** 2nd ed., 1972. ANA Library No. GA50 R4c.

Complete with glossary, illustrations of all coin designs, information about their creation, and how the U.S. Mint operates.

SCHWARTZ, TED. **Coins as Living History.** 1976.

Individual coins and their stories.

Selections from the Numismatist: United States Coins. 1960. ANA Library No. US20 A5.

This three-hundred-page book reprints articles on U.S. coinage that have appeared in *The Numismatist,* the monthly journal of the American Numismatic Association, from its founding in 1893 until 1960. Topics include everything from an introduction to coin collecting to articles on specific denominations, types, and series. An excellent one-volume work covering major aspects of American coinage.

STEWART, FRANK H. **History of the First United States Mint.** 1924, reprint 1974. ANA Library No. GA80 S7y.

An absolutely fascinating story of the creation of the first mint, the building, and the life and times of its early occupants, by the man who purchased it in the 1900s.

TAXAY, DON. **The U.S. Mint and Coinage.** 1966. ANA Library No. GA80 T3.

An expansive effort at researching the history of the U.S. Mint and the various coinage attempts (patterns and otherwise); told in a highly readable form.

VERMEULE, CORNELIUS. **Numismatic Art in America.** Cambridge, Mass.: Harvard University (Belknap Press), 1971. ANA Library No. GB40 V4.

If there is anything you wish to know about the artistic value of American coinage, this book supplies the answers. The author is a museum curator accomplished in the field of numismatic art; the information the book contains is exquisite in detail and presentation.

U.S. Coin Catalogues (all with valuations and additional information)

RAYMOND, WAYTE. **Standard Catalogue of United States Coins.** 1935–1957. ANA Library No. GA30 R3u.

Annual editions, each with a special supplement pertaining to a specific area (e.g., hard-times tokens; Washington medals; etc.), and rich data on coin types.

TAXAY, DON. **Scott's Catalogue and Encyclopedia of U.S. Coins.** 2nd ed., 1976. ANA Library No. GA30 T3.

Probably the finest tool in terms of varieties and data on mintage; goes beyond mere figures, though prices are outdated.

YEOMAN, R. S. **A Guide Book of United States Coins.** 34th ed., 1981. ANA Library No. GA50 W5.

More than 10 million copies in print.

———. **Handbook of United States Coins.** 37th ed., 1980. ANA Library No. GA50 Y4.

Lists dealers' buying prices.

Colonial Money and Prior Issues

CROSBY, SYLVESTER S. **The Early Coins of America.** 1874, reprint 1974. ANA Library No. GB50 C7.

This is the classic book for any collector of colonial coinages, for it was commissioned a century ago and traces at length not only the various types but also the correspondence between parties that helped create coin issues. Fascinating reading carefully presented colony by colony.

DURST, SANFORD J. **Comprehensive Guide to American Colonial Coinage.** 1976. ANA Library No. GB50 D8.

History of the various issues and their values; valuable chart listing auction prices; realized records on a coin-for-coin basis.

KESSLER, ALAN. **The Fugio Coppers.** 1976. ANA Library No. GB30 K4.

Gives the origins of Fugio cents and, more importantly, a means by which collectors can readily identify the many different varieties.

NEWMAN, ERIC P. **The Secret of the Good Samaritan Shilling.** 1959. ANA Library No. GB50 N4j.

NOE, SYDNEY P. **The Silver Coinage of Massachusetts.** Reprint 1973. ANA Library No. GB80 M4N6n, o, p.

Originally published as monographs by the American Numismatic Society. A "must" for those collecting the series.

Numismatic Notes and Monographs (American Numismatic Society). A fascinating tale.

_____, ed. **Studies in Money in Early America.** 1976. ANA Library No. QB70 T3.

A series of essays sponsored by the American Numismatic Society on colonial issues and their history.

SCOTT, KENNETH. **Counterfeiting in Colonial America.** 1957. ANA Library No. GB50 S3.

TAXAY, DON. **Money of the American Indians.** 1970. ANA Library No. QB70 T3. 153 pp., bibliography.

Commemorative Coins, Pattern Pieces, Type Coins

AKERS, DAVID W. **United States Gold Patterns.** 1975. ANA Library No. GB10 A3.

An expanded discussion, with price analysis, of all gold patterns.

BOWERS, Q. DAVID. **The History of United States Coinage as Illustrated by the Garrett Collection.**

Reportedly a requirement of Johns Hopkins University in the disposition of the magnificent Garrett collection was that it should be memorialized in book form.

This opus is a tribute to Garrett, and to American collecting at the turn of the century.

————. **Virgil Brand: A Man and His Era.** 1983.
Another major collection and its owner is discussed.

BREEN, WALTER. **Encyclopedia of U.S. and Colonial Proof Coins 1722–1977.** 1977.
An essential book for any student in the field.

BULLOWA, DAVID M. **The Commemorative Coinage of the United States.** 1938. ANA Library No. GB40 B8.

JUDD, J. HEWITT. **United States Pattern, Experimental and Trial Pieces.** 6th ed., 1977. ANA Library No. GA90 J8.
A complete catalogue and listing, along with history of creation of these 1,800 different distinctive coin types.

Numismatic Notes and Monographs No. 83. Well-researched history of commemoratives, including all legislation.

SLABAUGH, ARLIE R. **United States Commemorative Coinage.** 2nd ed., 1975. ANA Library No. GB40 S5.
History and valuations of all American issues.

STACK, NORMAN. **United States Type Coins.** 1977.
Offers a means to collect type coinage systematically. Color illustrations.

SWIATEK, ANTHONY, and WALTER BREEN. **Silver & Gold Commemorative Coins 1892–1954.** 1981.
Now the standard reference in the field.

YEOMAN, R. S. **Handbook of United States Type Coins.** 1943–1957. ANA Library No. GA50 Y4.
Illustrated; shows the differences among coins. Copper, nickel, silver only.

Special Areas

ADAMS, EDGAR. **Private Gold Coinage of California.** 1913. ANA Library No. GB80 C3A3.
Territorial gold; a standard reference book.

BOOSEL, HARRY X. **1873–1873.** 1964. ANA Library No. GB70 B6. 64 pp.
Reprinted from *Numismatic Scrapbook*, this is the story of the coinage of 1873, the year in which the Coinage Act revamped the monetary system and more coins were produced in more denominations than in any other year.

BREEN, WALTER. "Proof Coins Struck by the U.S. Mint, 1817–1921." **The Coin Collector's Journal**, March–April, May–June, 1953. ANA Library No. GA80 B7p.

————. "Silver Coinages of the Philadelphia Mint, 1794–1916." **The Coin Collector's Journal**, No. 159 (1958).

————. **Walter Breen's Encyclopedia of United States and Colonial Proof Coins, 1792–1977.** 1977.

Probably the most fascinating book on a single subject of American numismatics. It is comprehensively researched and complete with the pedigrees of various coins (hence showing their value). Chronologically presented.

GANZ, DAVID L. **14 Bits. The Story of America's Bicentennial Coinage, 1976.** 1975, 1976. ANA Library No. GB40 G3.

Originally published in *The Numismatist*, this gives the history of how the Bicentennial quarter, half, and dollar were created, complete with the legislative documents of Congress.

————. "Toward a Revision of the Minting and Coinage Laws of the United States." **Cleveland State Law Review**, vol. 26, pp. 175–253. 1977.

Research Triangle Institute. **A Comprehensive Review of U.S. Coinage System Requirements to 1990.** September 1976.

Consists of: (a) Project summary; (b) Final Report, vol. 1; Final Report, vol. 2. The six-hundred-page, two-volume study on the future of American coinage contracted for the Treasury Department.

SCHILKE, OSCAR, and RAPHAEL SOLOMON. **America's Foreign Coins.** 1964. ANA Library No. GB60 S3.

The fascinating story of the coins that had legal tender status in the United States until 1857 but were produced abroad, not made by the U.S. Mint.

SEYMOUR, DEXTER. **Templeton Reid. First of the Pioneer Coiners.** Museum Notes of the American Numismatic Society, No. 19 (1974). ANA Library No. GB15 S4.

A biography of the Georgia minter.

TREASURY DEPARTMENT. **Alternative Materials for One Cent Coinage.** December 1973.

The Treasury's search for an aluminum cent is explored.

————. **Annual Report of the Director of the Mint.** Produced annually since 1873.

A storehouse of information on the happenings of the previous fiscal and calendar years, with detailed examination of some issues.

————. **One Cent Coinage. A Summary of 1973–1974 Treasury–Federal Reserve Committee Studies.** October 1974.

Searching for a solution to the problem of the cent.

————. **A New Smaller Dollar Coin. Technical Considerations.** August 1976.

A major study on creating a small, 26.5mm dollar.

Various Denominations

Copper Coinage

GILBERT, EBENEZER. **The U.S. Half Cents from 1793 to 1857.** 1916. ANA Library No. GB30 G5v.

The classic study of half-cent varieties. Numbering system still used.

LAPP, WARREN A., and HERBERT A. SILBERMAN, eds. **United States Large Cents, 1793–1857.** Reprint 1975. ANA Library No. GB30 L3.

Covering large cents and half cents, this 645-page volume has virtually every article on the old large coppers that has appeared in *The Numismatist*. A treasure-house of information for the specialist.

NEWCOMB, HOWARD. **U.S. Copper Cents, 1816–1857.** 1944. ANA Library No. GB30 N4c.

The standard treatise on these coins. Newcomb devised a numbering system that is still used for varieties. Refer to this along with Dr. Sheldon's classic.

SHELDON, WILLIAM H. **Penny Whimsy.** 1958. ANA Library No. GB30 S5p.

The classic book on early American large cents, 1793–1814, complete with descriptions of hundreds of varieties, and the grading system now utilized for all American coins.

Silver Coinage

BEISTLE, M. L. **A Register of Half Dollar Die Varieties and Subvarieties.** 1929. ANA Library No. GB20 B4.

A standard reference.

BOLENDER, M. H. **The U.S. Early Silver Dollars.** 1950. ANA Library No. GB20 B6.

Covers the years 1794 to 1803.

BROWNING, A. W. **Early Quarter Dollars of the United States, 1796–1838.** 1925, reprint 1977. ANA Library No. GB20 B8.

This study is used by everyone to distinguish varieties and types.

HAZELTINE, JOHN W. **Early U.S. Silver Dollars, Half Dollars, and Quarter Dollars.** Reprint 1927. ANA Library No. GB20 H4e.

An early reference to the varieties and types of the field, with an interesting history of some key rarities.

IVY, STEVE, and RON HOWARD. **What Every Silver Dollar Buyer Should Know.** 1984.

A good introductory book on investing in silver dollars by principals of a firm that has made a market in them.

MILLER, WAYNE. **The Morgan and Peace Dollar Textbook.** 1983.

A major reference work by a market-maker in the dollar field.

NEWMAN, ERIC P. **The Fantastic 1804 Silver Dollar.** 1962. ANA Library No. GB20 N42.

An interesting tale of mystery and intrigue.

OVERTON, AL C. **Early Half Dollar Varieties, 1794–1836.** 1964. ANA Library No. GB20 O8.

Another standard reference book.

PIPER, RICHARD. **The Elusive 1836 Reeded Half Dollar.** 1976. ANA Library No. GB20 P5.

VALENTINE, DANIEL W. **United States Half Dimes.** 1941, reprint 1975. ANA Library No. GB20 V3.

A classic study, done for the American Numismatic Society (Numismatic Notes and Monographs). The 1975 reprint by Quarterman includes a supplement by Walter Breen and much additional data.

VAN ALLEN, LEROY C., and GEORGE A. MALLIS. **Comprehensive Encyclopedia and Catalog of U.S. Morgan and Peace Silver Dollars.** 1971, 1976. ANA Library No. GB20 V35.

All the known varieties and die strikes, plus general information, are contained in this major work.

WILLEM, JOHN. **The United States Trade Dollar.** 1959, 1965. ANA Library No. GB70 W5.

The classic study of America's "unwanted coin," giving its full legal history, legislative package, and congressional debate.

Gold Coinage

ADAMS, EDGAR H. **Adams's Official Premium List of United States, Private and Territorial Gold Coins.** 1913, reprint 1977. ANA Library No. GB15 A3.

The earliest known listing detailing all varieties of pioneer gold of the West and the South, along with other material on gold coins in general.

AKERS, DAVID W. **United States Gold Coins: An Analysis of Auction Records.** ANA Library No. GB10 A3g.

This multivolume study, published since 1975, offers photographs of each gold coin produced by the U.S. Mint, a brief commentary on the relative rarity and scarcity of each date, and an extensive analysis of each coin's various auction appearances (which is used to show rarity). An outstanding job of research, and a "must" for the enthusiast.

BOWERS, Q. DAVID. **United States Gold Coins: An Illustrated History.** 1982.

The magnificent Eliasberg collection of U.S. gold coins.

BREEN, WALTER. **Major Varieties of U.S. Gold Dollars.** 1964. ANA Library No. GB10 B7g.

_____. **Major Varieties of the U.S. $3 Gold Pieces, 1964.** 1964. ANA Library No. GB10 B7t.

_____. **Varieties of U.S. Quarter Eagles.** 1965. ANA Library No. GB10 B7q.

_____. **U.S. Eagles.** 1966. ANA Library No. GB10 B73.

Grading U.S. Coins

AMERICAN NUMISMATIC ASSOCIATION. **Official A.N.A. Grading Standards for United States Coins.** 1977.
Textual description at great length for all U.S. coin series and types; illustrations of various grades from about good to perfect uncirculated. Currently the standard used by most dealers and collectors.

BAGG, RICHARD, and JAMES JELINSKI, eds. **Grading Coins: A Collection of Readings.** 1977.
Offers a compilation of various means by which to grade coins from 1892 to the present. Reprints of articles published in selected journals on the subject.

BROWN, MARTIN R., and JOHN DUNN. **A Guide to the Grading of United States Coins.** 6th ed., 1975. ANA Library No. GA50 B7.
An analysis with drawings for each of several conditions for all coin series of regular U.S. issue.

NUMISMATIC CERTIFICATION INSTITUTE. 311 Market Street. Dallas, Texas 75202.
Heritage Numismatic's grading and certification service.

RUDDY, JAMES F. **New Photograde. A Photographic Grading Guide for U.S. Coins.** Rev. ed., 1972. ANA Library No. GA50 R8.
Photographs of all U.S. coins in each of several conditions, with descriptions of the accompanying grade.

Histories of Currency

GRIFFITHS, WILLIAM H. **The Story of the American Bank Note Company.** 1959. ANA Library No. US25 G7.
A corporate history, lavishly illustrated with engravings that were specially printed by American Bank Note.

TREASURY DEPARTMENT. **History of the Bureau of Engraving and Printing, 1862–1962.** 1962. ANA Library No. US25 U5.
Fascinating story of the making of U.S. paper money through the years, and other items.

Guidebooks on Particular American Currencies

NOTE: Most of the obsolete paper money catalogues are very large because of the vast number of wildcat or broken banks that issued paper money. Some of the catalogues are well illustrated, and some give a good history of the various banks that went broke. Titles are for the most part wholly descriptive of the book.

AFFLECK, CHARLES J. **The Obsolete Paper Money of Virginia.** 1968–69. ANA Library No. US80 V5A4.

Bowen, Harold L. **State Bank Notes of Michigan.** 1956. ANA Library No. US80 M5B6.

Carothers, Neil. **Fractional Money.** 1930. ANA Library No. US50 C3.

This is the classic study on all fractional money, including coins and fractional currency (paper). Frequently cited by economic authorities.

Curto, J. J. **Michigan Depression Scrip of the 1930's.** 1949. ANA Library No. US35 C8m.

Donn, Albert. **World War II Prisoner of War Scrip of the United States.** 1970. ANA Library No. US35 D6.

McGarry, Sheridan. **Mormon Money.** 1950. Reprinted from *The Numismatist.* ANA Library No. US75 M3.

Medlar, Bob. **Texas Obsolete Notes and Scrip.** 1968. ANA Library No. US80 T4M4.

Mumey, Nolie. **Colorado Territorial Scrip.** 1966. ANA Library No. US80 C6M8.

Includes the history and biographies of the issuers.

Pennell, J. Roy. **Obsolete Bank Notes of North Carolina.** 1965. ANA Library No. US80 N6P4.

Reprinted from *Numismatic Scrapbook.*

Rothert, Matt. **A Guide Book of U.S. Fractional Currency.** 1963. ANA Library No. US50 R6.

Sheheen, Austin M. **South Carolina Obsolete Notes.** 1960. ANA Library No. US80 S6S5.

Slabaugh, Arlie. **Confederate States Paper Money.** 1961. ANA Library No. US60 S5.

Wismer, D. C. **Descriptive List of Old Paper Money Issued in Ohio.** 1932. ANA Library No. US80 O6W5.

———. **New York Descriptive List of Obsolete Paper Money.** 1931. ANA Library No. US80 N5W4.

———. **The Obsolete Bank Notes of New England.** 1922–1935, reprint 1972. ANA Library No. US75 W5.

Originally run as a serial for thirteen years in *The Numismatist,* it is all pulled together in this reprint.

———. **The Obsolete Paper Money of New Jersey.** 1928. ANA Library No. US80 N4W5.

———. **Pennsylvania Descriptive List of Obsolete Bank Notes, 1782–1866.** 1933. ANA Library No. US80 P4W5.

BOOKS AND CATALOGUES ON U.S. PAPER MONEY

Unless otherwise noted, all the catalogues listed employ a numbering system and have bills arranged in an order that permits comparison and lists valuations. Some contain substantially more information than others.

CRISWELL, GROVER C. **Confederate and Southern States Currency.** 3rd ed., 1976. ANA Library No. US60 C7.

Monies of the Confederacy.

———. **North American Currency.** 2nd ed., 1969. ANA Library No. US20 C7.

Listings include broken bank notes and obsolete bank notes by state and city, all numbered.

FRIEDBERG, ROBERT. **Paper Money of the United States.** 8th ed., 1975. ANA Library No. US20 F7.

This is the standard guide to all American paper money, with a numbering system that is widely used. Arrangement is by type of note (Federal Reserve, Fractional Currency, National Currency, etc.), then by denomination.

HESSLER, GENE. **The Comprehensive Catalog of U.S. Paper Money.** 2nd ed., 1977. ANA Library No. US40 H4.

The approach taken is strictly by denomination, without regard to series or type. Lists quantities printed (a major first) and is fairly explicit in its treatment. A veritable encyclopedia that is most useful.

Hewitt-Donlon Catalog of U.S. Small-Size Paper Money. Annual edition from 1964. ANA Library No. US90 D6.

Checklist with additional information, prices.

KNOX, JOHN JAY. **United States Notes.** 1884, reprint 1978. ANA Library No. US20 K6.

This is the standard authoritative reference work by the former comptroller of the currency.

NEWMAN, ERIC P. **The Early Paper Money of America.** 2nd ed., 1976. ANA Library No. US40 N4e.

Although it lacks a numbering system, this comprehensive and fully illustrated catalogue is standard and essential for those seeking to collect colonial currency.

PICK, ALBERT. **Standard Catalog of World Paper Money.** 3rd ed., 1980. ANA Library No. UA33 P5s.

U.S. notes are covered in list form in the appropriate chapter.

SHAFER, NEIL. **A Guidebook of Modern United States Currency.** 7th ed., 1975. ANA Library No. US90 S5.

Modern (post–1929) currency only, arranged in checklist form with number printed, valuations, and other data.

BOOKS AND CATALOGUES ON PAPER MONEY OF THE WORLD

BERESINER, YASHA. **The Story of Paper Money.** 1973. ANA Library No. UA30 B4.

An excellent introduction to the field of "notaphily."

PICK, ALBERT. **Standard Catalogue of World Paper Money.** Multiple editions since 1975. ANA Library No. UA33 P5s. 720 pp.

This covers modern issues from about 1850 onward and is a catalogue listing.

NOTE: The American Numismatic Association's Library Catalogue lists more than sixty pages of books on various paper money fields, by country, time period, region, and topic. It is strongly suggested that, after a basic reference work such as the Pick guide is purchased, collectors acquaint themselves with books from the particular region in which they are specializing.

BOOKS AND CATALOGUES ON MEDALLIC ART OF THE WORLD

AMERICAN NUMISMATIC SOCIETY. **Catalogue of the International Exhibition of the Contemporary Medal.** Rev. ed., 1911. ANA Library No. RA10 A5c. 412 pp. Illustrated catalogue.

BAKER, WILLIAM. **Medallic Portraits of Washington.** 1885 (and numerous reprints). ANA Library No. RM80 W3B3.

A standard catalogue, fully illustrated.

BETTS, C. WYLLYS. **American Colonial History Illustrated by Contemporary Medals.** 1894. ANA Library No. RM50 B4.

COTT, PERRY B., ed. **Renaissance Bronzes . . . from the Kress Collection.** 1951.

Collection of the National Gallery of Art, Washington, D.C.

DUSTERBERG, RICHARD. **The Official Inaugural Medals of the Presidents of the United States.** 2nd ed., 1976. ANA Library No. RM85 P7D8.

FORRER, LEONARD. **Biographical Dictionary of Medallists.** 1904–1930 (8 vols). ANA Library No. RA30 F6.

The standard reference work on the subject.

FRANKLIN MINT. **Numismatic Issues of the Franklin Mint.** 1st ed., 1969 (covering 1964–1969), annually thereafter. ANA Library No. RM15 F7.
The complete catalogue of Franklin Mint products.

GORDON, MAJOR L. L. **British Battles and Medals.** 1947. 4th rev. ed., 1978, by Edward C. Joslin.
A standard catalogue for collectors of military memorabilia.

HEISS, ALOIS. **Medallists of the Renaissance (*Les Médailleurs de la Renaissance*).** 9 vols., 1881–1892. In French.

HIBLER, HAROLD E., and CHARLES V. KAPPEN. **So-called Dollars.** 1963. ANA Library No. RM30 H5.
A standard text and catalogue of medals that are dollar-size and which, but for legal tender statutes, would have served as currency.

HILL, SIR GEORGE FRANCIS. **Medals of the Renaissance.** 1920.
A superb volume.

HOCH, A., ed. **Canadian Tokens and Medals.** Quarterman reprint, 1974.
An anthology of articles reprinted from *The Numismatist.*

JULIAN, R. W. **Medals of the United States Mint: The First Century, 1792–1892.** 1977.
Archival research made this fully illustrated book a standard reference work in the field immediately. Covering not only armed forces' medals but also assay commission, Indian peace medals, school medals, and many others, the work carefully researches and describes each design.

KING, ROBERT P. **Lincoln in Numismatics.** 1924–1933. ANA Library No. GB40 K5.
Published in *The Numismatist* between 1924 and 1933, this work is considered the definitive study.

MacNEIL, NEIL. **The President's Medal, 1789–1977.** 1977. ANA Library No. RM85 P7M3.
A deeply historical study of inaugural medals done in association with the National Portrait Gallery of the Smithsonian Institution.

NORRIS, A., and I. WEBER, eds. **Medals and Plaquettes from the Molinari Collection at Bowdoin College.** 1976.
Some 1,500 medals from Pisanello to the late Renaissance artists are illustrated and catalogued. Full explanations of the work and style.

ROCHETTE, EDWARD C. **The Medallic Portraits of John F. Kennedy.** 1966. ANA Library No. RA60 K4R6.
A definitive study, fully illustrated.

The Salton Collection: Renaissance and Baroque Medals and Plaquettes. 1965. ANA Library No. RA10 B6.
An extraordinary collection of fine art medals, illustrated and explained.

Sculpture in Miniature: The Andrew S. Ciechanowiecki Collection. 1969. ANA Library No. RA10 C5. 222 pp.
Fully illustrated.

TOYNBEE, JOCELYN M. C. **Roman Medallions.** 1944. ANA Library No. RB50 T6.

Numismatic Notes and Monographs (American Numismatic Society).

Treasury Department. **Medals of the United States Mint.** Rev. ed., 1972. ANA Library No. RM15 U5.

This is a catalogue of current medals issued for sale on the regular mint list, but it is no mere listing of the items available. Each medal is illustrated, and each of the figures depicted is given a biographical sketch or, in the case of an event, historical record. A worthwhile book for collector and researcher.

BOOKS AND CATALOGUES ON COIN INVESTMENT

Bowers, Q. David. **High Profits from Rare Coin Investment.** Rev. ed., 1977. ANA Library No. GA55 B6.

By a popular coin dealer.

———. **Commonsense Coin Investment.** 1982.

An historical approach by a leading dealer.

Forman, Harry J. **How You Can Make Big Profits Investing in Coins.** 1972. ANA Library No. AA78 F6.

Another popular dealer.

Hoppe, Donald J. **How to Invest in Gold Coins.** 1970. ANA Library No. CC63 H65.

By a "gold bug" whose prognostications have proved correct.

Pritchard, Jeffery J. **Heads You Win, Tails You Win: The Inside Secrets of Rare Coin Investing.** 1983.

Turner, W. W. **Gold Coins for Financial Survival.** 1971. ANA Library No. CC63 T8g.

BOOKS AND CATALOGUES ON GOLD COINAGE

Friedberg, Robert. **Gold Coins of the World.** 5th ed., 1980. ANA Library No. CC63 F7 1980.

Standard catalogue used by collectors in numbering types of gold coins of the world. Appendix contains useful information about weight, fineness, and types of gold coins struck in contemporary times; the book covers coinage from A.D. 500 to the present.

Harris, Robert F. **Gold Coins of the Americas.** 1971. ANA Library No. FA23 H3.

A definitive study of Latin American, Central American, and North American gold coins.

Hobson, Burton. **Historic Gold Coins of the World.** 1971. ANA Library No. CC63 H6.

An attractive book for gold coin collectors.

SCHLUMBERGER, HANS. **European Gold Coins Guide Book.** Rev. ed., 1975. ANA Library No. JA63 S3e.

Prior to publication of the *Standard Catalogue of World Coins*, this was required reading for every collector; now it is of use principally to those collecting European gold. Includes dates, mintage figures, valuations.

BOOKS AND CATALOGUES ON FOREIGN COINS

The following are several standard catalogues used by collectors in their pursuit of foreign numismatic items. These are standard American catalogues that are part of most libraries where collectors are involved in the field in any depth. There are, of course, numerous volumes that deal with the coinage of foreign countries on a more specific basis. No attempt has been made here to elaborate on these, because of considerations of space and because it is difficult to evaluate distinctions among the many volumes in foreign languages and in English.

CRAIG, WILLIAM D. **Coins of the World, 1750–1850.** 3rd ed., 1976. ANA Library No. CC83 C7.

Comprehensive treatment of coins by type, though individual dates and mintage figures are not given. This is a standard catalogue for the early field, and coins are frequently sold with little more identification than their actual date of issue, country of origin, and Craig number.

KRAUSE, CHESTER L., and CLIFFORD MISHLER. **Standard Catalogue of World Coins.** 11th ed., 1984. ANA Library No. CC87 K7.

The size of a large city telephone book, this volume attempts to cover all coin issues the world over from 1800 on. Some 563 coin-issuing countries are included, with nearly 60,000 coins listed by date (and accompanied for identification purposes by 30,000 photographs). The catalogue employs the standard numbering systems of Craig and Yeoman, described in this section.

YEOMAN, R. S. **A Catalogue of Modern World Coins, 1850–1950.** 13th ed., 1984. ANA Library No. CC87 Y4m.

Picking up where Craig leaves off (though this catalogue was first published many years earlier) the "Y number" catalogues type coins of the world for this important century. The Krause and Mishler standard catalogue, along with nearly all collectors of world coins, utilize the Yeoman numbering system for types. Arthur and Ira Friedberg revised this volume, last issued in 1976.

———. **Current Coins of the World.** 7th ed., 1976. ANA Library No. CC87 Y4c.

Completes the trilogy described above; even for current coinages this is widely used by type and other collectors. Western Publishing updates it periodically.

BOOKS AND CATALOGUES ON PRIMITIVE MONIES

EINZIG, PAUL. **Primitive Money in its Ethnological, Historical and Economic Aspects.** 1948 and 1951. ANA Library No. QB40 E3.

This is one of the classic books on the subject, giving in vast detail everything that a collector, sociologist, and historian might want to know about the unusual monies of the world. Thoroughly analytical, it is also a technical publication with scholarly references.

HERSKOVITZ, MELVILLE J. **Economic Anthropology.** 1952.

An illustrated, thoroughly scholarly presentation by a man who knew black Africa well.

QUIGGIN, A. HINGSTON. **A Survey of Primitive Money: The Beginning of Currency.** Rev. ed., 1963. ANA Library No. QB40 Q5.

An extremely well-written reference work for the field; an excellent place to start research or collecting.

SIGLER, PHARES O. "The Primitive Money of Africa." **The Numismatist**, vol. 65 (1952), vol. 66 (1953), vol. 67 (1954).

Monthly installments in various issues; intended primarily for the collector. Individual volumes in the ANA Library.

TAXAY, DON. **Money of the American Indians and Other Primitive Currencies of the Americas.** 1970. ANA Library No. QB70 T3.

For earliest monies of North America, this is the authoritative reference book, by a skilled researcher and writer.

NUMISMATIC BIBLIOGRAPHIES

A Bibliography of American Numismatic Auction Catalogues, 1828–1875. 1876, reprint 1976. ANA Library No. AA50 A8.

The only book of its type giving good annotations on the catalogues of the period; unfortunately, there is no such book for subsequent catalogues.

CLAIN-STEFANELLI, ELVIRA. **Select Numismatic Bibliography.** 1965. ANA Library No. AA50 C55.

Lists nearly 5,000 items, including books, magazine articles, pamphlets, and the like, in an annotated format that makes it relatively easy for noncollectors to use because it is country or region oriented, and because the subject matter (coin, to-ken, medal, or paper money) is similarly divided, as is the time frame covered in each listing. Technical aspects and "special topics" are also dealt with.

Coin World Almanac. First ed. 1976; annually thereafter.

The "book edition" chapter is an invaluable source of information for many areas. For those interested in purchasing out-of-print books, this is the sole source for the going market price. (Some of these books are very costly.)

COOLE, ARTHUR B. **A Bibliography on Far Eastern Numismatics.** 1940. ANA Library No. KB10 C6.

Dictionary Catalogue of the Library of the American Numismatic Society. 1962.

A seven-volume set giving the complete listing of all items in the catalogue of the ANS through 1962. There has been a substantial number of additions since then, but through the use of *Numismatic Literature*, the semiannual publication of the ANS, it is possible to glean additions selectively. ANA Library (reference collection does not circulate).

Library Catalogue of the American Numismatic Association. 1st ed. 1972; 2d ed. 1978.

Lists books from 1575 to the present, along with periodicals, auction catalogues, and articles that have been reprinted in pamphlet form. The catalogue also contains the call numbers used in the library (neither the Dewey decimal system nor the Library of Congress classifications), and as such is necessary for those seeking to borrow books from the library that circulate by mail. The total cost to the borrower is postage both ways. The library's address is: P.O. Box 2366, Colorado Springs, Colo. 80901.

MOSSER, SAWYER M. **A Bibliography of Byzantine Coin Hoards.** 1935. ANA Library No. BE50 M6.

Numismatic Notes and Monographs No. 67 (American Numismatic Society).

New York Public Library. **Listing of Works Pertaining to Numismatics.** 1914. ANA Library No. AA50 N4. Approximately 200 pages.

NOE, SYDNEY P. **A Bibliography of Greek Coin Hoards.** 1925 and 1937. ANA Library No. BB45 N6.

Numismatic Notes and Monographs Nos. 25 and 78 (American Numismatic Society).

Numismatic Literature.

This semiannual publication of the American Numismatic Society lists approximately 1,000 articles, books, and pamphlets issued on all varieties and phases of numismatics, and surveys numerous journals (some of which regularly carry articles on coins, others which only occasionally do so). The publication dates to 1947 and currently numbers some 100 issues. A complete series is available from the ANS, 156th Street and Broadway, New York, N.Y. 10032.

Index

Index

Fisher, Mel, 41
fish hook money, 11
Flanagan, John, 199
flying eagle cent, 155
Ford, Gerald, inaugural medal of, 110
Fort Knox, 81, 201–2
France
  medieval coins of, 19
  paper money in, 88
Franklin, Benjamin, 86
  commemorative medallions authorized by, 106
  paper money design by, 129–31
Franklin half dollar, 208–9
Franklin Mint, 27, 29
  coin medals of, 112, 115–16
  museum of, 247
Fraser, James Earle, 2, 108
  Buffalo nickel of, 194–95
  Fraser, Laura Gardin, 199
Fugio cents, 133–36

Galvanno, 24
Garfield, James A., 162
Gasparro, Frank, 213, 231, 233
German coins, 19
Getz, Peter, 137
Gobrecht, Christian, 148–49
gold coins
  ancient, 14–18, 69–70
  collection of, 73–74
  counterfeit, 32–33
  double eagle, 2, 72–74, 169
    high relief, 38–39, 60, 62, 191–93
    of 1933, 199–201
  eagle, 72, 144, 147–48, 194
  1834 devaluation of, 146–48
  half eagle, 50–51
  in Fort Knox, 201–2
  investment value of, 75–80
  modern issues of, 75
    American Gold Arts Medallion, 77
  monetary stability of, 25, 71, 72, 125
  1933 confiscation of, 200
  Olympic commemorative, 29

pioneer, 145, 150
price of, 51, 60, 62, 69
  bullion value and, 56–58, 74, 75–80
  pre- *vs* post-1834, 147–48
rarity of, 50–51, 71–72, 144–45
under 1792 act, 140–42
Spanish colonial, 70
"Stella," 180–81
$3 gold piece, 184
Gold Reserve Act of 1934, 25
Grace President Commission Report, 26
grading standards, 32, 52–54
Grant, Ulysses S., 3, 166, 177
Greece (ancient)
  coins of, 14–16
  medallic art of, 101–3
Grey Sheet. See *Coin Dealer Newsletter*
Guide Book of United States Coins, A (Yeoman), 5, 147, 174

half cent, 153–54
  elimination of, 26
half dollar
  1838-O, 62, 64–65
  1892-O, 187–88
  Franklin, 208–9
  Kennedy, 212–13, 215
  1970-D, 222–23
half eagle, 50, 51
Hamilton, Alexander, 71
  mint report of, 138–39
hammered coinage, 19, 22
hard-times tokens, 118–21
Hepburn vs *Griswold* (1870), 91–92, 165–66
History of the American People (Wilson), 97
hogge money, 125–26
Huntington, Seth R., 226, 231

inaugural medals, 108–10
Indian head design, 151–52
  on small cent, 156
  type set collection of, 153
"In God We Trust" motto, 163–65, 193–94
investment coins. *See* coin collecting and collections, for investment
Iowa State Centennial, 236

Index

Index

Index

Vatican, medal art of, 104–5
V.D.B. cent, 44, 193
vending machines, 30
Vermeule, Cornelius, 149
Victor Emmanuel II, King of Italy, 3
Vigdor, Luis, 39

wampum, 7, 12, 126–27
war nickels, 205–6
Washington, Booker T., 236
Washington, George, xvi, 137, 142, 237
Washington, Martha, 142, 233
Washington quarter, 198–99
Watkinson, M. R., 163

Weinman, Adolph, 108, 195
West Point depository, 203
whale teeth currency, 11
Williams, Dennis R., 226, 231
Wilson, Woodrow, 96–98
   and monetary reform, 98
Windsor, Duke of, coin collection of, 3–5
Wood, William, 128
World Coin News, 244
World War II, coinage of, 206–7

Yeoman, Richard S., 5, 174

zinc content in 1-cent coin, 26, 238